THE BATTLE OF
PIEDMONT
AND HUNTER'S RAID ON
STAUNTON

The 1864 Shenandoah Campaign

SCOTT C. PATCHAN
SERIES EDITOR DOUGLAS BOSTICK

Charleston London

THE
History
PRESS

Published by The History Press
Charleston, SC 29403
www.historypress.net

First published 2011

Manufactured in the United States

ISBN 978.1.60949.197.0

Library of Congress Cataloging-in-Publication Data

Patchan, Scott C., 1966-
The Battle of Piedmont and Hunter's raid on Staunton : the 1864 Shenandoah
campaign / Scott Patchan.
p. cm.
Includes bibliographical references and index.
ISBN 978-1-60949-197-0
1. Piedmont, Battle of, Piedmont, Va., 1864. 2. Shenandoah Valley Campaign, 1864
(May-August) 3. Staunton (Va.)--History, Military--19th century. 4. Hunter, David,
1802-1886. I. Title.
E476.6.P36 2011
975.5'6--dc22
2011000914

This book is dedicated to the memory of the American soldiers who fought and died on the bloody fields of Piedmont on June 5, 1864. May the sacrifices of all American soldiers never be forgotten, especially those who are now putting their lives on the line to protect the freedoms we enjoy today.

Contents

Acknowledgements

Many individuals contributed much to this book. But no one has contributed as much as my wife, Nancy. She provided constant encouragement and helped make the Battle of Piedmont come to life. It is the result of her influence that this book is more than a mere tactical discussion of the battle. Nancy took the time out of her busy daily routine (three kids and a full-time job) to read my manuscript and smooth over the rough spots.

On the research front, Mike Miller of Fairfax, Virginia, shared his research files at Marine Corps History Institute at Quantico, Virginia. Mike consistently offered sound advice and posed questions that helped unlock some of the mysteries of Piedmont. Gary Ecelbarger of Annandale, Virginia, reviewed an early draft of my manuscript and suggested several changes. Gary and I have made numerous research trips together to archival institutions across the country. His presence enlivened the usually mundane task of poring through archival records.

Mr. E.B. Vandiver of McClean, Virginia, reviewed a draft of this book and provided many useful suggestions that were incorporated into the text and layout. Colonel John P. McAnaw, U.S. Army (retired), took time out of his busy schedule to spend several hours analyzing the Battle of Piedmont. John's military experience and immense knowledge of the Civil War prompted many questions that greatly improved this book. I also want to thank my editors, Hannah Cassilly and Ryan Finn, for their patience and dedication to this project.

ACKNOWLEDGEMENTS

The late Armstrong Shifflet and his son Larry, longtime residents of the Piedmont area, permitted access to their portion of the battlefield. They also shared their in-depth knowledge of the local history and the battle itself. A number of other historians assisted in gathering material used in this book. Jeff Weaver of Arlington, Virginia; Bob Driver of Brownsburg, Virginia; Johnny L. Scott of Franklin County, Virginia; Don Bible of Mohawk, Tennessee; Nick Picerno of Bridgewater, Virginia; and John Hoffman of the Illinois Historical Survey provided copies of manuscripts and saved the author much time in obtaining these items. Thanks are in order for Jim Burgess and the staff at Manassas National Battlefield Park for the use of the park's library. Jim also shared his extensive knowledge of Civil War weaponry. In the years since I first wrote on this battle, many descendants of Piedmont veterans have contacted me and shared accounts on the Battle of Piedmont, and to them I am most grateful.

I would also like to take the time to thank two individuals whose influence of many years made the successful completion of this book possible. My parents, Ray and Anne Patchan of Salem, Virginia, instilled the value of faith, hard work, patience and perseverance for as long as I can remember. Thanks to their exemplary work as role models, I have been able to achieve success in all of my endeavors.

Prologue

The Shenandoah Valley has long been recognized as one of the great scenic wonders of the United States. For centuries, it provided fertile farmland and hunting grounds for American Indians. By the mid-1700s, European settlement had arrived in the form of the English from eastern Virginia and then large numbers of Germans and Scotch-Irish moving into the Great Valley from Pennsylvania. Throughout its history, the Shenandoah Valley served as a natural transportation corridor, whether it was Cherokee from the south ranging northward to hunt or make war on opposing tribes or Europeon settlers heading southward to settle in Kentucky or Tennessee.

During the Civil War, the valley served as the granary and a workshop for the primary Confederate army operating east of the Blue Ridge. But its most lasting legacy during the war was the Confederate usage of the valley to disrupt the strategic balance in Virginia. In 1861, Confederate General Joe Johnston moved his army from the valley to Manassas Junction, where it played the decisive role in the Battle of Bull Run. In 1862, General Thomas J. "Stonewall" Jackson baffled and defeated the Federals in the valley, prompting President Abraham Lincoln to withhold critical reinforcements from Major General George B. McClellan's campaign against Richmond, allowing Lee to save the Confederate capital from capture. In 1863, the Shenandoah served as an avenue for invading the North. Dick Ewell crushed the hapless Robert Milroy at the Second Battle of Winchester before moving on to his rendezvous with destiny at Gettysburg. From Lincoln and the Union cause, the Shenandoah Valley had indeed become the "Valley of Humiliation."

The unalterable geographical features of the Shenandoah Valley lent themselves naturally to a Confederate army fighting on the defensive. The valley stretched southwestward for 150 miles from the Potomac River at Harper's Ferry to the James River in Rockbridge County. The rugged Allegheny Mountains formed the western wall of the valley. To the east, the scenic Blue Ridge separated the valley from the central Virginia Piedmont region. With its numerous gaps and passes, the Blue Ridge allowed defenders to slip in and out of the Shenandoah Valley, befuddling opponents as Stonewall Jackson had done in 1862. Massanutten Mountain rose up from the valley's floor, hovering over the valley for nearly fifty miles from Front Royal to Harrisonburg. This steep, wall-like ridge cut the Shenandoah into two parts, with the eastern valley known as the Luray or Page Valley and the main Shenandoah Valley to the west. The North and South Forks of the Shenandoah River flow through the Shenandoah and Luray Valleys, respectively, coming to a confluence at Front Royal. It then continues northward until it spills into the Potomac River at Harper's Ferry.

The geographical positioning of the Shenandoah Valley favored the Confederacy. Its location forced Federal armies operating there to uncover Washington, D.C., to a potential counterstroke from the Virginia Piedmont east of the Blue Ridge. Additionally, any force marching south in the Shenandoah Valley moved away from Richmond, the primary Federal objective in Virginia. Conversely, the valley formed an excellent corridor for any Confederate force invading the North. A Confederate force emerging from the northern extreme of the Shenandoah Valley found itself in an ideal position to threaten important Northern cities such as Washington, Baltimore, Philadelphia and Harrisburg.

In the spring of 1864, President Abraham Lincoln and the people of the North placed their hopes for victory in the hands of newly appointed Lieutenant General Ulysses Simpson Grant. He planned a simultaneous offensive from Virginia to the Mississippi River, and the Shenandoah Valley figured into those arrangements. Previously, uncoordinated Federal efforts permitted the Confederacy to reinforce threatened areas from inactive theaters of war. In 1863, the Confederate victory at Chickamauga became possible when the Army of the Potomac's inaction in Virginia allowed Lieutenant General James Longstreet's two divisions from the Army of Northern Virginia to reinforce the Confederate Army of Tennessee. In 1864, Grant intended his coordinated offensive across the eastern half of the United States to prevent another Chickamauga. He included every able-bodied soldier in the scheme, significantly limiting the usage of large forces to defend strategic points such as Washington. He reasoned that the garrison forces "guarded their special trusts when advancing from them as well as when remaining at them."[1]

Grant's strategy called for Major General William T. Sherman's army to press General Joseph E. Johnston's Confederate Army of Tennessee in north Georgia. Grant hoped that Sherman would defeat Johnston and capture Atlanta, arguably the most important city remaining in the Confederacy outside of Richmond. The Union's military chieftain also instructed Major General Nathaniel Banks to assemble his forces at New Orleans and then advance on Mobile, Alabama, a key Confederate port situated on the Gulf Coast. The final and perhaps most important part of Grant's strategy would unfold in Virginia.[2]

In the Old Dominion, Grant planned four simultaneous advances. Major General George G. Meade led the Army of the Potomac across the Rapidan River against Lee's army. Major General Benjamin Butler's Army of the James operated against General Pierre Gustave Toutant Beauregard's force along the James River line. From the mountains of West Virginia, General George Crook's Army of the Kanawha descended upon southwest Virginia to sever the crucial Virginia & Tennessee Railroad, which connected Virginia with the Deep South. After severing the railroad, Crook was to march north to the Shenandoah Valley and join forces with General Franz Sigel at Staunton. Sigel's Army of the Shenandoah advanced up the valley from Martinsburg, West Virginia, against General John C. Breckinridge's Army of the Valley District. If Grant's plan succeeded, it would prevent the Confederates in Virginia from reinforcing one another through constant pressure in all departments. Grant's plan proved to be the most comprehensive one that the Union unveiled during the war. Yet as in most military campaigns, unforeseen difficulties and failures made strategic and tactical adjustments a necessity.[3]

Lee's Army of Northern Virginia stayed one step ahead of Meade. Butler made things tense in Richmond for a while, but a reinforced Beauregard "corked" the "Beast" in a bottle at Bermuda Hundred. Breckinridge thrashed the inept Sigel at New Market on May 15, forcing the German to retreat to the northern side of Cedar Creek, fourteen miles south of Winchester. George Crook achieved the only clear-cut Union victory of May when he routed General Albert Gallatin Jenkins's force at Cloyd's Mountain and severed the Virginia & Tennessee Railroad at New River Bridge. A captured telegram reporting Lee's purported victory over Grant in the Wilderness convinced Crook to return to his base in West Virginia instead of moving into the Shenandoah Valley.

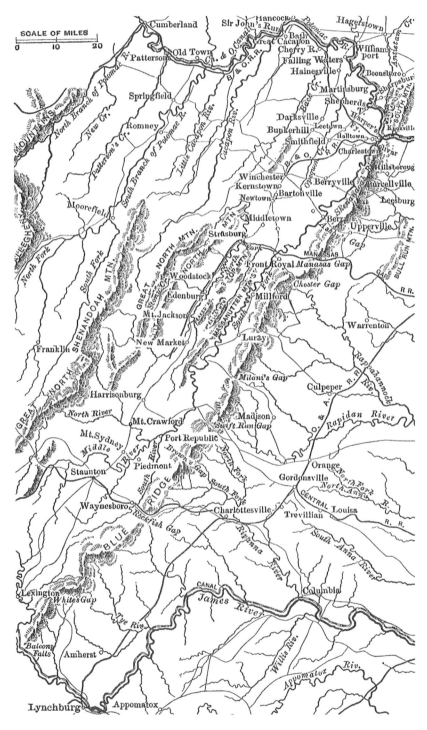

The Shenandoah Valley.

Sigel's defeat quickly enlightened Grant to the impact of operations in the Shenandoah Valley on the overall military situation in Virginia. Within days, Breckinridge reinforced Lee in the defense of Richmond, where the Kentuckian's division played a key role in Lee's victory at Cold Harbor on June 3, 1864. Additionally, the valley continued to supply Lee's army with food, clothing and other desperately needed material without the interference of invading Union forces. To achieve victory in Virginia, Grant realized that he needed to prevent the Shenandoah Valley from becoming a thorn in his side. Only two years before, Stonewall Jackson's Valley Campaign played a key role in disrupting General George C. McClellan's Peninsula Campaign.

The situation looked slightly better in the west. By May 15, Sherman had fought Johnston to a standstill at Resaca, Georgia, but Johnston's army remained intact and continued its defense of Atlanta. The situation in Banks's department verged on disastrous. Banks had barely escaped from his ill-fated Red River Campaign, which had started before Grant assumed command. Banks's debacle and bedlam created by Nathan Bedford Forrest in Tennessee eliminated Grant's intended operations against Mobile for the foreseeable future, and the Gulf Coast port ultimately remained in Confederate hands until April 1865.

Overall, Grant's spring offensive in Virginia produced heavy casualties but fell far short of final victory. Many politicians in the North reacted by calling for an end to the war, and more importantly, the number of citizens sharing that sentiment was growing along with the Federal casualty lists. Many people wondered aloud if the cost of preserving the Union was simply too high. Republicans openly debated dumping Lincoln from their ticket in the 1864 presidential election. In the South, Lee successfully fended off Grant's ferocious attacks but lost a high number of irreplaceable men and forfeited the initiative to the tenacious midwesterner.

Ultimately, operations in the Shenandoah Valley would play a critical role in determining the outcome of the epic Grant-Lee struggle in Virginia. While the two giants maintained the status quo along the Petersburg and Richmond fronts, the more fluid and wide-ranging operations in western Virginia and Maryland ultimately changed the strategic balance in Virginia. The Battle of Piedmont served as the catalyst that upped the ante on the operations in the Shenandoah Valley and led to several months of constant campaigning in the valley that did not end until the Battle of Cedar Creek four months later.

Chapter 1

"We Too Must Be in Earnest"

The spring of 1864 in the Shenandoah Valley of Virginia came with the usual sowing of crops and the splashes of flora blossoming throughout the country and along the mountainsides. Since the Civil War erupted, springtime in the Shenandoah also brought military activity to the region. More often than not, the campaigns resulted in much embarrassment to the Union cause. The appointment of Lieutenant General Ulysses S. Grant to supreme command of all United States forces in 1864 provided hope that victory would be forthcoming. However, his appointment provided President Abraham Lincoln with no immediate relief from the embarrassing trend in the Shenandoah Valley. This time, spring began with the Battle of New Market on May 15 where Confederate Major General John C. Breckinridge, the former vice president of the United States and former U.S. senator from Kentucky, routed Union forces led by German-born Major General Franz Sigel. This stinging defeat hurt all the more because it was lost as much through Sigel's incompetence as it was by any spectacular Confederate tactics. "The campaign," noted Colonel David Hunter Strother of Sigel's staff, "was conducted miserably." He was, concluded Strother, "merely a book general…having no capacity to fight with troops in the field." If the Union was to achieve victory in the valley, another change in leadership was desperately needed, and Grant knew it.[4]

As the brilliant rays of sunshine beamed eastward across the Shenandoah sky on the evening of May 21, 1864, a group of Sigel's staff officers stood on the portico of Belle Grove manor house near Middletown, Virginia. Inside the stately limestone manor, Sigel stewed over his defeat, while a party of horsemen galloping south on the Valley Pike caught Strother's eye. When the riders reached Belle Grove, Strother immediately noticed that one officer wore a major general's insignia on his coat. An anxious Captain Thomas Putnam inquired of Strother, "What does this mean?" Strother smugly retorted, "It means our Captain [Sigel] is relieved." Not everyone shared Strother's satisfaction at Sigel's relief. Many soldiers like Putnam were fond of the doting Sigel. One soldier wrote that he was "a good officer [and] kind to the men under his command." Their opinions mattered not; Sigel's tenure as commander of the Department of West Virginia had ended.[5]

Strother quickly recognized the approaching general as his cousin, David Hunter, and descended the stairs to welcome him. The two men exchanged warm greetings, and the general pulled Strother aside. Hunter confided: "I have come to relieve General Sigel; you know it is customary with a general who has been unfortunate to relieve him whether he has committed a fault or not." They entered the mansion, and Hunter politely informed Sigel of

Major General David Hunter was a militant abolitionist who implemented a harsher brand of warfare in the Shenandoah Valley than was previously seen. At war's end, he served as the president of the military commission that tried the Lincoln assassination conspirators. *Library of Congress.*

the change in command. The German's spirit sagged. "It were better to have died on that battlefield than to have suffered this disgrace," lamented Sigel as tears welled up in his eyes. It was no time for self-pity, as Sigel had failed to fulfill his role in Grant's grand strategy to keep the pressure on the Confederacy on all fronts. That job and more now belonged to the determined General Hunter.[6]

At sixty-one years of age, Hunter possessed good health and vigor. He had lived a clean and active life and reaped the benefits of his lifestyle in his later years. One officer observed that Hunter's "still white and perfect teeth give evidence of a stomach never disarranged by strong potations, a mouth never misused as a receptacle for tobacco or its fumes." Hunter stood five feet, eight inches tall and possessed broad and powerful shoulders, a deep chest and sinewy arms and legs. His face was "swarthy and Indian-like," with gray eyes that dilated "into blackness and brilliancy" when excited. He was, in fact, a down-to-earth officer who preferred "comfort instead of show" in his choice of uniform. On the campaign, he donned "a pair of government trousers and shoes, lined coat and an old black slouch hat, penetrated with air holes." Major Charles Halpine summed the general up as a "finer ideal of a veteran soldier."[7] Not everyone agreed with that assessment. An enlisted man described his new commander as "a large dark visaged stern man of severe aspect; a man not at all of a sympathetic or genial disposition."[8]

The "Lost Cause" mythos portrayed Hunter as a renegade Virginian who went against his family and state, but nothing could be further from the truth. His grandfather emigrated from Ireland sometime before 1750, while his father, Andrew, was born in York, Pennsylvania. Andrew became a prominent Presbyterian minister, an ardent patriot and a chaplain in the Continental army during the Revolutionary War. His mother was Mary Stockton, the daughter of New Jersey's Richard Stockton, a signer of the Declaration of Independence. As for the general himself, he was born a full-blooded Northerner on July 21, 1802, in Princeton, New Jersey. He had a sister and a brother, Lewis, who was a surgeon in the U.S. Navy during the Civil War.[9]

Hunter graduated from West Point in 1822, ranked twenty-fifth out of forty cadets, and received a commission in the 5th U.S. Infantry. In 1833, he became a captain in the 1st U.S. Dragoons serving with future Confederate president Jefferson Davis. Comrades dubbed Hunter "Black Dave" due to his jet-black hair and dark complexion. As Hunter aged, his hair maintained its ebony hue, convincing colleagues that he dyed it to preserve its color. During the Mexican-American War, Hunter served as General Zachary Taylor's paymaster throughout the conflict, a role that continued for many years in the postwar army. While stationed at Fort Leavenworth, he witnessed the growing sectional strife during the "Bleeding Kansas" crisis.[10]

Politically, Hunter had been a Whig and then a Republican in an army dominated by Democrats. As a result, he considered himself "persecuted on account of my love of Freedom and the Whig and Republican parties." Upon Abraham Lincoln's election to the presidency, Hunter corresponded with the president-elect, expressing concern for his safety and security with open talk of assassination brewing among fire-eating Southerners. Lincoln invited Hunter to serve on his security detail during the train ride from Illinois to Washington. Hunter also secured the White House with a makeshift militia, sleeping on the floor of the East Room in the early days of the Lincoln administration. In an army dominated by Democrats, Hunter's Republican ideology and association with Lincoln secured a commission as the fourth highest-ranking general of the volunteer army.[11]

At the First Battle of Bull Run, a Southern bullet removed Hunter from the battle early on and allowed him to largely avoid the stigma of defeat. Upon recovery, Lincoln subsequently appointed him to commands in Missouri and then Kansas. In March 1862, Lincoln appointed Hunter to command the Department of the South, which encompassed South Carolina, Georgia and Florida. In the only major military operation conceived during his tenure, his forces failed to capture a Confederate stronghold at Secessionville, South Carolina. His term oversaw the successful reduction and capture of Fort Pulaski on the Savannah River, but Hunter left his mark more so by his actions on behalf of his department's enslaved African American populace. On May 9, 1862, Hunter brashly abolished slavery in his department, but Lincoln nullified the zealous abolitionist's proclamation ten days later. Ironically, Lincoln issued the Emancipation Proclamation just four months later. Hunter also organized the first regiment of African American troops, the 1st South Carolina Infantry, composed of freed slaves in the department. Lincoln attempted to dissolve the unit, but Radical Republicans in Congress interceded on behalf of the 1st South Carolina and saved the unit. Before the war's end, 180,000 African Americans had served the Union cause. As a result of Hunter's premature emancipation declaration and the creation of a black regiment, the Confederates declared Hunter a "felon to be executed if captured."[12]

Hunter's tenure in the Department of the South revealed the stormy side of his personality and shortcomings in his military ability. In late 1862 and early 1863, Hunter received the support from Major General John Foster, commanding the neighboring Department of North Carolina. Hunter then used his political influence to wrench control of Foster's troops and have Foster returned to his own department. Hunter also ran afoul in his dealings with Captain Samuel F. DuPont, commander of the naval forces cooperating with Hunter's operations, complaining bitterly to the Lincoln administration on several occasions. Lincoln soon tired of Hunter's rants and admonished: "I would dare to make a suggestion; I would say you are adopting the best possible way to ruin yourself. Act well your part, there all the honor lies."[13]

Finally, after a year of few accomplishments and much complaining, the administration relieved Hunter of command. In the fall of 1863, the War Department sent Hunter to Chattanooga to monitor Grant's actions in lifting the Confederate siege there. The two men hit it off and quickly became confidants, with Hunter commending Grant in his reports to Washington. Hunter also acted as an unofficial inspector and afterward presided over the court of inquiry investigating the conduct of several general officers at Chickamauga. Hunter's association with Grant was a second key factor in his subsequent reassignment to a combat command in the valley, making him an ally of not only the president but also the future commanding general of the United States Army.[14]

Although still mingling with the Union's high commanders, Hunter yearned for another combat command. In February 1864, he asked Secretary of War Stanton, "Please give me command of one of the corps in the Army of the Potomac." Hunter apparently had overplayed his hand, and nothing came of the request. However, by April Grant had entrusted Hunter to deliver personal messages to Mrs. Julia Grant and to act as Grant's eyes and ears in Nathaniel Banks's Department of the Gulf on the heels of the disastrous Red River Campaign.[15] The latter assignment had placed Hunter in New Orleans on May 2, where he wrote his report on the situation to Grant. By May 16, the day after Sigel's New Market defeat, Hunter reached Grant's headquarters near Spotsylvania and personally briefed him on the situation in the Gulf. Given Hunter's ensuing appointment to command in the Shenandoah, the two men surely must have discussed the situation in the valley. Two days later, Grant asked Secretary of War Stanton to replace Sigel. When Stanton suggested Hunter as the German's replacement, Grant "heartily assented."[16]

Hunter has gone down in history largely as a tyrant or arch villain. However, this image was, and still is in some quarters, overly influenced by the hard war that he conducted against the Confederacy. His advocation of the emancipation of slaves and usage of African Americans as combat troops made him a pariah not only in the South but in Northern Democratic circles as well. However, like anyone, there were many aspects to Hunter's personality. His good friend Charles G. Halpine recalled that Hunter was "of sensitive and choleric tempers" and possessed "a heart overflowing with kindliness, though liable to sudden fits of rage." A naval officer who had worked with Hunter in South Carolina echoed that same sentiment, noting that Hunter was "both gentle and fierce." Upon Hunter's arrival in the valley, Colonel George D. Wells of the 34th Massachusetts found Hunter to be "very kindly and pleasant."[17]

From Washington, Major General Henry Halleck telegraphed Grant's blueprint for operations in the Shenandoah Valley. Grant instructed Hunter to clear the valley of Confederate forces and eliminate Staunton as a logistical center for Lee's Army of Northern Virginia by destroying the town's workshops and factories along with the coveted Virginia Central Railroad. If Hunter accomplished that, Grant then wanted Hunter to cross the Blue Ridge and raid Charlottesville and Gordonsville. There Hunter was to do more damage to the Virginia Central and Orange & Alexandria Railroads, severing Confederate supply lines and communications between Richmond and the valley. However, upon the heels of Sigel's debacle, Grant would consider it "good Service" if Hunter simply held an equal Confederate force at bay in the valley.[18]

Immediately upon assuming command, Hunter assessed his officer corps and did not like the findings. Major General Julius Stahel-Szamvald led the Army of the Shenandoah's mounted arm, and if anything happened to Hunter, Stahel was next in line to command the army. Born in Szeged, Hungary, in 1825, he joined the Austrian Army as a private and rose to the rank of lieutenant. He joined the revolutionary forces in the unsuccessful 1848 Hungarian uprising and was forced to flee his native land. Stahel lived abroad for some time but eventually settled in New York City, where he found employment with a German-language newspaper. When the war broke out, he became colonel of the all-German 8th New York Infantry. By 1862, he had risen to brigade command and suffered the indignation of having the 8th New York nearly annihilated at the Battle of Cross Keys, fought at the Second Battle of Bull Run and eventually rose to division command in the 11th Corps. More recently, he had ineptly led Sigel's cavalry at New Market contributing much toward that defeat.

Hunter's infantry commander, Brigadier General Jeremiah Cutler Sullivan, had amassed a mundane record thus far in the war. Lieutenant Colonel William Lincoln of the 34th Massachusetts first met Sullivan at Thanksgiving dinner in Harper's Ferry. With his "large size, stout build…

Major General Julius Stahel, the much-maligned Union cavalry leader who exceeded expectations at Piedmont and was later given the Medal of Honor for his services in that battle. *Library of Congress.*

and a keen black eye," Sullivan "looked more the soldier than he actually is," observed Lincoln. Born the son of an Indiana Supreme Court justice, Sullivan grew up and attended school in Madison, Indiana. He later joined the United States Navy in 1848, serving a stint aboard the USS *Constitution*. He resigned in 1854 and returned to Indiana to practice law until the Civil War erupted. Before 1864, his military career was lackluster at best, with his most in-depth action coming at the Battle of Iuka, Mississippi, in 1862. After being relieved of command in the West, Sullivan was transferred to his current position, which he owed to his father-in-law, Major General Benjamin F. Kelley, Sigel's predecessor in the Department of West Virginia.

The shortcomings of both Stahel and Sullivan were obvious to Hunter, and he wanted them replaced. Shortly after arriving at Belle Grove, Hunter telegraphed Halleck: "If you can send me two energetic and efficient brigadiers it will add greatly to the availability of this command." He also requested

Brigadier General Jeremiah Sullivan commanded Hunter's infantry at Piedmont and was likely seeking a measure of redemption, as some in the army had questioned his leadership during Sigel's brief campaign. *USAMHI.*

a promotion to brigadier general for Major Samuel Stockton a member of Hunter's staff. On May 22, Hunter wired Halleck once more, emphasizing Stahel's deficiencies: "Our cavalry is utterly demoralized from frequent defeats by inferior forces and retreats without fighting, and it most urgently needs a commander of grit, zeal, activity and courage." He added, "It would be impossible to exaggerate the inefficiency of General Stahel."[19] Two days later, Halleck replied, "Energetic and efficient brigadiers are scarce. Name any you want who are available and you shall have them." He added that there were no vacant positions for promoting Stockton. Hunter quickly realized that no one was available and was forced to undertake his campaign with the personnel at hand. However, as Hunter noted in his original dispatch to Halleck, his army contained several "excellent colonels" at the brigade level.[20]

In the infantry, German-born Colonel Augustus Moor provided some of the veteran leadership, experience and initiative that Sullivan lacked. Major Theodore F. Lang of Hunter's staff observed that Moor was "an intelligent and efficient officer and gallant soldier who was well liked by officers and men." He had received military training at the Royal Academy of Forestry in Germany and was actively involved in democratic activities aimed at the ruling monarchy. The latter resulted in an eight-month prison sentence and two-year banishment from the fatherland. Upon release from prison, Moor immigrated to the United States, settling in Philadelphia. During Florida's Second Seminole Indian War, he served as an officer in a Philadelphia

Dragoon Company. He subsequently moved to Cincinnati, where he opened Moor's Garden, a popular bakery, coffeehouse and tavern. He also joined the local militia and founded the city's German Democratic Club, gaining prominence among Cincinnati's burgeoning German population. During the Mexican-American War, he saw action under both Zachary Taylor and Winfield Scott and rose to the rank of colonel. After the war, Moor returned to his family and prosperous business in Cincinnati until the outbreak of the Civil War.[21]

In 1861, Moor organized the 2nd German Regiment (or 28th Ohio Infantry) and led it through the 1861 West Virginia campaigns. He rose to brigade command in 1862 but was captured while leading an advance patrol during the Battle of South Mountain. After returning to West Virginia, Moor experienced his greatest tactical success of the war leading his small brigade in a victorious charge in November 1863 at the Battle of Droop Mountain, the largest ever fought in West Virginia.[22] During the New Market Campaign, Sigel broke up Moor's brigade and sent his reduced force twenty miles in advance of the main army. Moor knew that Sigel had committed a "great mistake" in splitting his force but dutifully followed orders. He drove Confederate cavalry from New Market and waited for Sigel to arrive. When he finally showed up, he posted his main force beyond supporting distance of Moor. The Confederates attacked and drove his outnumbered force from the field in confusion. Although Sigel was a fellow German, Moor mockingly described Sigel's efforts as a case of "beautiful management." When Hunter assumed command, Moor's responsibilities increased as his brigade was strengthened so that it contained nearly two-thirds of the army's entire infantry strength.[23]

Hunter's second infantry brigadier was Colonel Joseph Thoburn, born in County Antrim, Ireland, in 1825. As a child, his family immigrated to America and settled on a farm near Saint Clairsville, Ohio, not far from the Ohio River. He had no military training or experience before the Civil War but had attended medical school and ultimately established his own practice at Wheeling, Virginia, in 1853. There he became a respected physician, highly regarded by all in the partisan border state atmosphere of Wheeling. When war came in 1861, Thoburn enlisted as the regimental surgeon for the 1st Virginia (U.S.) Infantry (three months' service).[24]

When that regiment reenlisted for three years, its soldiers chose the popular Thoburn to be their colonel. He had gained familiarity with the Shenandoah Valley in 1862 when he led his regiment against Stonewall Jackson in battles at Kernstown and Port Republic, receiving a serious wound in the former engagement.[25] After serving in Major General John Pope's Army of Virginia at the Second Battle of Bull Run, he returned to West Virginia to protect the vital B&O Railroad and chase down Confederate raiders and partisans in the fall of 1862. In 1864, he returned to the Shenandoah under Sigel as an acting brigadier at New Market, where his troops covered the retreat and endured heavy losses.[26]

In the cavalry, Hunter had a rising star initially leading his first brigade. Colonel William B. Tibbits was born in 1837 at Hoosick Falls, New York. He graduated from Union College and became intricately involved in the area's growing manufacturing industry. At the outbreak of the war, he recruited a company that became part of the 2nd New York Infantry. He fought at Big Bethel in 1861 and subsequently received a promotion to major. He participated in the Peninsula Campaign, Second Bull Run, Fredericksburg and Chancellorsville and was then mustered out when his two-year enlistment expired. In February 1864, Tibbits returned to duty as colonel of the newly raised 21st New York Cavalry, a unit that included many veteran soldiers. Unfortunately, the pedestrian Colonel Andrew McReynolds of the 1st New York Lincoln Cavalry (1st New York hereafter) returned to the army after the battle and superseded Tibbits as the brigade commander due to seniority to the detriment of the Union cause.[27]

Hunter also possessed several talented officers at the regimental level, such as colonels Jacob Campbell, 54th Pennsylvania, and William D. Wells, 34th Massachusetts, as well as a competent staff that would play a key role in what promised to be an arduous campaign. Hunter appointed his trusted friend Lieutenant Colonel Charles G. Halpine assistant adjutant general. The general's nephew, Lieutenant Samuel Stockton, served as Hunter's aide-de-camp. The capable Lieutenant John R. Meigs, who had graduated at the top of the West Point class of 1863, stayed on board as the army's chief engineer and cartographer. He was also the son of General Montgomery Meigs, the quartermaster general of the U.S. Army. But the most influential member of Hunter's staff was David H. Strother, the newly appointed chief of staff.[28]

Strother played an influential role as Hunter's confidant throughout the campaign, more so than any other officer in the army. Strother's knowledge of the Shenandoah Valley's topography and people provided the Union a most valuable asset. He also displayed a strategic vision that guided the course of Hunter's campaign. Strother, a prewar artist and a native of Bath, Virginia (now Berkeley Springs, West Virginia), attempted to remain neutral at the outset of the war. Although he did not want to take up arms against the South, he openly sympathized with the Union. In 1861, Confederate authorities arrested Strother, as they considered his pencil and sketch pad the obvious equipment of a spy. On another occasion, a Confederate conscription detail appeared at Strother's door, but the Virginian promptly turned the men away with a loaded pistol. In the end, these incidents turned him from Northern sympathizer to Union soldier.[29]

Hunter quickly turned his attention to security matters and worked vigorously to eliminate the guerrilla attacks that plagued the army. He strengthened the picket line south of Cedar Creek, extending it east toward the Shenandoah River. To the west, mounted pickets patrolled the Back Road and scouted in the direction of Wardensville, West Virginia, to the west. Detachments of Stahel's cavalry covered the crossings of the Shenandoah River near Front Royal to alert the army of any Confederate movements out of the Luray Valley to the east. By Hunter's order, pickets detained any unauthorized civilians who came within the Union lines to limit espionage. It quickly became apparent that Hunter ran a much tighter ship than Sigel. Major Harry Gilmor, commander of the Confederate 2nd Maryland Cavalry Battalion, complained that Hunter "had his front so well picketed that I found it impractical to get through his lines." Instead, he made a circuitous march around Hunter and operated against Hunter's supply line between Middletown and Martinsburg.[30]

Hunter also convened a military court to rid the army of negligent and cowardly officers. A major and a captain of the 15th New York Cavalry, whose picket post was surprised and captured, found themselves cashiered from the service. As a warning to other potential scofflaws, Hunter decreed that "all officers commanding guards, outposts, and pickets will be held strictly responsible for the performance of their duties." He accepted no excuses from officers found guilty of negligence or misconduct before the enemy. He considered such actions "a crime against the whole command," which endangered "the lives of thousands of our fellow soldiers." Hunter also dishonorably discharged an officer from the shaky 12th West Virginia Infantry who had abandoned his command during the heat of combat at New Market. To some these measures seemed drastic, but the army's combat efficiency rendered them necessary.[31]

Hunter also recognized that discipline had been lacking under the benevolent Sigel and was determined to change that. Hunter challenged the mettle of his troops, telling them that

> [i]t is of the utmost importance that this army be placed in a situation for immediate efficiency. We are contending against an enemy who is in earnest,

and, if we expect success, we, too, must be in earnest. We must be willing to make sacrifices, willing to suffer for a short time, that a glorious result may crown our efforts. The country is expecting every man to do his duty; and this done, an ever kind Providence will certainly grant us complete success.

To that end, he modeled his army after the light marching forces led by Grant at Vicksburg and Sherman in Georgia. All tents and unnecessary baggage not explicitly permitted by orders were turned in and sent to Martinsburg for storage. He allowed only one wagon per regiment to "transport spare ammunition, camp kettles, tools and mess-pans." Every soldier would carry one hundred rounds of ammunition in his knapsack, along with an extra pair of shoes and socks, rations and "nothing else." Hunter's army would also live off the bounty of the Shenandoah Valley to limit the amount of food and forage that had to be carried.[32]

This order created stir among the rank and file of Hunter's army and highlighted his stylistic differences with Sigel. One staff officer noted: "The troops are very much dissatisfied at losing General Sigel."[33] For the enlisted men, this order convinced some that Hunter governed the army with an "iron hand." Private Charles Lynch of the 18th Connecticut and his comrades thought him rather "stern looking" and concluded: "We don't like his looks."[34] Colonel Thoburn observed that there was not one hundred rounds of ammunition per man available and concluded that although "Hunter appears to be very energetic and active…he has spoken too fast. He begins to work before he knows the material he has to work with." However, as noted by Captain Henry A. DuPont of Battery B, 5th U.S. Light Artillery, once Hunter "made up his mind either as to present events or as to a forecast of those to come, he never swerved, and nothing but the cold logic of accomplished facts could induce him to modify his opinions in the slightest degree."[35]

Colonel George Duncan Wells, commander of the 34th Massachusetts Infantry, sensed some discord among his troops as a result of Hunter's orders. Wells explained: "Great things are expected of this army. You will be expected to conduct yourselves as usual and keep you[r] former reputation." He then noted that when the army left Strasburg, "its communications will be cut off with the outer world. The valley is abundantly supplied with food for the Southern army and he [Hunter] is resolved to subsist this army on a portion of it and destroy the rest." Much to the soldiers' satisfaction, Wells declared that "cattle and hogs will stand but a slim chance if they come near us." He assured the men that "[t]he officers and myself will live as you live and die as you die. Whatever we get you will share with us." After hearing Wells, the Bay State soldiers well understood their mission and called for "[t]hree cheers for Wells, Thoburn and Hunter, and we are off for Lynchburg!"[36]

As in all campaigns, logistics played a major role in Hunter's advance. Hunter planned to rely on foraging to feed his army, but clothing, ammunition and other important supplies came from his supply depot. In spring of 1864, the Army of the Shenandoah used Martinsburg, West Virginia, as its supply base. Its location astride the Baltimore & Ohio Railroad and the macadamized Valley Turnpike made it the ideal spot for supplying Union troops in the Shenandoah Valley. There the department's quartermaster corps had

Captain Henry A. DuPont, Hunter's young chief of artillery. *USAMHI.*

established extensive warehouses that the railroad kept filled with supplies for the army. Harper's Ferry also served as an ancillary supply base.

From Martinsburg, the Federals transported supplies in wagon trains over the Valley Turnpike. The road had been preceded by an old Indian trail that was later developed into a rough wagon road. In 1834, the Valley Turnpike Company was incorporated to construct a sixty-eight-mile pike from Winchester to Harrisonburg for Shenandoah Valley farmers to haul crops and livestock to the markets. A second company undertook a similar project between Harrisonburg and Staunton, and the two ventures ultimately merged, forming a ninety-three-mile turnpike. By the time of the Civil War, the road extended from the Potomac River to Lexington in the southern extreme of the valley. The builders constructed the road's surface from a macadamized or crushed-stone surface, which lent itself well to the passage of wagons, even in poor weather. Not many army commanders had the good fortune to possess a dependable supply route such as Hunter had.[37]

The pike had one significant drawback—guerrilla activity. The macadam road ran through forested patches and rolling areas that furnished partisans with excellent opportunities to strike at Federal supply trains. These Confederate guerrillas preyed on small groups of Union soldiers and wagon trains. Earlier in May, Captain Hanse McNeill and Colonel John Singleton Mosby successfully distracted Sigel from his primary mission and significantly delayed the German's progress. As the Federal forces advanced south, the supply line lengthened and, with it, the odds of a guerrilla attack. Aside from large detachments to guard the wagons, which also reduced combat strength, no effective means existed to stop the unseen but deadly bushwhackers. Constant vigilance and large escorts provided Federal soldiers and supply trains the only true means of protection on the Valley Pike.

On May 23, a small party of Confederate horsemen attacked a Union wagon train rolling up the Valley Pike as it passed through Newtown. After a brief exchange of gunfire, the partisans retreated after the wounding of a sergeant of the 28th Ohio Infantry. When Hunter learned of the incident, he sent Major Timothy Quinn's 1st New York (Lincoln) Cavalry to Newtown to exact retribution for the attack. Quinn ascertained the houses from which the train was fired upon, burned them and distributed a warning from Hunter:

> *You are hereby notified that for every train fired upon, or soldier of the Union wounded or assassinated by bushwhackers in any neighborhood in reach of my cavalry, the houses and other property of every secession sympathizer residing within a circuit of five miles from the place of the outrage shall be destroyed by fire.*

Fortunately for the people of Newtown, Quinn only burned three homes that day. Tales of Hunter's penchant for burning homes quickly spread throughout the Shenandoah Valley, invoking fear among the civilian populace.[38]

In an effort to smooth things over with Hunter, four respected men of Newtown requested a meeting with him at Belle Grove Plantation. Sentries halted them at the Federal picket line and sent word of the townsmen's arrival to Hunter's headquarters. Hunter dispatched his newly appointed chief of staff, Colonel Strother, to meet with them on the picket line. The men apprised Strother that only one of the burned homes destroyed belonged to a known guerrilla. Strother said nothing but handed them Hunter's broadside warning of the consequences to towns in which guerrilla activity took place. Strother warned that the only way to avoid Hunter's wrath was to indicate who the guilty parties were. The men immediately identified the attackers as members of Major Harry Gilmor's unruly 2nd Maryland Cavalry Battalion, a semiregular unit that operated in the valley. In particular, the townsmen named Captains George E. Shearer and W.Y. Glenn. These Marylanders had terrorized the residents of the area and had already been the source of complaints to the Confederate authorities. The townsmen further informed Strother of Mrs. Wilson, who had allowed the partisans to use the house that she rented as a gathering point.[39]

Many residents of the Lower Shenandoah Valley disdained these unruly Marylanders. In August 1863, seventeen Winchester residents sent a letter of protest to the Confederate government regarding the Marylanders' unruly behavior. The Confederate civilians wrote that Gilmor's command rode "about the country in small parties very frequently intoxicated, many of them stealing horses, or whatever else they may want, sometimes arresting citizens, and in fact doing as much, if not more injury to us than the Federals." Perhaps the citizens of Newtown secretly hoped that Hunter might have accomplished what the Confederacy failed to do.[40]

Returning to headquarters, Strother briefed Hunter on the meeting. Not surprisingly, Hunter immediately ordered the arrest of Mrs. Wilson. A Federal contingent arrived at her leased dwelling and then arrested and charged her with feeding and harboring guerrillas. When the Federals removed her furniture and personal belongings from the house, she and her daughter readily assisted them and thanked the officer for removing her possessions before burning the home. To her utter astonishment and dismay, the Union troopers, who knew that she was simply a tenant and not the property owner, promptly set the furniture aflame. Mrs. Wilson then walked the six miles back to the Federal camp, where she was placed in the custody of the provost marshal along with several others who had been detained as a security precaution after they had entered the Union lines.[41]

The man initially charged with stopping Hunter was John Daniel Imboden, who was born in 1823 near Fishersville in Augusta County, Virginia, and grew up in the heart of the valley. In 1849, he attended Washington College in Lexington for two years and then taught at the Virginia Institute for the

Brigadier General John D. Imboden, commander of the Valley District, suddenly found himself facing long odds when Hunter quickly resumed the offensive. *Library of Congress.*

Education of the Deaf, Dumb and Blind in Staunton. He studied law and subsequently started his own practice and served two terms in the Virginia House of Delegates. In 1861, Imboden campaigned to represent the Staunton area at the Virginia Secession Convention. However, his fervent pro-secession stance led to defeat in this strongly Unionists section of Virginia.[42]

When secession and war ultimately came, Imboden signed on as captain of the Staunton Artillery and fought bravely at First Manassas. In the winter of 1861–62, he raised the 1st Virginia Partisan Rangers among the highly divided populace of the Allegheny Mountains, leading it in Jackson's 1862 Valley Campaign. This unit ultimately formed the foundation for the regiments that became Imboden's Brigade. It consisted primarily of the 18th and 23rd Virginia Cavalry, the 62nd Virginia Mounted Infantry and McClanahan's Battery of horse artillery. Promoted to brigadier general in January 1863, Imboden cooperated with Brigadier General William E. Jones in a successful raid into Union-held West Virginia during the spring of 1863. Imboden made his greatest contribution to the Southern war effort during the Confederate retreat from Gettysburg. He fended off pursuing Federal cavalry who had attempted to capture Lee's wagon train while it was stranded on the northern bank of the rain-swollen Potomac River. As a reward, General Lee appointed Imboden commander of the Valley District, a position the latter considered a great honor, as Stonewall Jackson was the district's first commander. In the spring of 1864, Imboden harassed and successfully delayed Sigel's advance up the valley. His actions bought Breckinridge the time needed to concentrate the forces that carried the day at New Market.

Now, with Breckinridge having left the valley, Imboden soon found himself in the same situation, facing an advancing Federal army with few resources to oppose it.[43]

With Breckinridge now in Lee's army, the Confederate War Department sought a suitable replacement for the Department of Western Virginia and Eastern Tennessee. The ranking officer in that department, Brigadier General William E. Jones, remained uncertain of his position. On May 20, at his headquarters near Abingdon, Virginia, Jones received a telegram from General Samuel Cooper ordering the retention of Brigadier General John C. Vaughn's Tennessee cavalry brigade in the department. The tone of the order implied that Jones was the acting commander of the department but failed to enumerate any specifics. To clarify the situation, Jones telegraphed Cooper: "Must I assume command of the Department of Western Virginia?"[44] Cooper ordered Jones to take command of the Department of Western Virginia and Eastern Tennessee, and he promptly set about to fulfill his duties.[45]

Born on the middle fork of the Holston River on May 9, 1824, William Edmondson Jones grew to manhood in Washington County, Virginia, near the Tennessee border. During the American Revolution, his Edmondson forebears had been "Overmountain" men who had turned the tide of that conflict at the Battle of Kings Mountain in 1780. Jones grew up learning the tough ways that allowed the Appalachian pioneers to survive in the rugged mountain terrain. At the same time, he received an extensive education at Emory and Henry College before attending West Point; he graduated from the U.S. Military Academy in 1848, ranked twelfth out of forty-eight cadets. One Confederate officer observed that Jones had "a fine squeaking voice, was misanthropic despising parade and every man that indulged in it; never courting any man's favor."[46]

After spending three years in Oregon as a lieutenant in the U.S. Army, the young officer returned home to marry Eliza Dunn. On the return trip to Jones's new duty post, the young couple was sailing from New Orleans to Texas when a violent storm wrecked their ship. When they attempted to land in a lifeboat, a wave swept Eliza from the small vessel. Only the heroism of Thomas B. Edmondson, the lieutenant's cousin, saved Jones from the same fate. The whirling waters literally washed away his dreams and hopes for a long and happy life together with his wife. Eliza's body was recovered and buried at Glade Spring Presbyterian Church back in southwest Virginia. Stunned by his tragic loss, Jones returned to his post with a heavy heart. The young widower immersed himself in his duty in order to avoid the pain of his loss and became "embittered, complaining and suspicious." He eventually became known to comrades as "Old Grumble Jones" and could

Brigadier General William E. "Grumble" Jones, the West Point graduate and commander of Confederate forces at Piedmont who lost his life attempting to rally his broken troops. *William Turner Collection.*

be "a disagreeable customer when crossed." Finally, in September 1856, he resigned from the army and returned to his estate on the Holston River.[47]

Politically, Jones strongly believed in antebellum Southern society and states' rights, seeing slavery as an economic necessity beneficial to both master and slave. In 1857, Jones visited Europe on military business for the State of Virginia, arranging for the procurement of arms in case of sectional conflict, which Jones believed would soon engulf the United States. When John Brown raided Harper's Ferry in an attempt to stimulate a slave insurrection in 1859, Jones urged Virginians to revitalize the commonwealth's ability to defend itself through military means. "It is as much our duty to prepare for the coming dangers," declared Jones, "as to defend our assailed rights and none but the obstinate blind can fail to see the dangers great and most horrible in our future."[48]

When the war broke out in 1861, Jones raised a company of cavalry from Washington County christened the Washington Mounted Rifles and served as its first captain. The company joined Colonel James E.B. "Jeb" Stuart's 1st Virginia Cavalry Regiment and took part in the First Battle of Bull Run under Jones's able guidance. He ultimately rose to the rank of colonel, but in

April 1862, Jones fell out of favor with Stuart, and the regiment voted him out of office due to his harsh disciplinary practices and embittered attitude. With competent officers in short supply, Jones soon received an appointment as the colonel of the 7th Virginia Cavalry in July 1862, replacing the fallen Turner Ashby. Jones instilled discipline in Ashby's rowdy horsemen and displayed the aggressive streak that Stonewall Jackson admired. In early August, Jones encountered and attacked a vastly superior force at Orange Courthouse. He reported, "No time could be afforded for inquiries—to fight or run were the only alternatives; I chose the former."[49]

By September, Confederate authorities had promoted him to brigadier general at the request of Stonewall Jackson. The latter had Jones placed in command of the Valley District, but his personality and military ways elicited complaints from local civilian leaders. In May 1863, the crotchety Virginian led his brigade on a raid into Union-held West Virginia in a joint mission with Imboden. This highly successful raid destroyed sixteen railroad bridges and two trains, seized one thousand head of cattle and 1,200 horses and captured seven hundred prisoners. Upon returning to Virginia, Jones rejoined Stuart's cavalry with the Army of Northern Virginia near Culpeper Courthouse. On June 9, his vigilance at Brandy Station while Stuart conducted a dress parade saved the cavalry from defeat. Jones's command withstood repeated Union assaults and played a decisive role in preventing disaster there. However, his icy relations with Stuart continued. When Jones warned Stuart of approaching Union troopers, the cavalry chief replied, "Tell General Jones to attend to the Federals in his front, and I'll watch the flanks." When Jones received the reply, he snarled, "So he thinks they ain't coming, does he? Well, let him alone, he'll damned soon see for himself."[50]

Jones attempted to resign from the service instead of continuing his service under Stuart, but General Lee withheld the resignation. Nevertheless, Jones continued his consistently dependable efforts throughout the Gettysburg Campaign. Although Stuart purposely assigned the capable Jones to rear echelon duty, he effectively led his brigade in several combats throughout the campaign, including actions at Upperville and Fairfield. His command twice crossed swords with the 6th U.S. Cavalry during the campaign. After inflicting 242 casualties on that regiment and defeating it on two separate occasions, Jones wryly reported, "The Sixth U.S. Cavalry numbers among the things that were."[51]

Jones's feud with Stuart boiled over as Lee's army returned from Gettysburg. Jones took exception with something that Stuart did and wrote his commander "a very disrespectful letter." In spite of their differences,

Stuart had considered Jones "the best outpost officer" in the Army of Northern Virginia. Stuart recognized that Jones's "watchfulness over his pickets and his skill and energy in obtaining information were worthy of all praise." Stuart's praises for Jones were matched only by his desire to have him removed from his command. When he received Jones's letter, Stuart promptly relieved Jones of his command and placed him under "close arrest." This incident resulted in a court-martial and ended Jones's service with the Army of Northern Virginia.[52]

In the aftermath of the court-martial, General Lee wrote to Confederate president Jefferson C. Davis:

> *I consider Jones a brave and intelligent officer, but his feelings have become so opposed to General Stuart that I have lost all hope of his being useful in the cavalry here…he says he will no longer serve under Stuart and I do not think it would be advantageous for him to do so, but I wish to make him useful.[53]*

As a result of Lee's recommendation, the Confederate War Department assigned Jones to east Tennessee. There he received command of a brigade of undisciplined Virginia cavalry regiments. Jones instilled these men with discipline and drastically improved their combat efficiency. In November, Jones routed a Union force at Rogersville, Tennessee, capturing 700 prisoners with their wagons and equipment. On January 2, 1864, Jones captured 385 men and three pieces of artillery by surrounding a Federal force at Jonesville, Virginia. During February, his troopers defeated the 11th Tennessee (U.S.) Cavalry at Wyerman's Mill and apprehended 265 Union soldiers, eight wagons and one hundred horses. The *Richmond Whig* declared Jones to be the "Stonewall Jackson of East Tennessee," aptly summing up his abilities as a leader of men.[54]

Jones had built his reputation with vigilance using scouts and patrols to obtain accurate information on enemy movements. He quickly assessed the situation and then aggressively went on the offensive, never ceding the initiative and hoping that his own celerity would catch his opponents with their guard down. From Orange Courthouse to Wyerman's Mill, Jones had done just that. Most of the time, his belligerence was rewarded with success and outright failure was unknown. In the Shenandoah Valley, Hunter's advance placed Jones and his methods to the ultimate test against a rejuvenated opponent intent on victory. No longer would Jones be leading a brigade or two of cavalry. For the first time in the Civil War, Jones was leading a combined arms force in which the infantry, not the cavalry, would be the primary combat arm.

Chapter 2

"We Shall Get This Road Pretty Well Learn't"

Late on May 23, Grant informed Hunter that Breckinridge's Division had indeed joined Lee in the defense of Richmond. This information eliminated any doubt as to the strength, or more appropriately the weakness, of the Confederate force opposing Hunter in the valley. Breckinridge, by virtue of his decision to join Lee's army, had forfeited the initiative won at New Market. Eager to add some luster to his tarnished reputation, Hunter grabbed the initiative and determined to advance on May 26. In accordance with Grant's wishes, Staunton was the Union army's immediate objective, and Hunter hoped to reach it without a fight. Once there, he intended to join forces with George Crook's little Army of the Kanawha, which still remained one hundred miles away near Lewisburg, West Virginia, awaiting supplies.[55]

The soldiers of the Army of the Shenandoah awoke early on the morning of May 26, 1864. An overcast sky infused the men with feelings of gloom as they ate breakfast and packed their equipment for the march. As the army moved out from its camps around Belle Grove, the temperature and the humidity rose with the morning sun. At eight o'clock, the 1st New York Cavalry trotted out ahead of the main army to screen the advance, accompanied by a company of mounted pioneers and a section of horse artillery. Thirty minutes later, Stahel followed with the main body of his cavalry division, and Sullivan's infantry and DuPont's artillery marched in column behind the horsemen. With half rations and one hundred rounds of ammunition to the man, the Army of the Shenandoah set out on an excursion up the Shenandoah Valley for the second time in less than one month. That their commander was subject to execution if captured symbolized the desperation felt by Unionists in 1864.[56]

The column moved south along the familiar Valley Turnpike, which many of the men had traveled before with Sigel, Milroy, Fremont and other such men. Private Chapin Warner of the 34th Massachusetts quipped, "I think we shall get this road pretty well learnt." The 2nd Maryland Eastern Shore's Colonel Robert S. Rodgers observed, "The trees are in full leaf and the fertile fields are covered with thick white and red clover." The blue hues of Massanutten Mountain highlighted the eastern horizon with the sparkling clear waters of the Shenandoah River running along the base of the mountain. The troops noticed several fertile and well-kept farms as they journeyed southward. Colonel George Wells of the 34th Massachusetts described the scene as "lovelier than a dream." Beautiful while it lasted, the serene setting quickly gave way to the ugliness of war. Hunter ordered the burning of the Borden farmhouse to retaliate for the murder of five Union soldiers by Confederate partisans at that location.[57]

The army then marched through Strasburg, where the residents stood gazing sullenly at the United States' soldiers. Only a few "shrill-tongued females" dared to speak up. They reminded the blue-coated soldiers of the fate of their predecessors: "We've seen men with your colored clothes go up this valley afore; and we've seen 'em come back this way a mighty sight faster than they went up." Most of Hunter's troops had been up the valley at least once, and the cold truth behind such comments likely inspired many to resolve to make this journey different than any prior Union excursion in the Shenandoah. The army marched nine more miles until it reached Pugh's Run, where it camped in the fields along the banks of that stream two miles north of Woodstock.[58] While on the march, Hunter received Grant's expanded vision for operations in the valley. He directed Hunter "to push on if possible to Charlottesville and Lynchburg and destroy railroads and [the James River] canal beyond possibility of repair for weeks" and then to either "join Grant via Gordonsville" or return to the valley. Grant further instructed Hunter to "live as much as possible on the country" in an effort to deplete Confederate resources in the Shenandoah Valley.[59]

While the Union army camped at Pugh's Run, Imboden informed the Confederate War Department in Richmond of the renewed Federal offensive. He believed that Sigel still commanded the U.S. Army of the Shenandoah and promised to give him "the best fight my means afford." Imboden's means, however, were very limited at the time, and he could do no more than screen Hunter's advance until reinforcements arrived. The next day, Imboden telegraphed General Lee and informed him of the long odds facing the Southern troops in the valley: "There is no point this side of Mount Crawford where I can successfully resist him, and there it is very doubtful, though I will do my best." Alarmed, Lee notified Imboden, "Keep commanding officer in Southwestern Virginia [Jones] informed of enemy's movements in this district, and co-operate in driving him back." Although Imboden lacked the manpower to seriously contest the Federal advance, logistical problems soon slowed Hunter's progress.[60]

When the army went into camp along Pugh's Run, Hunter realized that many of his soldiers had marched without shoes, one officer placing the number at two thousand men. The day's march had brought them great suffering; a sergeant from the 116th Ohio told his family that "it was really a pitiful sight to see them marching along, leaving marks of blood on the ground."[61] Food and forage were also running short even at this early stage of the campaign. To rectify the situation, Hunter detailed men from each regiment to gather wheat and grind it into flour at local mills, issuing it to the troops. The soldiers mixed the flour with water, forming bread dough, which they wrapped around their bayonets and baked over a campfire. Forage parties also seized cattle from the local farms, drove them to the camp, slaughtered them and distributed the meat among the troops. The foragers also brought a number of fine dairy cows into camp that produced gallons of milk and cream for the enjoyment of the officers and a few privileged men.[62]

Horses for the cavalry and wagon train were also in great demand, and Hunter's army procured them from the countryside, giving Unionists receipts for reimbursement and leaving the secessionists empty-handed. As far as the shoes were concerned, Hunter had no choice but to wait for a supply train from Martinsburg. While he waited, several army bands serenaded the sixty-one-year-old army commander while he watched from the porch of his headquarters in Woodstock. When they played "Just in Time for Lanigan's Ball," a quick-paced Irish tune, the irascible Hunter suddenly came to life. Frank Reader Smith, a headquarters orderly, recorded that "the old fellow skipped around over porch to it and it was real amusing." It was a human side of the general that the average soldier had not seen previously.[63]

Hunter's march up the valley stretched out his supply lines, which presented an inviting target to the Confederate raiders operating in the area. As fate would have it, partisans hit Hunter's supply lines at Newtown again. On May 29, Lieutenant Colonel Augustus J. Root and his detachment of eighty-three men from the 15th and 21st New York cavalry regiments escorted a small wagon train carrying supplies to the army from Martinsburg. A few miles north of Newtown, Confederate Major Harry Gilmor had concealed his fifty-three Marylanders in Barton's Woods, along the west side of the Valley Pike. Gilmor and his men watched Root's convoy roll past and then shadowed it to Newtown. Once the train was confined in the narrow streets of the village, Gilmor attacked. With many of his men dressed in blue to deceive the Federals, the Marylanders got exceedingly close to the wagons without detection and charged the rear of the convoy.[64]

Root wheeled his small rear guard into line of battle and fired at the Confederates. The New Yorkers stood their ground, but the Marylanders charged into their midst and fought with their sabers. The trains raced southward in confusion, and Root's rear guard followed rapidly. The trains made it across a "muddy run" south of Newtown, with the exception of two that overturned on the bridge. Root regrouped his men on the south side of the creek and repulsed Gilmor's lead company. However, Captain Nicholas Burke led a reserve company forward and drove off the Federals. Gilmor's men quickly overtook the train, plundered the wagons and set them afire. Gilmor also claimed the capture of thirty-three men and sixty horses. Root placed losses among his escort detachment at ten wounded and ten captured. The survivors retreated southward and encountered an empty wagon train headed back to Martinsburg escorted by Colonel Cyrus Reasoner's 160th Ohio Infantry.[65]

Reasoner had heard the firing and rushed his troops toward the scene of the attack. They found only burning wagons but salvaged a single wagon loaded with medical supplies. Root and Reasoner's commands camped at Newtown, and Gilmor remained in the area and attacked the camp guards early the next morning. A sharp encounter ensued, but the Ohioans drove the partisans off, losing one man wounded. The convoy then hurried to Martinsburg without incident.[66] News of the attack enraged Hunter, and he resolved to fulfill his promise to burn Newtown. "Black Dave" sent Major Jospeh Stearns with two hundred men from the 1st New York Cavalry to Newtown "for the purpose of burning every house, store and out-building in that place, except the churches and houses and out-buildings of those who are known to be loyal citizens of the United States." Hunter also exempted the home of Dr. Owens, who had tended to wounded U.S. soldiers after Gilmor's attack.[67]

The New Yorkers promptly rode out of camp in the predawn darkness of May 31, only a few select officers knowing their purpose. Most troopers simply speculated on the latest move. Major Stearns's battalion covered forty miles that day and bivouacked for the night along the banks of Cedar Creek. Early on June 1, Stearns revealed the purpose of the mission to the men, who sullenly rode toward Newtown, "more like a funeral procession than a marching army."

The enlisted men talked of nothing other than refusing to carry out Hunter's heinous order. When they reached the village, elderly citizens and young children stood in "mute helplessness" as the Federals rode past their homes.[68]

Stearns's arrival did not surprise the residents of Newtown, who had anxiously awaited the fiery consequences of Gilmor's attack. Before taking any action, Stearns conferred with Newtown's leading citizens. They informed the sympathetic major that they held no sway over the attacking Confederates and emphasized the kindness and care given to Federals wounded in Gilmor's attack. After talking to the men and hearing the mournful prayers of the tearful women, Stearns courageously spared the innocent people of Newtown from Hunter's vengeance. In return, the townspeople took an oath of allegiance to the United States. The New Yorkers then turned around and marched back to the army. When Stearns rejoined the army on June 2, he informed Hunter that he had refused to burn the town. Hunter launched a savage verbal barrage at Stearns, but in the end Strother convinced Hunter that Stearns had acted properly. Once they were away from the general, Strother even commended Stearns for his humanity and said that Hunter would get over it.[69]

Meanwhile, Hunter's army had resumed its march on the same day as the attack at Newtown. The heat and humidity made the soldiers miserable, and the road dust choked the men and clung to their sweaty skin. As the Northerners moved southward, hunger began to plague the army. One infantryman complained in his diary: "We were pretty hungry and had nothing to eat." Samuel Ely of the 20th Pennsylvania Cavalry lamented: "Rations scarce and if it were not for foraging parties we would starve." These teams swarmed through the bountiful agricultural country on both flanks of the army, herding in sheep, hogs and cattle to feed the troops.[70] Hunter's advance guard encountered Imboden's outposts at Rude's Hill between Mount Jackson and New Market. Major Timothy Quinn's 1st New York Cavalry charged and easily dispersed the few Southerners in their front, following them southward and establishing a picket line one mile south of New Market.[71]

Hunter's renewed advance grabbed Imboden's attention. From Lacey Springs nine miles south of New Market, he promptly telegraphed General Jones in southwest Virginia at 4:00 p.m. Imboden told Jones that Hunter had just passed through Mount Jackson. Imboden also passed on an erroneous report that the enemy, supposedly Crook, was "in force at McDowell," intimating that Crook was ninety miles nearer Staunton than he actually was. Most importantly, Imboden let Jones know that he needed help, asking, "Is it possible for you to aid me?"[72]

Chapter 3

"We Can Ruin Him"

While the Union army rested at New Market, General Lee ordered Jones to "[g]et all the available forces you can and move at once to Imboden's assistance" in the valley. The available force in Jones's department consisted of one infantry brigade, five cavalry brigades, five artillery batteries and several unattached infantry regiments. These 8,200 troops guarded the mountainous regions of east Tennessee and southwestern Virginia, protecting the Virginia & Tennessee Railroad, Wytheville's lead mines and Saltville's salt mines. Not all of these troops could be sent to the valley, but Jones set out to build an army from the disparate commands in his department.[73]

Jones's largest contingent camped near Christiansburg, Virginia, 110 miles southwest of Staunton. There, Colonel Beuhring H. Jones of the 60th Virginia commanded a brigade of veteran infantry. On May 9 at Cloyd's Mountain, these troops had fought desperately against Crook's much larger Union force until a Union flank attack drove them from the field. In spite of heavy losses incurred there, Colonel Jones's veteran brigade still numbered 1,300 effective enlisted men. Captain Thomas A. Bryan's Lewisburg Artillery supported the foot soldiers with its six-gun battery.[74] Ten miles farther south, Colonel William E. Browne's 45th Virginia Infantry bivouacked on the south side of the New River in Pulaski County near the remains of the railroad bridge that Crook's raid had rendered useless for the time being. Being native southwest Virginians, some of Browne's men obtained three-day passes and went home after the fight at Cloyd's Mountain. Proximity to home kept the soldiers relatively well fed and adequately clothed for the present. As a result, the morale in these units improved following the setback at Cloyd's Mountain, and they would form the bedrock of General Jones's nascent army.[75]

Jones possessed additional troops stationed across a wide front from West Virginia to Tennessee. His own 1,600-man cavalry brigade rested near Wytheville after driving off a Federal cavalry raid in early May. Colonel James Love's Thomas Legion garrisoned Saltville, supported by two Tennessee batteries. Brigadier General John C. Vaughn's mounted infantry brigade occupied the environs around Bristol on the Virginia-Tennessee border. The recently promoted Brigadier General John McCausland's 1,200-man cavalry brigade kept tabs on Crook's force in conjunction with Colonel William L. "Mudwall" Jackson's 1,000 troopers. Additionally, numerous partisan bands and home guard units patrolled the vast expanse of this mountainous region. Although scattered throughout the Department of Western Virginia and East Tennessee, these troops shared a common lifeline: the Virginia & Tennessee Railroad.[76]

Jones gathered in his troops and used this vital rail line to transport them to Lynchburg, from which they headed north on the Orange & Alexandria Railroad until reaching Charlottesville. There, they took the Virginia Central westward through the Blue Ridge Tunnel into Staunton. It had not been easy, but General Jones had moved his forces hundreds of miles from southwest Virginia in time to confront Hunter's advance up the Shenandoah Valley. The troops near Christiansburg journeyed two hundred miles on the trains, while Vaughn's detachment left its horses in Bristol and rode the rails for three hundred miles. Without the railroad, Jones would not have been able to reach the valley in time to contest Hunter's advance toward Staunton. Jones's reinforcements arrived in Staunton over a period of several days. When each contingent arrived, it disembarked from the trains and marched north on the Valley Pike to join Imboden at Mount Crawford.[77]

While Jones's troops rode the rails to the Staunton, he received a message from General Imboden:

> General:
> This will be handed to you by Gen'l. Means of Shenandoah who goes to meet you at my request, and will state to you fully the condition of affairs in the Valley. I am holding out every inducement I can to Hunter to follow me up as far as Mount Crawford. If he does not and you can get him "on a run," we can ruin him. He is playing devilish cautious however, and may not take the bait. Colonel [William L.] Jackson telegraphed me last night that the enemy in Greenbriar was moving, he believed in the direction

of Staunton. If I can, with [the] *North River in my front, hold Hunter,*
till you thrash Crook and Averell, and we can pay our respects to Hunter.[78]

Meanwhile, Hunter rested his army just north of New Market, near
Rude's Hill. Hunter determined that he would not advance any farther until
he heard from Crook, then advancing toward Staunton from West Virginia.
While the army waited, many Union troops visited the battlefield at New
Market, where they had been defeated under Sigel. The aftermath of the
battle horrified the Northerners. When Breckinridge left the valley, his
troops hastily buried the Union dead, leaving decomposing arms and legs
protruding from the ground. The Confederates' lack of respectful burials
accorded to the fallen Northern soldiers angered their comrades. In some
cases the dead were buried so hastily that skulls stared out of the ground.
The sight burned itself into the memories of all who saw it, and many swore
revenge. Federal burial details dug graves and gave their comrades a proper
burial. In addition to the partially buried Federals, rotting carcasses of dead
horses lay skinned on the battlefield, with their hides and shoes having been
removed by the hard-pressed Confederates.[79]

At five o'clock on the morning of June 2, 1864, not having heard from
Crook, the Army of the Shenandoah marched south from New Market,
leaving many wounded behind. The troops marched to music from several
bands and exchanged cheers with their sick and wounded comrades who
"were able to drag themselves to the doors or windows of their temporary
hospitals." The advance moved so slowly that Imboden sent a dispatch back
to Staunton: "My videttes four miles this side [south] of New Market have
just reported the appearance of a column of cavalry on the pike this side
of New Market advancing. They had come so short a distance that it is
yet undecided whether they are coming on, or merely seeking pasture or
making a scout up the road." The 1st Maryland Potomac Home Brigade
(PHB hereafter) Cavalry attacked pickets from the 18th Virginia Cavalry near
Lacey Springs where skirmishing commenced. The 1st New York Veteran
Cavalry (1st Veteran hereafter) joined the fray and forced the Virginians back
after a brief fight. They retired to another position, where the skirmishing
flared up until the Unionists again drove the Virginians back again in a
pattern that repeated itself throughout the day. When the Marylanders and
New Yorkers finally reached Harrisonburg, they charged and cleared the
Southerners out of town.[80]

At the southern edge of Harrisonburg, Imboden had deployed a battalion
of troops that included local Rockingham County reserves. The retreating

Confederate cavalry fell back behind this line, and their pursuers abandoned the chase upon seeing the awaiting reinforcements. Imboden dismounted one of his cavalry regiments and deployed it in front of the reserves, where they skirmished with the Union cavalry. Before the main body of Union cavalry arrived, Imboden carefully conserved his forces and withdrew before they were overwhelmed by the tide of blue-coated soldiers streaming into Harrisonburg. As Imboden's small force began falling back to Mount Crawford, a single Confederate cannon fired a couple of shots at the Union vanguard to cover the withdrawal.[81]

At Mount Crawford, Imboden organized the miscellaneous detachments that he had assembled in the valley. Through Special Orders No. 148, Imboden assigned Colonel Kenton Harper command of the Valley Reserves composed of men from Augusta, Rockbridge and Rockingham Counties who had been called into the field "for the present emergency." Imboden had pressed many of them into the service against their will and in spite of their loyalty to the United States. Harper, a native Pennsylvanian, originally served as colonel of the Stonewall Brigade's 5th Virginia Infantry, which he commanded at First Bull Run. Harper resigned his commission when Jackson denied the colonel a brief furlough to visit his dying wife. Imboden assigned Captain Thomas J. Smith to command the 2nd Maryland Cavalry Battalion's (CSA) dismounted men, other miscellaneous Maryland line troops who had been gathering in Staunton and the convalescents from Staunton's several military hospitals.[82]

Harper's Valley Reserves dug in along the North River near Mount Crawford, just south of Harrisonburg. Harper placed one company on duty at the bridge, which carried the Valley Pike over the water. Despite the long odds, Imboden determined to hold off Hunter at Mount Crawford, as Lee's orders made it clear that Imboden must defend Staunton. In anticipation of battle, he also appointed a surgeon "to establish a field infirmary, organize an ambulance corps and do whatever else" the newly appointed medical director considered necessary "for the efficient discharge of his important duties." All the surgeons in the Valley District were instructed to report to this medical director.[83]

Back in Harrisonburg, the Federals found that some of their wounded comrades from the Battle of New Market had been aided by some of the townspeople. Colonel Lincoln of the 34th Massachusetts and 90 other Union soldiers had enjoyed their care in both hospitals and private homes of Harrisonburg. Lincoln informed the Union commanders which families had aided wounded Union soldiers, and Hunter reciprocated by not confiscating food or provisions from them. As the army would soon be moving on, Hunter supplied the wounded Northerners with food, medical supplies, clothing and boots. Even more reassuring than the supplies, the wounded took hope in "Hunter's solemn promise" that he would send a train of ambulances to carry "those poor fellows" to Martinsburg. Hunter also provided ample provisions for 150 wounded Southerners who were in the town's hospitals.[84]

The efforts of the Harrisonburg Unionists who fraternized with Federal officers or cared for wounded Union soldiers raised the eyebrows of their pro-Confederate neighbors. Even worse, Hunter used the Gray family's home for his headquarters, adding to the antipathy felt toward the Grays. "The people there [Harrisonburg] speak bitterly of Algernon and Robert Gray [and] say they shall bring them to an account," observed Jed Hotchkiss when he passed through a few weeks later. When Confederate partisans murdered a local pacifist on June 15, they declared "Colonel Gray next," so he fled to Baltimore with his brothers.[85]

Colonel Joseph Thoburn made the acquaintance of Reverend David Irwin, a Presbyterian clergyman, whose mother, sister and two brothers

Colonel Joseph Thoburn. This Wheeling, West Virginia doctor maintained a detailed journal of Hunter's campaign in which he detailed his observations and opinions on the impact of operations in the valley. *USAMHI.*

lived in Wheeling, West Virginia, Thoburn's hometown. The Wheeling Irwins remained loyal to the United States, while the Harrisonburg Irwin became a bitter secessionist. Ironically, Irwin's nephews served in Thoburn's command and paid their uncle a friendly visit. Upon greeting his Unionist kinsmen, Irwin proclaimed to them that "he did not know whether he ought to shake hands with them." Although he dutifully inquired about his mother, he refused to mention his brothers and sister. Such actions puzzled Thoburn, and he wondered what forsaken cause had made this man forgo "his humanity and Christianity" toward his own family.[86]

While the Army of the Shenandoah occupied Harrisonburg, Confederate reinforcements filtered into the defenses along the North River several miles south of town. Hunter had not realized that substantial reinforcements from Jones had joined Imboden at Mount Crawford. On June 4, Strother noted that Imboden had only 2,500 men in his command. In reality, Imboden's force numbered at least 5,000 men by the end of the day. The three days Hunter had spent at Woodstock and the two days at New Market had provided Jones enough time to transport his troops to Staunton before Hunter arrived. In hindsight, Hunter's dawdling advance up the Shenandoah Valley cost him the opportunity to capture Staunton and join Crook without any serious opposition. He would have been better served if he had remained at Belle Grove until his army was resupplied before moving south and revealing his intentions to Imboden.[87]

On June 3, Hunter and his staff formulated a strategy for avoiding Imboden's strong position behind the North River at Mount Crawford. Strother recommended that Hunter move "by way of Port Republic, cross the river there, and take Waynesboro with his cavalry, thereby cutting off stores and railroad stock from Staunton. He would also cut off the enemy [from Richmond] that way, which would greatly demoralize him." Hunter adopted Strother's plan and ordered his army to march for Port Republic early on June 4.[88] Frank S. Reader, an orderly on Hunter's staff, had watched the increased activity at Hunter's headquarters and knew that something was afoot. Back in his tent that evening, he recorded his thoughts in his diary: "We will have a fight tomorrow…Everything is in good order for a Va. muss and we'll give Imboden a trial of abolition skill."[89]

At 5:00 a.m. on June 4, the Army of the Shenandoah broke camp at Harrisonburg and marched southward on the Valley Pike. Lieutenant John R. Meigs, Hunter's chief engineer, pleaded with Hunter to send a cavalry regiment toward Mount Crawford as a diversion to the flanking march to Port Republic. Hunter consented, and young Meigs personally showed the men the way. This diversion made sound military sense, but sending Meigs along as the guide cost Hunter the services of his chief engineer at a crucial time later that day. Hunter had plenty of officers capable of leading the diversionary action, but Meigs was his most competent engineer and his skills would be needed later on.[90]

After moving only a short distance on the pike, the army turned east and headed down the Port Republic Road. Lieutenant Colonel John S. Platner's 1st Veteran Cavalry didn't follow the column but instead rode southward on the Valley Pike toward Mount Crawford, guided by Meigs. Platner sent a detachment toward Bridgewater, giving the appearance of an advance across a wider front. Before long, the New Yorkers attacked pickets from the 18th Virginia, driving them toward the North River. Platner's diversion froze the Southerners in position at Mount Crawford, as they dubiously assumed that Platner's horse soldiers were the vanguard of Hunter's advancing army.[91]

While the Confederates waited for an attack that never came, Hunter's army hastened eastward to Port Republic, passing sites already famous from Stonewall Jackson's renowned 1862 Valley Campaign. The army moved past the spot where Jackson's cavalry commander Turner Ashby fell at the Battle of Harrisonburg and then marched through the fields of conflict at Cross Keys. The latter place likely rekindled sullen memories for Major General Julius Stahel. Almost precisely two years earlier, Confederate General Isaac Trimble had laid waste to Stahel's brigade at the Battle of Cross Keys, killing and wounding numerous men whom Stahel had recruited into the Union army.[92]

Leading the way to Port Republic was Colonel John Wynkoop's cavalry brigade. When the army turned off the Valley Pike, most Union personnel remained uncertain of their ultimate objective now that they were marching away from Staunton. Speculation ran rampant through the ranks. Colonel Rodgers of the 2nd Maryland Eastern Shore Infantry surmised that Hunter had changed the army's objective to Charlottesville, an important stop on the Virginia Central Railroad, east of the Blue Ridge. As the Federals marched toward Port Republic, the families along the road informed the bluecoats that all men capable of bearing arms had been impressed into the Confederate army. Thoburn noted in his diary that "from what we can learn along the road the majority have gone in much against their will and we have many friends in the rebel army." Imboden had indeed impressed many men into the ranks. In Staunton, one Unionist avoided impressment by hiding in his room until the Union army arrived.[93]

Brigadier General William E. "Grumble" Jones arrived at Mount Crawford a little after sunrise and immediately assumed command of the

Contentment, or the Grattan house, served as Confederate headquarters and is where Jones arrived and assumed command of Confederate forces on June 4. *Scott C. Patchan.*

Army of the Valley District from Imboden. Within the confines of the Grattan house, Jones reviewed and approved the dispositions that Imboden had made to meet Hunter's advance. Both officers agreed that they needed "to fight Hunter at the earliest moment, and possibly defeat him, and then turn upon Crook and Averell and do the best we could." Jones expressed much confidence that "he could whip Hunter" at Mount Crawford. The only problem was that Hunter and his staff had realized that very same thing and had made alternative arrangements.[94]

As the sun rose higher in the morning sky, the stir created by Platner's feint on Bridgewater and Mount Crawford died down. By 10:00 a.m., Imboden dispatched his brother, Colonel George W. Imboden, with the 18th Virginia Cavalry to ascertain what Hunter was doing north of the river. Sometime around noon, a courier from Colonel Imboden galloped back to headquarters at the Grattan house to notify Jones of Hunter's flank march.[95] Jones "did not put full confidence in the reports of the scouts." He worried that Hunter was only buying time for Crook's force to reach Staunton. However, confirmation soon came from another source. Captain

Hanse McNeil and his partisan rangers from West Virginia's South Branch Valley had been lurking on the flanks and rear of Hunter's army. McNeil had passed through Harrisonburg after Hunter's departure and proceeded to Confederate headquarters at Mount Crawford, and Jones belatedly accepted the fact of Hunter's flank movement to Port Republic. As Imboden told it, this news "disappointed and somewhat disconcerted General Jones." However, it is difficult to picture a veteran officer with Jones's combat experience and innate fortitude becoming flustered because his opponent did not walk into an obvious trap.[96]

More accurately, Jones could hardly believe that Hunter would position his army at Port Republic "with a deep and rough ford" at his back. The North and South Rivers joined at Port Republic to form the South Fork of the Shenandoah River. This junction created a peninsula onto which Hunter had placed his army. Hunter's position there presented Jones with an opportunity to trap Hunter with "bad crossings" forming his only avenues of escape. If Jones could interpose his forces between Hunter and Waynesboro, an opportunity existed for Jones to drive Hunter back onto the narrow peninsula at Port Republic. Such a move would also protect Waynesboro and the crucial Blue Ridge Tunnel, where the Virginia Central Railroad passed through the mountains. The loss of this tunnel would have been just as damaging to the Confederate interests in the valley as Staunton itself. If the tunnel was destroyed, the town held little value without a railroad connecting it to eastern Virginia. Jones decided to allow Hunter to cross the river at Port Republic so that he could attack him and force his beaten army back across the rain-swollen rivers.[97]

Jones then called on General Imboden's intricate knowledge of his native region. Although Jones had spent significant time in the valley, his understanding of its roads and topography was limited to the vicinity of the Valley Turnpike, while Imboden had grown up in the environs where their army was operating. Imboden described Hunter's route for Jones and drew him "a crude map showing the streams and roads, distances, etc."[98] In Imboden's postwar account of these events, he claimed that he proposed moving the Army of the Valley District to Mowry's Hill, located eight miles northeast of Staunton. That position offered an excellent tactical position on which to fight a defensive battle, but the position was vulnerable to flanking. According to Imboden, Jones endorsed the proposed scheme as he could offer no alternative at the time. However, the version of events penned by Major J.J. Lafferty of Imboden's staff shortly after the battle does not mention the selection of Mowry's Hill as the chosen field of battle.

In Lafferty's contemporary account, Jones and Imboden did not select a specific position for battle on June 4 as Imboden claimed. Rather, the plan was to interpose their forces between Hunter and Waynesboro in the rolling farmland of eastern Augusta County.[99]

At one o'clock in the afternoon of June 4, Imboden's cavalry rode out of Mount Crawford, heading south along the Valley Pike until reaching Pleasant Grove Church. There they turned southeast on to the Forge Road toward Mount Meridian, located four miles south of Port Republic. Imboden posted vedettes at the intervening fords along the North River to provide early warning should the Federals attempt to cut off Imboden from Jones's main force on the Valley Pike. At three o'clock, Jones's infantry and artillery marched south from their fortified position at Mount Crawford. Harper's Valley Reserves remained as the rear guard at the river until the army's wagon train had safely passed through Mount Sidney eight miles southward.[100]

Jones wired word of Hunter's flank movement to Colonel Edwin G. Lee, commandant of the military post at Staunton. Colonel Lee, a cousin of Robert E. Lee, had assumed command of the Staunton post only several hours earlier. Lee quickly prepared "the heavy stores and official papers" for evacuation. The vast assortment of supplies stored in Staunton included a large cache of ammunition, weapons, wool, leather, flour and salt. Unable to save all of the commissary supplies, Lee opened the warehouses to the civilian populace, who eagerly took the flour and salt to their homes. The town's residents quickly followed the military's example and began to send off their slaves and personal belongings to the Blue Ridge, where they would be beyond the immediate reach of the Union military if Staunton fell.[101]

Meanwhile, Hunter's vanguard reached Port Republic around half past two o'clock that afternoon. Colonel John Wynkoop led his brigade across the swiftly flowing South River at a rough ford upstream from the road. Troopers from the 20th and 22nd Pennsylvania Cavalry fanned out and encountered a Confederate wagon train. During the crossing, one of Wynkoop's troopers fell from his horse and was swept away by the powerful current, casting a pall over the thousands of onlooking soldiers. The Pennsylvanians entered the village, charged and captured twenty prisoners and eight wagons loaded with supplies and fifty horses after a wild chase.[102] Two local women emerged from their house and cheered the Union troops, saying, "That's right; the rebels starved us and let us go almost naked, and this serves them right." After capturing the wagon train, the Pennsylvanians torched the woolen mills in Port Republic that supplied cloth for the Confederate army.[103]

The main column of the Union army arrived at the North River crossing at 3:00 p.m. The river was running high and swift as a result of recent heavy rains, making it impossible for the infantry to ford. Fortunately for the Federals, Hunter had the foresight to bring along a canvas pontoon bridge. Conversely, at least three hours were lost, as the only engineer who knew how to assemble the bridge, Lieutenant Meigs, was far to the rear, having guided the early morning feint against Mount Crawford. The delay annoyed Hunter, and he personally oversaw the engineer troops who assembled the cumbersome pontoon bridge. Hunter had good reason to be annoyed; precious time had slipped away, preventing his cavalry from "making a dash to Waynesboro."[104]

At 6:00 p.m., the engineers belatedly completed the bridge, and the troops formed up for the crossing. Private Lynch of the 18th Connecticut noted that the bridge "was a frail thing for an army to cross on." As the Union soldiers marched over it, Hunter sat astride his horse on the riverbank, calling out, "Men, break step" in order to distribute the weight equitably on the bridge. Lynch wrote, "That seemed to be a duty that the General would not trust to any one else."[105]

As dusk settled over the Shenandoah Valley, the Union army marched southward through Port Republic. The village rekindled more unpleasant memories of Jackson's 1862 Valley Campaign. Colonel Thoburn and the 1st West Virginia had fought at the Battle of Port Republic when Jackson defeated General James Shields. Although the colonel hoped for victory this trip up the valley, his prior experience tempered his optimism. One mile south of the village, Hunter established his camp in the woods and brush fields alongside the Staunton and Port Republic Road (Staunton Road hereafter). The U.S. troops trudged into camp until late in the evening and spent a "rainy and disagreeable" night without tents. The artillery and its escorts did not reach camp until 11:00 p.m. after a difficult time crossing the river.[106]

Three miles south of Hunter's bivouac, Imboden went into position at Mount Meridian and successfully interposed his brigade between the Union army and Waynesboro. Jones's effort to bring Hunter to bay before he reached Waynesboro or Staunton had succeeded. Imboden established his headquarters at Bonnie Doon, the stately farm of Samuel Crawford, a prominent Augusta County citizen. Imboden deployed twenty Virginians on picket duty at Alexander Givens's farm, where the Staunton Road forked northward to Port Republic and eastward to Weyer's Cave. His brigade's encampment stretched for two and a half miles along the Staunton and Port Republic Road from Bonnie Doon back toward the village of Piedmont, where Captain John Opie, a veteran captain from Jeb Stuart's cavalry, and Captain Henry Peck, the Augusta County sheriff, encamped with their companies of Augusta County mounted reserves on the Shaver Farm near Piedmont.[107]

Over on the Valley Pike, Jones's Confederate foot soldiers encamped for the night south of Mount Sidney. Like their Union counterparts, these men "slept in the rain without tents, blankets, or rations."[108] During the night, Robert E. Lee informed Jones that no additional troops would reach the valley for several days and urged him to "fight Hunter as quickly as possible, and beat him back before Crook's and Averell's advent on the scene." Lee's orders suited Jones perfectly, and he adopted his usual aggressive strategy that had earned him the sobriquet "Stonewall Jackson of East Tennessee."[109]

On June 4, Jones disregarded the Mowry's Hill plan, if indeed he had ever agreed to it. If the Confederate forces fell back to Mowry's, they would uncover several byroads that Hunter could use to flank back to the Valley Pike. The Mowry's position also gave Hunter an opportunity to flank Jones to the east and head toward Waynesboro and the vital Blue Ridge Tunnel. Jones had seen enough of Hunter's flanking and determined to advance toward Port Republic and fight Hunter wherever found. If Jones could hold his ground and force Hunter to retreat, Jones might severely damage the Union army as it attempted to recross the difficult rivers at Port Republic. It was a tall order under the circumstances, but Jones had defied the odds before, and with a little luck he just might pull it off.[110]

Chapter 4

"I Would Just as Soon Fight Him Now"

As a steady rain fell from the dark, early morning sky, Julius Stahel's cavalry formed its column for the coming day's march. Major Timothy Quinn's 1st New York Cavalry from Colonel Andrew McReynolds's brigade led the way. At 5:00 a.m., Quinn's advance scouts moved out on the muddy Staunton Road, followed by the rest of the regiment. Captain George J.P. Wood's detachment of the 1st Maryland PHB Cavalry deployed in skirmish order on the New Yorkers' right flank. Although Hunter's plan had anticipated an open road to Waynesboro, all indications were that this would be a day of battle, as Jones and Hunter were on a collision course.[111]

Hunter and his entourage rode between the main cavalry column and Quinn's advance. Colonel William B. Tibbits's 21st New York Cavalry and Captain Ashbell F. Duncan's battalion of the 14th Pennsylvania Cavalry (serving under Tibbits) formed the head of the Stahel's main column, and Lieutenant Colonel John Platner's 1st Veteran Cavalry brought up the rear of McReynolds's brigade.[112] Colonel John Wynkoop's diminutive brigade followed McReynolds's troopers. Wynkoop's brigade consisted of his own two-hundred-man 20th Pennsylvania Cavalry and a one-hundred-man detachment from the Ringgold Cavalry (a part of the 22nd Pennsylvania Cavalry). The three hundred men of the 15th New York Cavalry were guarding the wagon trains and were not with Wynkoop.[113]

At 5:30 a.m., Sullivan's infantrymen trudged along behind Stahel's horse soldiers after having stood waiting in the rain for ninety minutes. It had mattered little, as they had no tents to shelter them and had spent a dreary, wet night under the clouds. Colonel Augustus Moor's brigade marched on the west side of the

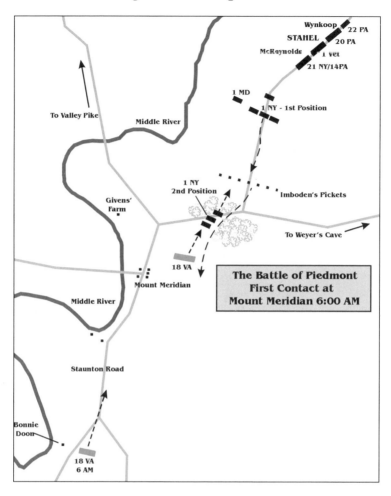

Staunton Road, while Thoburn's brigade took the east side. At Moor's direction, Major Henry Peale led two companies each from the 18th Connecticut and the 5th New York Heavy Artillery as the infantry's advance guard. Peale's skirmishers fanned out and followed closely behind the advancing cavalry. Captain Henry DuPont's twenty-two-gun artillery brigade moved along on the muddy road between the two infantry brigades. The army's wagon train came next, escorted by the 123rd Ohio and 4th West Virginia marching alongside the vehicles, with the 15th New York Cavalry forming the army's rear guard.[114]

As the Union army moved up the Staunton Road, Colonel Rodgers of the 2nd Maryland Eastern Shore noticed the changing cultivation in this section of the valley. The open woods and farmland that dominated the Valley Pike were replaced by denser forests that were more difficult for the troops to traverse. Out in front, Captain James Stevenson's company of the 1st New York Cavalry scouted the route aided by the small battalion of the 1st Maryland PHB Cavalry. At 6:00 a.m., Stevenson's scouts peered through the mist and spotted Imboden's pickets on the Givens Farm just east of the junction of the Staunton Road with a country track that led from the vicinity of Weyer's Cave westward to Pleasant Grove Church on the Valley Pike. Immediately, the New Yorkers opened fire, and the rattle of carbine fire shattered the early morning silence as a steady skirmish ensued. Stevenson rushed a courier back to Quinn, notifying him that they had located the enemy.[115]

Imboden's rain-soaked troopers had been resting in their bivouacs near Bonnie Doon waiting for orders when the staccato crack of carbines echoed up the cloud-covered valley from the Givens Farm. Even though General Jones had dispatched Imboden to Mount Meridian to slow Hunter's advance, the appearance of Stahel's cavalry surprised Imboden. He dashed to his nearest regiment, the 18th Virginia, and directed its commander, Colonel George Imboden, to advance and support the pickets. The general also likely sent orders to Colonel Robert White to saddle up the 23rd Virginia Cavalry and Captain T. Sturgis Davis's battalion and prepare for combat. A courier carried orders to Captain John Opie to hurry to Imboden's support at Mount Meridian. That would take time, however, as Opie's two hundred mounted reserves were camped at Piedmont, more than two miles south of Mount Meridian.[116]

The troopers of the 18th Virginia raced through Mount Meridian and continued northward a short distance before halting in the road. General Imboden ordered the Virginians to deploy in the adjoining field east of the road. Several gray-coated troopers leapt from their saddles and quickly ripped down a fence that obstructed their way. With the barrier cleared away, the regiment trotted into the field and formed a line of battle on an open hill that sloped toward timbered ground in front. Then the Virginians sat in their saddles and waited anxiously as they listened intently to the gunfire from the Givens Farm, less than half a mile in front of them.[117]

When Quinn learned of the Confederate presence, he rushed two companies of the 1st New York Cavalry to reinforce the advance and deployed the three companies into line of battle astride the road. Stevenson's company shifted into the woods on the west side of the road, and Captain Abram Jones's command went to the east. Captain Franklin Martindale's company formed its line across the road to spearhead the advance. The balance of the regiment remained in column on the road a short distance behind Martindale's men. Quinn ordered a charge, and the battalion surged ahead, driving the Virginians on picket back toward Mount Meridian. The

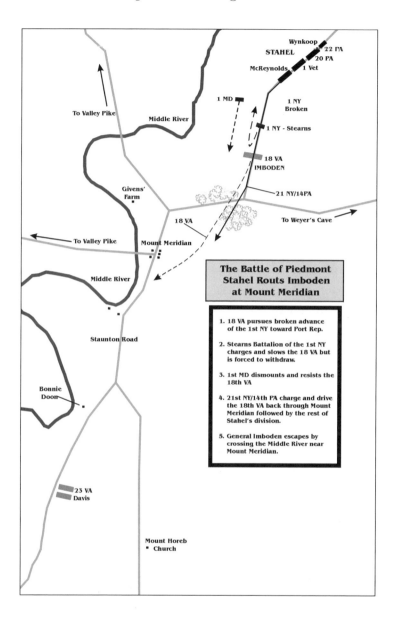

The Battle of Piedmont
Stahel Routs Imboden
at Mount Meridian

1. 18 VA pursues broken advance of the 1st NY toward Port Rep.

2. Stearns Battalion of the 1st NY charges and slows the 18 VA but is forced to withdraw.

3. 1st MD dismounts and resists the 18th VA

4. 21st NY/14th PA charge and drive the 18th VA back through Mount Meridian followed by the rest of Stahel's division.

5. General Imboden escapes by crossing the Middle River near Mount Meridian.

New Yorkers chased them down the Staunton Road past its junction with the road from Weyer's Cave and into the woods beyond.[118]

The flying Confederate pickets soon emerged from the opposite side of the woods in front of the 18th Virginia and raced up the hill, passing through the Virginians without halting. Colonel Imboden's men cocked their rifles and carbines and then waited for the Federals to momentarily emerge from the trees. Almost immediately, Martindale's company dashed recklessly into the clearing directly in front of the 18th Virginia and suddenly found its way blocked by a rail fence. Colonel Imboden's men saw them instantly and leveled a devastating volley into the New Yorkers, emptying many saddles with that initial blast and throwing the survivors into chaos. Before Martindale could regain control of the situation, Jones's company burst into the clearing and received the same rough greeting. The Virginians continued blazing away at the Federals struggling to regain the cover of the trees.[119]

Colonel Imboden sensed the confusion in the Union ranks, raised his sword above his head and led the 18th Virginia down the hill in a classic mounted charge. The Virginians yelled like "fiends" and discharged their revolvers at close range as they slammed into the beleaguered Federals. The sudden gray onslaught routed the 1st New York Cavalry's advance squadron and shoved it back through the woods toward Port Republic. The Virginians continued their advance across the road from Weyer's Cave and routed the second battalion of the 1st New York.[120] On the left, the Virginians struck skirmishers from Captain Wood's 1st Maryland PHB Cavalry, who checked the initial Confederate onslaught for "a short time." However, Imboden's numbers quickly swelled, and the Virginians forced the Marylanders back to a rail fence.

Wood rushed reinforcements forward who jumped from their horses and dashed toward the fence. They quickly picked their targets and fired on the advancing Virginians, slowing their attack. On the right, the Virginians pressed their attack against the New Yorkers but encountered more obstinate resistance once they crossed the road from Weyer's Cave. There Major Joseph Stearns made a "splendid" charge with his battalion of the 1st New York Cavalry. Although he temporarily checked the 18th Virginia, the Confederates ultimately forced Stearns back, causing confusion in the Union ranks. In the chaos of the mounted melee, Lieutenant Edwin Savacool of the Lincoln Cavalry lost control of his horse and became entangled among the Confederates. Wearing a light-colored raincoat, Savacool calmly intermixed with the Southerners in their advance. Later, when the tide of battle again favored the North, the crafty Savacool rejoined his comrades.[121]

Hunter and his staff had galloped rapidly to the head of the column as the 18th Virginia nearly overwhelmed the 1st New York Cavalry. He immediately ordered Stahel to "attack the enemy and check his advance." Then Hunter and his staff wheeled their mounts and "moved rapidly to the rear." Stahel dashed up to Tibbits commanding the 21st New York and 14th Pennsylvania and shouted excitedly in broken English, marred by his thick Hungarian accent, "For God's sake Colonel Tibbits, charge and if possible hold them in

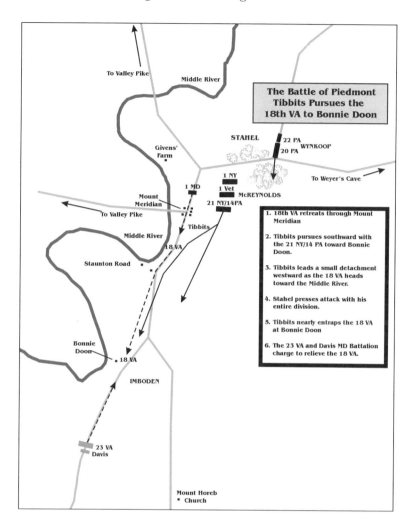

The Battle of Piedmont
Tibbits Pursues the
18th VA to Bonnie Doon

1. 18th VA retreats through Mount Meridian

2. Tibbits pursues southward with the 21 NY/14 PA toward Bonnie Doon.

3. Tibbits leads a small detachment westward as the 18 VA heads toward the Middle River.

4. Stahel presses attack with his entire division.

5. Tibbits nearly entraps the 18 VA at Bonnie Doon

6. The 23 VA and Davis MD Battalion charge to relieve the 18 VA.

check." The combative Tibbits quickly wheeled his troops out of column into a line across the road and "charged to help [the] 1st New York Cavalry."[122] With Tibbits in the lead, the Union horse soldiers drew their sabers and charged the 18th Virginia. Quinn and Stearns rallied the 1st New York and quickly joined the attack on the left, while Wood's Marylanders followed suit on the extreme right.

The Virginians had lost their momentum when they struck the Marylanders and Stearns's battalion, becoming somewhat scattered and strung out from their explosive advance. Seeing Tibbits's hard-charging Union cavalry backed by infantry, Colonel Imboden and his troopers suddenly found themselves greatly outnumbered and did not wait to receive the charge. Instead, they wheeled their mounts and headed back toward

Mount Meridian in such wild disorder that one Virginia trooper "declared himself ashamed of his regiment" after its poor showing on June 5, 1864.[123]

General Imboden found himself cut off from his command and pursued by an entire company of Federals. He later recalled, "I owed…my escape to the speed and great power of my horse, a gift stallion from my command, who carried me at a bound over a post and rail fence into the river road below the village." The Federal horses could not negotiate the obstacle, and Imboden raced up the road, rejoining the 18th Virginia just above the hamlet.[124] Racing over the numerous dips and hillocks, the Virginians engaged the New Yorkers and Pennsylvanians in a running fight that nearly destroyed the 18th Virginia. At one point, a Union trooper dashed at General Imboden, blasting away with his revolver. Imboden attempted to draw his pistol but could not extricate it from his holster, so he yelled to one of his men, "Kill the Yankee!" The Virginia trooper "leveled his carbine, [fired] and the Yankee tumbled-dead."[125]

The Union cavalry charged after the Virginians in the open ground at Mount Meridian. Colonel Imboden led his men through the fields and up the Staunton Road. They clattered over a bridge that spanned a small stream and headed toward their bivouac near Bonnie Doon. When Tibbits reached the top of a hill, he saw the Virginians racing diagonally across the field toward the road and the Middle River. Tibbits and Captain Duncan reined in their mounts and stopped a squad of men from the 21st New York/14th Pennsylvania Cavalry. Tibbits shouted and waved his sword to the men of the 21st New York, motioning for them to change their course and follow him. Then he dashed after the Virginians with the few troopers at his immediate disposal. Most of the Union cavalry continued straight ahead across the field and threatened to cut off the 18th Virginia's line of retreat.[126]

To escape the surging Federals, the endangered regiment turned up a farm lane leading to the Bonnie Doon house. In front of the house, a board fence lined both sides of the lane leading from the road. When the head of the regiment reached the far end of the lane nearest the house, the Virginians closest to the road spotted Tibbits's small squad advancing on them and turned to fight. The panic-stricken Virginians in the middle continued to press up the lane toward the house in their efforts to escape from the approaching Federals. The continued jostling created a logjam that wedged their horses between the tall post and rail fence on either side of the lane. Stahel's horse artillery opened fire, increasing the confusion and significantly damaging the Bonnie Doon house as well. As the Virginians struggled to escape, Tibbits's troopers poured into the melee at the lane's entrance, the Confederate situation worsening as more Union cavalry joined the attack.[127]

Tibbits and his men blocked the opening of the lane and summoned the Virginians to surrender. Those closest to him complied with the order, but most of the nearby Virginians belonged to Captain Frank Imboden's company, and they chose to fight. The rest just struggled to get away. A hand-to-hand saber fight swirled at the east end of the lane, while many men of the 18th Virginia rode to safety at the opposite end. Tibbits personally wielded his saber until his wrist gave out, and then he switched over to his revolver. At one point in the contest, a Virginian struck Lieutenant William W. Murphy of the 14th Pennsylvania on the head, slightly wounding him. As the Virginian raised his sword high in the air to finish off the Pennsylvanian, Tibbits fired his revolver into the Confederate at point-blank range, killing him and two others before the melee ended.[128]

At length it looked as if Tibbits might trap the 18th Virginia in the lane. However, the timely arrival of reinforcements saved the 18th Virginia from severe losses. White's 23rd Virginia surged forward and exploded into the midst of the Federal horsemen. Davis's Maryland Battalion attacked to the left of White's Virginians, adding its weight to the fight. Davis's command included two companies of mounted reserves from Rockingham County, Captain George Chrisman's "Boy Company" and Captain Henry Harnsberger's "Old Men." The combined force of White's Virginians and Davis's Battalion slammed into the Union cavalry, preventing them from completely surrounding the 18th Virginia.[129] Under cover of the Confederate countercharge, the 18th Virginia broke free of the logjam in the lane and narrowly avoided disaster. As it was, Tibbits's command captured twenty-six men of the 18th Virginia, including an excited Captain Frank Imboden, another of the general's brothers. Some members of the 18th Virginia halted to join in the stand of the 23rd Virginia and Davis's Battalion, but most galloped southward in wild confusion. Although the Confederate counterattack had stalled the Union momentum, more bluecoats were pounding up the road to join the fight.[130]

When Tibbits first commenced his charge, Stahel ordered the balance of his troops into the fight. He sent Wynkoop into the woods on the far Union left flank, where the Pennsylvanians moved steadily but slowly through the trees. The Hungarian personally led the balance of McReynolds's brigade through Mount Meridian and deployed it into line of battle just north of Bonnie Doon. Platner's five-hundred-man 1st Veteran Cavalry formed the larger portion of the approaching Federal reinforcements. When it encountered a fence blocking the way, Platner shouted, "Halt! First squadron; dismount and take down the fence to the right of the road." Several troopers

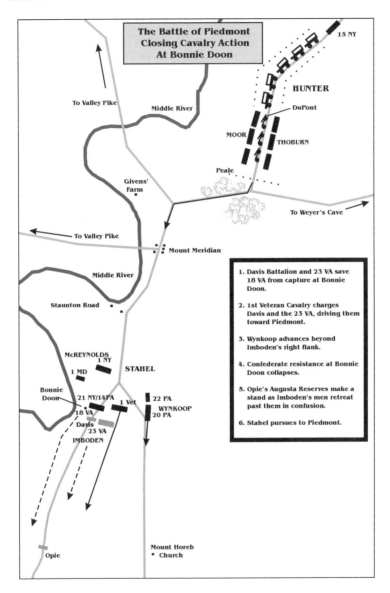

jumped from their horses and ripped away the obstructions. The men of the 1st Veteran Cavalry spurred their horses, dashed through the opening and rushed forward to energize Stahel's sagging advance. Wood's Marylanders joined Platner's troopers, charging on the extreme right next to the river.

For several minutes, General Imboden's Virginians and Marylanders engaged the Union cavalry in the fields just south of Bonnie Doon. When Platner's Veterans shot toward White's 23rd Virginia and Davis's Marylanders and Reserves, the Southerners fled as the Federal horsemen threatened to overwhelm the Confederates. Private Washington Marsh of Platner's 1st Veteran recalled: "The Johnnies immediately started on southward and a sort of go-as-you-please fight conducted at all velocities from a dead stop to a rattling gallop ensued." In the fast-paced action between Mount Meridian and Piedmont, the Union horsemen captured eight men from Davis's Battalion and six of the 23rd Virginia. The "Old Man" and "Boy" companies lost heavily in killed and wounded as well. At one point, Captain Chrisman saw several of his "boys" about to be overwhelmed and charged back into the fray to save them from capture or worse. By seven o'clock in the morning, Stahel's cavalry had put Imboden's Brigade to flight and subsequently encountered little resistance from the Confederate cavalry.[131]

While the battle ebbed and flowed near Mount Meridian, Captain John Opie heard the brisk gunfire from Imboden's fight growing increasingly louder as the Federals pressed the stricken Confederates. Opie had already directed his men to eat "a hasty breakfast and saddle up." As they ate their food, Imboden's courier dashed into Opie's camp with orders to advance and assist the besieged Confederate horsemen. Opie's greenhorns mounted their horses and rode rapidly toward Mount Meridian, two and a half miles northward. Before they reached their destination, hundreds of Imboden's demoralized troopers fled past them in confusion. The reserves called for them to rally, but the regular cavalrymen kept going, yelling, "Yes, you go and try it." An embarrassed Lieutenant Colonel Charles O'Ferrall of the 23rd Virginia "was abusing and swearing at his men, and asking them if they couldn't 'stand as long as the _____ Home Guards?'"[132]

Remarkably, the Augusta County Reserves maintained their composure and continued on their way as the veterans retreated toward Piedmont. More ominously, Opie spied Stahel's column of blue horsemen advancing along the Staunton Road through open woods and fields. With no time to waste, Opie immediately dismounted his command and sent every fourth man rearward as a horse holder. Then he arrayed his men, armed with infantry muskets, behind a brush-covered rail fence at the edge of a clearing. With Imboden's veterans still galloping rearward in retreat, Opie observed that the sight of the regular soldiers falling back rattled his raw troops and took preventive measures. Opie shouted to his greenhorns, "Now men, if it is necessary to run, I will start first, but, if any man runs before I do, I will shoot him!"[133] Not a man flinched.

Tibbits detected the Confederate presence and charged Opie's 150 dragoons, who fired into the New Yorkers and stopped their advance cold. Opie matter-of-factly reported, "The enemy charged through the open field, in our front, several times, but each time withdrew under our fire." Although Opie repulsed the frontal assault, Stahel had advanced Wynkoop along the South River or Rockfish Road half a mile from Tibbits's left. These blue-coated horse soldiers now threatened to turn Opie's right flank and sever his line of retreat if he held his position too long.[134] A Confederate staff officer stationed on a hill behind Opie's position spotted the Federal flanking force, mounted his horse, dashed down the road and warned Opie. The veteran cavalryman adroitly pulled his men back before the Union troopers attacked and went into position on a bluff behind a stream named Polecat Draft, which prevented the Union cavalry from attacking. When the Augusta Reserves fell back, Tibbits slowly followed them at a respectful distance. Opie briefly maintained his new position until he was ordered to withdraw and support a section of McClanahan's Battery that was going into position near the village of Piedmont.[135]

While Stahel followed the Confederates toward Piedmont, some of the Union cavalry halted in the fields south of Bonnie Doon to regroup and rest their horses. Several troopers took advantage of the lull in the action to eat breakfast. First, they had to locate food, as their rations had run out. Near the Middle River, Sergeant William McIlhenny of the 1st Maryland PHB and six comrades approached a small house occupied by a kind elderly woman. She did not recognize the men as U.S. troops and inquired as to the whereabouts of "the hated Federals." McIlhenny replied that they "had driven the Yanks out of the country." She thankfully cried out, "God bless you!" The Marylanders did not dissuade her from her mistaken notion but instead asked if "she had anything good to eat." She went inside and returned with fresh bread and butter for her "Confederate" heroes.[136]

While the Southern cavalry was falling back in confusion, General Jones arrived at Piedmont and learned of Imboden's discomfiture at Mount Meridian. Jones ordered Captain John McClanahan—a native Texan and commander of a six-gun battery composed of four three-inch ordnance rifles and two howitzers—to hurry one section (two guns) forward to bolster Imboden's sagging cavalry. McClanahan assigned Lieutenant Carter Berkeley's rifled section the job.[137] Jones sent Major Richard Henry Brewer, commander of five hundred dismounted Virginia cavalrymen from Jones's own brigade and other assorted troops, to deploy in front of Berkeley's artillery on the slope of Northwest Hill, three-quarters of a mile north of Piedmont. Jones rode down the Staunton Road to personally examine the situation. In the distance ahead, he soon spotted Imboden and Colonel White riding in retreat and galloped up to them.[138]

Jones greeted the downtrodden Imboden and requested a summary of the morning's combat. Imboden gave his commander the details and relayed

Major Brewer's battalion of dismounted cavalrymen from "Grumble" Jones's Brigade occupied a line approximating the trees lining the lane. *Scott C. Patchan.*

the report of a trusted scout who had incorrectly estimated that Hunter had 9,000 infantry and 2,500 cavalry in camp at Port Republic the previous night (the Army of the Shenandoah numbered about 7,800 officers and fighting men). Jones informed the Augusta native that Brewer and Berkeley were moving into position and would be on the scene in five minutes. Jones then remarked that the rest of the army was only short distance to the rear and would soon be there as well. According to Imboden's self-serving recollections, this news astounded him, as he believed that Jones would challenge Hunter's advance at Mowry's Hill.[139]

As Imboden later told the story, he first thought that Jones's guide had misled him. The Staunton lawyer exclaimed, "My God General! You are not going to fight here, and lose all the advantage of position we shall have at Mowry's Hill?" Grumble roared back, "Yes! I am going to fight right here, if Hunter advances promptly to the attack. If he don't I will go over there and attack him where he is." Imboden inaccurately pleaded, "We have no advantage of ground here, and he out numbers us nearly three to one, and will beat us." An infuriated Jones retorted, "I don't want any advantage of ground, for I can whip Hunter anywhere," according to Imboden.[140]

Imboden then entered a "solemn protest against fighting" at Piedmont. Jones reminded the Staunton lawyer, "By G-d, Sir! I believe I am in command here today." Imboden, somewhat suspectly, claimed that he responded, "You are Sir! And I now ask your orders and will carry them out as best I can; but if I live, I will see that the responsibility for this day's work is fixed where I think it belongs." While it is clear from contemporary sources that Imboden disagreed with Jones's decision to fight at Piedmont, the accuracy and tone of his portrayal of the incident is questionable. Imboden's historical writings often exaggerated his own self-importance and misstated events to his own advantage, something that was not uncommon among officers' postwar recollections.[141]

While the two generals debated the matter, Berkeley arrived on the scene with his two rifled guns. Fighting in their home county gave his gunners a sense of urgency and desperation that they had not previously shown. Berkeley never forgot the scene, and many years later recounted:

> *We passed through the village, our horses on the run, and our boys yelling enthusiastically as they always did when going to the front. My boys were inspired by the glory of battle, and when that feeling takes possession of men, all fear vanishes…We all had that feeling that day, and were inspired by one still stronger, for behind us were our mothers, wives, sisters and sweethearts. At home bright eyes were sparkling for us, and we would defend them to the last. There were some ladies standing in a porch, waving their handkerchiefs and cheering as we passed, as was usual with the noble women of the valley, when they saw our men going into battle. One of them cried out, "Lieutenant, don't let your men make so much noise, they will scare all the Federals away before you can get a shot at them."*[142]

Eclipsing the village, Berkeley continued on until reaching Northwest Hill. There, the two guns were wheeled into battery and dropped trail. Berkeley surveyed the front and saw Tibbits's and Platner's cavalry immediately in front, with the rest of the Union army approaching in the distance. The country appeared blue with Federals as the smoke from a burning mill at Mount Meridian mushroomed into the sky to the north.[143]

Following close behind Berkeley, Brewer's Battalion hustled through Piedmont and up the Staunton Road. The men deployed west of the road in the wood line on the northern face of Northwest Hill. Brewer placed his men behind a breastwork of fences, rails and fallen timber on the northern face of the hill. In front, an open field extended for several hundred yards, offering a clear field of fire. Crawford Run and Polecat Draft flowed through the field and into the Middle River, creating obstacles to any Federal advance. Brewer posted a strong skirmish line in front and deployed two niter mining companies on his left flank inside of the sweeping bend of the Middle River to cover a crossing on his left. On Brewer's right, Opie's Augusta County Reserves covered the road, and regrouped elements of Imboden's Brigade held the ground on the east side of the road. The line was barely in position when the Union cavalry appeared in front of the Confederates.[144]

On the opposite side of the battlefield, Stahel surveyed the new Confederate position and concluded that his cavalry could not drive Brewer and Berkeley from their strong position. As such, the Hungarian secured his position until Hunter arrived with the infantry. On the west side of the Staunton Road, McReynolds's brigade cautiously approached Brewer and Berkeley's strong position on Northwest Hill. When Berkeley's guns and Brewer's Battalion opened fire at 9:00 a.m., the Union cavalry halted and dismounted. "It did not pay for us to sit on our horses and have them firing at us," related Charles F. Wisewell of the 1st Veteran Cavalry. That regiment sheltered itself from the Confederate fire in a ravine formed by Polecat Draft and Crawford Run. Stahel's mounted regiments each deployed skirmishers to cover their fronts.[145]

On his right, Tibbits's troopers were stationed on the flood plain of the Middle River, terrain that offered little shelter. Brewer felt out the strength

Colonel William B. Tibbits aggressively led the 21st New York and 14th Pennsylvania Cavalry in the morning cavalry action at Mount Meridian. *USAMHI.*

of Tibbits's position by slowly advancing his skirmish line down the hill. Tibbits countered by advancing troopers from the 21st New York and 14th Pennsylvania to engage Brewer's Virginians. The Confederates slowly fell back up the hill, drawing the Northerners after them. As the Federal troopers followed, Berkeley's two guns fired from their hilltop position, sending the Northerners scurrying to the rear. Then Brewer's troopers advanced, and the whole scenario played itself out once more.[146]

To counter the stiffening Confederate resistance, Stahel shifted Wynkoop's brigade from his far left flank to the right, but that would take time. For more immediate assistance, he deployed his horse artillery. Lieutenant Samuel J. Shearer's two-gun section of Battery G, 1st West Virginia Light Artillery, rolled up the Staunton Road to support Tibbits and Platner. The West Virginians wheeled into battery, unlimbering their guns in a wheat field. From the Confederate position on Northwest Hill, Lieutenant Berkeley's quick eye spied Shearer's section as it went into battery on the heights immediately south of Polecat Draft. The Augusta native promptly ranged in and commenced pounding the Federal artillerists. Shearer tried to respond but could not effectively operate his guns under the accurate Confederate

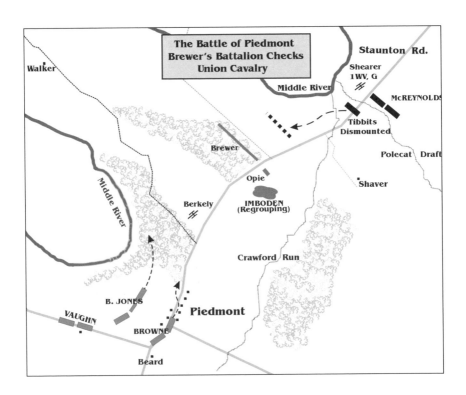

fire. Berkeley had the advantage of already being in position and hammered away at the Federal battery. A single shot killed two horses and wounded several more. Berkeley recalled that the Federal horse artillery "seemed to be excited and fired wildly" under the precision fire of the Virginia gunners. Although Shearer was unable to effectively respond to the Confederate barrage, his presence aided the Union cavalry by drawing Berkeley's fire away from the dismounted Union troopers.[147]

For almost two hours, Brewer and Berkeley held Stahel's cavalry at bay. In fact, Brewer's bold front convinced Tibbits that the Southerners were going to launch a counterattack. Brewer's stand purchased enough time for the balance of the Confederate army to reach Piedmont. Jones used the time gained to deploy his infantry, dismounted cavalry and artillery. These units had marched to the battlefield via the Cross Road, an east–west thoroughfare that connected the Valley Pike with eastern Augusta County and intersected the Staunton Road just south of Piedmont. Jones surveyed the terrain and selected the area north of the Cross Road and west of the Staunton Road to place his veteran infantry and dismounted men.[148] Sergeant Milton Humphreys, a Confederate participant as well as a postwar scholar and artillery expert, aptly described the battlefield:

> *West of the East* [Staunton] *Road and south of the Cross Road the land was timbered and north of it was open land* [a wheat field at the time] *for some 300 yards north, and west till it was broken by a hollow and then descended to Middle River. This stream bends to the east and curves northward around to the west and all around this curve there is a high, almost vertical bluff. The woodland, north of the cross road and the wheat field, extended from the toe of this horse-shoe bend to the East Road. The woodland was about three hundred yards broad, measured on a north and south line and its length on an east and west line was considerably greater. Its southern edge was almost straight, but the northern edge was considerably convex toward the north.*[149]

Jones deployed his infantry along the northern edge of the woods about half a mile north of the Cross Road on the west side of the Staunton Road. His battle line also approximated the course of Walker's Lane, running through and along the northern course of the woods from the Staunton Road to the Walker home one mile to the west. The line rested just inside the northern fringe of a timbered area. Nearer the Staunton Road, the line rested one hundred yards behind an open rise. In the center of this line, open ground offered the defenders an excellent field of fire. On the left flank, the Confederates occupied the military crest of the Middle River bluffs. These allowed the defenders to deliver a plunging fire on any attacking troops, rendering this part of the Confederate line virtually impregnable to a direct attack.

General Jones directed Colonel Beuhring H. Jones (no relation), commander of the Confederate 1st Brigade, to quickly deploy his brigade into a line with "the left resting on the Middle River bluffs at a bend which he [General Jones] pointed out." The commanding general told Beuhring Jones that the lay of the land "would suggest the position." Colonel Jones's Virginians marched through the woods to the designated position. Leaving his troops concealed in the woods, the Virginian rode across the field into the opposite timber. There he saw Brewer's men holding the Federal cavalry at bay. After examining the terrain, Jones understood his assignment and galloped back across the field to his brigade.[150]

Jones positioned his brigade in line of battle along the northern edge of the wood with Lieutenant Colonel William E. Fife's 36th Virginia Infantry anchoring the army's left flank on the bluffs. Numbering about five hundred effectives, the 36th Virginia was a veteran outfit that had seen much action in West Virginia, as well as at Fort Donelson. Although most of the regiment was concealed in the woods, the companies on its left flank occupied an open field atop the steep bluffs that negated any possibility of the Federals turning the Confederate left flank. One Virginian recalled the bank to be "something like seventy or a hundred feet high [and] covered with a dense undergrowth of brush." The woods did not fully extend all the way to the bluffs, so the 36th Virginia's left flank companies occupied an open field.[151]

Lieutenant Colonel Henry Beckley's 150-man 45th Battalion Virginia Infantry filed into line along the edge of the woods on the right flank of the 36th Virginia. Most of these Mountaineers hailed from the heart of West Virginia coal country. The unit's roster included seventeen Hatfields and eleven McCoys—families whose postwar feud earned them lasting infamy in American history. On Beckley's right flank, Captain James W. Johnston's 60th Virginia Infantry deployed along the wood line where it, too, built rail breastworks. Company F of the 60th Virginia deployed a skirmish line across the brigade front. These Virginians crossed the field and entered the opposite wood line to the left of Brewer's position. Once in the woods, the skirmishers halted, took whatever cover was available and waited for the expected attack.[152]

As soon as the troops reached their designated positions, they quickly converted a rail fence lining the wood line into a breastwork. The soldiers left the fence posts in the ground and kept the top rails in place. The Virginians laid the remaining rails and timber vertically on the top rail. The top end of the vertical rails slanted back over the heads of the defenders, who dug a slight entrenchment behind the rail structure. When complete, it "formed a very good breastwork to shield" the Confederates from Minié balls. Private Isaac Prillaman of the 36th Virginia felt so secure in this position that he "squatted down behind a rail pile at one time & went fast asleep."[153]

On Colonel Jones's right flank, Colonel William H. Browne deployed the Confederate 2nd Brigade, extending the battle line to the Staunton Road. The twenty-five-year-old Virginian was among the best-trained officers in General Jones's army. Browne would have graduated from West Point in the second class of 1861 but resigned from the academy on April 22, 1861, when Virginia seceded. Returning to his home in Jeffersonville (now Tazewell), Virginia, Browne received a captain's commission in the Confederate army. Browne, now the colonel of the 45th Virginia Infantry, commanded the 2nd Infantry Brigade of General Jones's army. Browne's Brigade included the 45th Virginia, the Thomas Legion and Brewer's Battalion.[154]

The six hundred men of Lieutenant Colonel Alexander Davis's 45th Virginia defended the center of the Confederate left wing. Davis, a graduate of Emory and Henry College, formed his veteran troops on the right flank of the 60th Virginia of Colonel Beuhring Jones's brigade. Davis's soldiers defended the wood line protected by a hastily erected rail breastwork. Brewer's Battalion eventually occupied the position on the left of the 45th Virginia but was initially deployed on the skirmish line. Colonel James R. Love's Thomas Legion anchored the right flank of Browne's Brigade. Love was a veteran officer from the Army of Northern Virginia's 16th North Carolina and had been wounded at the Battle of Seven Pines in 1862. His Thomas Legion consisted of an eight-company regiment commanded by Major William W. Stringfield and a five-company battalion led by Lieutenant Colonel James McKamy, numbering 390 men in all. Love's rugged Tennessee and North Carolina Mountaineers defended an elevated position "facing cleared fields [to the] north, west and east." The legion's line formed a gradual arc that extended from the right flank of the 45th Virginia to the Staunton Road. By the time the arc reached the road, the Legion's line veered southward for a short distance and paralleled the Staunton Road.[155]

On Love's right flank, four guns from Captain James C. Marquis' Augusta Reserve Battery went into position. One gun deployed in the Staunton Road, and the remaining three unlimbered in a plowed field immediately adjacent to and east of the road. Marquis had organized the battery at

Colonel William G. Ely returned to the 18th Connecticut shortly before the Battle of Piedmont, having been captured at the Second Battle of Winchester in June 1863. *USAMHI.*

Staunton in April. Young men ages sixteen to eighteen fleshed out its ranks, earning it the moniker of the "Boy Battery." At Piedmont, these "boys" manned a twenty-four-pound howitzer, a twenty-pound Parrott gun, a three-inch rifle and a twelve-pound howitzer. Regardless of their age and experience, General Jones had posted Marquis' Battery in a key position on the battlefield and expected it to deliver. The four remaining guns of McClanahan's Battery dropped trail east of the Staunton Road near the northern fringe of Piedmont.[156]

A large unoccupied gap (six hundred yards wide) existed in the Confederate line between Browne's right flank and the next body of Confederates, Vaughn's Brigade. These one thousand Tennesseans deployed their line just south of Piedmont. This position occupied the Beard family farm, situated in the southeast quadrant of the intersection of the Staunton and Cross Roads. Vaughn's left flank rested near the junction of the two roads, and his Tennesseans hastily constructed rail breastworks from nearby fences and other suitable material. Vaughn's Brigade consisted of both cavalry and mounted infantry who had been recruited in Unionist-dominated east Tennessee. However, when the brigade departed for the Shenandoah Valley, the men left their horses in Bristol and fought as infantry for the next six weeks.[157]

John Crawford Vaughn was born in Roane County, Tennessee, in 1824, and had served as a captain in the 5th Tennessee Infantry during the Mexican-American War. Following that conflict, Vaughn returned to Tennessee, where he became a successful businessman. While on business in Charleston, South

Carolina, he witnessed the bombardment of Fort Sumter. When he returned to Tennessee, his prior military service brought him the rank of colonel in the 3rd Tennessee Infantry. He guided this unit at First Manassas, where it participated in the Southern counterattack that collapsed the Federal right flank. By the fall of 1862, Vaughn had received a commission as a brigadier general and commanded a brigade of Tennessee infantry. This command suffered the misfortune of being on the receiving end of Grant's highly successful Vicksburg Campaign, which gutted his brigade's integrity. The brigade that Vaughn commanded at Piedmont was cobbled together from the remnants of two infantry brigades that were mounted and combined with several cavalry commands during the winter of 1863–64 to make it a respectably sized unit.[158]

Overall, Vaughn and his men had earned a poor reputation thus far in the war. In April 1864, Lieutenant Colonel Archer Anderson inspected Vaughn's command for the Confederate War Department and concluded, "This brigade is in deplorable condition," adding that it was "almost a band of marauders." Anderson blamed Vaughn, writing that "General V. has no idea of discipline." Anderson recommended that Vaughn take his infantry and join an infantry division with a strict commander. This last suggestion unintentionally became a reality to some extent when Vaughn's brigade dismounted and went to the Valley of Virginia with Grumble Jones, a renowned disciplinarian.[159]

Like Imboden, Vaughn had questioned Jones on the army's position for the coming battle. Vaughn attempted to convince Jones that the ground was unfavorable and that "the line [was] too extended to be successfully occupied by the troops in hand." Unlike Imboden, Vaughn accepted his commander's decision without dissent. Both men, however, staked their claims after Jones died on the battlefield.[160]

While the Confederate foot soldiers solidified their position, Jones and Imboden rode along the front of the infantry battle line posted in the edge of the woods. The generals surveyed the situation and cheered the men as they trotted down Walker Lane toward the Middle River. Imboden related the scene:

> *The men were in high spirits and cheered us as we rode along their front, where, for a part of the distance, they had torn down fences to form breastworks of the rails. Jones was gleeful and often repeated as we passed from one command to another: "Aim low, boys, aim low, and hit 'em below the belt. And be sure you see them before you shoot. Aim low and make every shot tell."*[161]

While General Jones's infantry deployed, Brewer and Berkeley continued to hold the Union cavalry at bay, Stahel having decided to wait for Hunter's infantry to arrive. Several hours of fighting and skirmishing diminished the Union troopers' ammunition to dangerously low levels. Tibbits had already distributed his reserve ammunition to the men on the firing line, but even that was running out now. To compensate for his dwindling rate of fire, Tibbits aggressively advanced his skirmishers, hoping to deceive the Confederates as to his strength and intentions. Luckily for Tibbits, Brewer did not call the New Yorker's bluff. While the cat-and-mouse maneuvering played itself out, Tibbits rode rearward in search of reinforcements but learned that Sullivan's infantry would soon be taking over the front line.[162]

When Brewer's Battalion initially stopped Stahel's advance north of Piedmont, the Hungarian hurried a courier to the rear, telling Hunter of the stiffening Confederate resistance. Hunter listened intently to the orderly's words and then calmly replied, "Damn them, I would just as soon fight him now as at any other time." The army commander ordered his chief of artillery, Captain Henry A. DuPont, to send more artillery forward and subdue the Confederate guns holding up the Union advance. Hunter then rode to the front and began deploying his army for the pending battle.[163]

DuPont led Lieutenant Charles Holman's Battery B, 5th U.S. Artillery, and Captain Alonzo Snow's Battery B, 1st Maryland Light Artillery, forward to assist the cavalry. The artillerists pulled out of column, sped to the front and went into position on the west side of the Staunton Road and north of Polecat Draft. The 5th U.S. unlimbered its guns nearest the road immediately to the left of Shearer's guns. Snow's Marylanders positioned their guns farther to Shearer's right, almost inside a sweeping bend of the Middle River. Shearer's damaged section limbered up and went to the rear to make repairs before rejoining the battle. Snow's and Holman's artillerists set their sites on Berkeley's section and yanked their lanyards. Holman's gunners simultaneously fired all six cannons, resulting in a tremendous blast that shook the battlefield and sent clouds of thick sulphuric smoke into the air. Snow's guns also opened fire, and the concentrated bombardment from DuPont's twelve rifled guns was more than the Virginians could endure. Fortunately, Captain McClanahan recalled Berkeley to the main Confederate position, and Berkeley rejoined McClanahan's Battery near Piedmont.[164]

When Berkeley withdrew, Snow and Holman trained their guns on Imboden's troopers posted in the open ground of the Shaver Farm on the east side of the Staunton Road. The mounted Confederate horse soldiers made inviting targets for the Union gunners. When Jones and Imboden returned to the road, the latter saw his brigade standing in the open, needlessly exposed to the Federal artillery fire. Imboden requested orders, and Jones replied, "Move your men back. You will find Vaughn dismounted just back of the village. Dismount your men, sending your horses to the rear in the woods, and take position on Vaughn's right." At the same time, Jones pointed toward Round Hill, a commanding eminence on the far right and rear of the Confederate position. Jones added, "You see that hill over there, throw out flankers to the foot of that hill, and protect my right flank. Hunter will try to turn my position there and if you can prevent that, it is all I shall ask of you. I'll attend to the rest of the field." Imboden replied, "Your orders will be carried out fully," and saluted Jones before dashing off to Piedmont.[165]

As the conflict heightened, General Jones established his headquarters behind the Thomas Legion's right flank on elevated ground just west of the Staunton Road. This position offered Jones a panoramic view of the battlefield. As he studied it, the gap between Browne's and Vaughn's Brigades troubled him. At the same time, the strength of his left flank resting on the commanding Middle River Bluffs allowed it to be easily defended by a smaller number of troops. As such, he ordered Colonel Beuhring Jones to detach half of his command from the left and send it to the right to fill the gap between Browne and Vaughn. The brigade commander immediately dispatched the five hundred men of Captain Johnston's 60th Virginia Infantry. When the Virginians reached the Staunton Road, General Jones directed them to form their line of battle parallel to the road in the center of the gap. The Virginians deployed near the village with their left flank 300 yards from the Thomas Legion and 175 yards north of Vaughn's brigade. From this position near Jones's field headquarters, the 60th Virginia overlooked the Crawford Run ravine. Grass and clover covered the hillside in front of the Virginians, and woods covered the ground east of the stream below.[166]

Meanwhile, Sullivan's infantry reached the battlefield and relieved Stahel's cavalry. The U.S. infantry had marched in the wake of the horsemen through dense underbrush in the woods and tall grain growing in the fields that had made the march exceedingly fatiguing for the infantrymen and slowed their progress. When Imboden's Brigade challenged the Union advance, the foot soldiers halted at the edge of a wooded lot just east of Mount Meridian, where they watched the swirling cavalry action. After Stahel routed the gray horsemen, the infantry continued on toward Piedmont.[167] Colonel Moor deployed his regiments into columns of battalions, each fronting the width of a company line of battle, leaving enough space between columns for the regiments to form their line of battle. The brigade marched for one mile toward Piedmont through fields and woods, with shells from the Confederate cannons whistling overhead through the treetops.[168]

As the brigade advanced, Hunter rode up to the 18th Connecticut Infantry on Moor's right flank. Colonel Ely halted his regiment and called his men to attention. Hunter addressed the New Englanders in a "direct and soldierly" manner, informing them that the Confederate army lay just ahead. He encouraged them to do their duty this day and remove the tarnish from New Market that had sullied the 18th Connecticut's reputation. Hunter's sardonic but honest remarks offended the New Englanders, and they "scarcely got up a decent cheer in response." Sergeant George C. Setchell recollected, "We were all as mad as hoppers before he got through, as we did not think it was any fault of ours that Sigel got licked. I think every man made up his mind then that if we did come up against the Rebs that day some of them would get hurt." While Hunter's oration gained him few friends, he did raise the fighting spirit of the men in the 18th Connecticut as intended.[169]

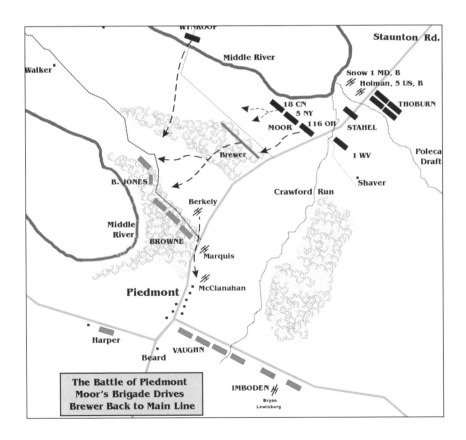

The Battle of Piedmont
Moor's Brigade Drives
Brewer Back to Main Line

After the brief pause, Colonel Moor's columns renewed their advance, clearing the woods and entering into an open meadow bisected by two streams flowing into the Middle River. Major Peale's skirmishers crossed this field and advanced toward the Confederate position on the timbered slope in their front. While the skirmishers moved forward, Moor wheeled his regiments into line of battle on the west side of the road and followed Peale's men into the meadow. Ely's 18th Connecticut anchored Moor's right flank near the east bank of the Middle River. Lieutenant Colonel Edward Murray's 5th New York Heavy Artillery deployed on the left of the New Englanders, and Colonel James Washburn's 116th Ohio extended Moor's line to the Staunton Road.[170]

Colonel Joseph Thoburn's brigade took position on the east side of the Staunton Road, deploying into a double line of battle. Thoburn positioned Colonel William B. Curtis's 12th West Virginia on the right of his front line, while Colonel George D. Wells's 34th Massachusetts aligned itself on the left of the West Virginians. Colonel Robert S. Rodgers's 2nd Maryland Eastern Shore Regiment manned the right of the second line, and Colonel Jacob Campbell's 54th Pennsylvania held the left. When it became apparent that the enemy lay in strength on Thoburn's right flank, he halted his brigade. Out in front of Thoburn's brigade, the 1st West Virginia had been in the advance, with two companies deployed as skirmishers. Sullivan placed the remaining eight companies behind the 116th Ohio on Moor's left flank.[171]

West of the road, Captain Alfred Von Kleiser's 30th New York Independent Battery, a unit composed of German Americans, arrived to support the infantry with its four twelve-pound Napoleons. The German battery unlimbered and deployed behind Moor's line. Moor assigned his own 28th Ohio troops to support their countrymen manning the four-gun battery. A feeling of unease ran through the minds of the soldiers of the 28th Ohio as they stood waiting for the battle to begin. This regiment's term of service expired before the month's end. The men anticipated joyous reunions at home with family and friends—if they survived the coming battle. When orders came to support the artillery instead of joining the attack, these men surely breathed a sigh of relief.[172]

Von Kleiser's Napoleons fired at Brewer's line posted in the woods on the slope in Moor's front. The artillery fire forced the Confederates to hug the earth for shelter. With artillery projectiles sailing overhead, Major Peale's skirmishers deployed about fifteen to twenty feet apart and cautiously advanced toward Brewer's position. A bugle soon sounded, and Moor's brigade trudged toward the Confederate line in the woods. Sergeant Setchell of the 18th Connecticut recalled the "beautiful sight" created as the blue line advanced with flags unfurled. Marquis' Confederate battery fired, but its shells initially fell short of the advancing Union troops. As the bluecoats pressed on, the shells exploded among the skirmishers but inflicted little damage among the loosely arrayed Federals. With these shells detonating around them, Peale's men ascended the hill toward Brewer's concealed line of battle.[173]

Brewer's rugged troopers fired and forced Peale's men to recoil. Moor observed the repulse and ordered the skirmishers to cede the firing line to the main force. The ground in Moor's front contained numerous obstacles, including small rivulets and a sturdy rail fence. Moor's troops negotiated the streams with little delay and steadily closed in on Brewer's position. When the Northerners reached the fence, Brewer's men opened fire from the woods, while Moor's men struggled to rip down the obstruction. As the brigade progressed, the closed end of a horseshoe bend in the Middle River jutted in front of the 18th Connecticut on Moor's right flank, disrupting its formation. After the New Englanders negotiated the disruptive bend, they veered westward into the open end of another horseshoe bend in the river. As they did so, the Confederates of Captain James F. Jones's Niter and Mining Battalion troops fired into the 18th Connecticut. Some of Captain Jones's skirmishers had deployed in the woods on the right flank of the New Englanders. Concealed in the trees, these Confederates picked their targets and fired into the exposed Federal flank. Sergeant Setchell informed Ely of the Confederates' position. He expressed skepticism at the report, but the raking Confederate fire quickly changed his mind.[174]

Ely ordered Sergeant Robert Kerr's Company G to clear out the Confederates on the right flank. In a voice that "must have made all the Rebs within two miles of us think the Day of Judgement had come," Ely shouted, "Company G, deploy as skirmishers! Forward! Double Quick! March!" With "vim and snap," Kerr's men obeyed and drove the offending Southerners away from the exposed Federal flank. After deploying Kerr's Company, Ely ordered his men to crawl up the hill on their stomachs to avoid the biting rifle fire from Brewer's troops. With the New Englanders literally slowed to a crawl, the Federal advance looked elsewhere for success. In the center, the rookie foot soldiers of the 5th New York encountered heavy resistance and failed to provide the impetus needed for the attack to succeed. However, the situation looked more promising on Moor's left flank.[175]

There, Colonel James Washburn's 116th Ohio overlapped the Confederate right flank. The Ohioans in front of Brewer's line engaged the Southerners in the woods, but those nearest the Staunton Road charged unopposed and wrapped around the Confederate right. These Buckeyes poured a heavy enfilade fire into Brewer's right and rear, and confusion soon reigned in the Confederate ranks. On the opposite flank, the 18th Connecticut crawled up to the brow of the hill, where Ely ordered the men to rise and fire. As the men stood up, the Confederates fired a volley at point-blank range into the Federal ranks, striking one officer and a dozen men. Motivated by memories of New Market, the Connecticut troops charged the Southern position in the wood line. As the Confederates scrambled to reload, Ely's regiment closed in on Brewer's butternuts, who steeled themselves for the impact. Before the 18th Connecticut made contact, the enfilade fire from the 116th Ohio on Moor's left made Brewer's entire line untenable. The gray troopers on his right streamed rearward in confusion as the Ohioans closed in from the east, supported by the 1st West Virginia. The 5th New York hastened its pace in the center, and the 18th Connecticut pressed hard on the right. Brewer's entire line rapidly unraveled from right to left.[176]

Supporting Moor's right flank was Colonel Wynkoop's 20th Pennsylvania Cavalry. These horsemen had crossed the winding Middle River and drove off Confederate skirmishers on the west bank. Reaching the next bend in the river, Wynkoop crossed back over to the east bank and charged Brewer's left as it retreated. Wynkoop's Pennsylvanians disorganized what had been a relatively orderly retreat by Brewer's left flank troops and captured several prisoners along the way. The fragments of Brewer's command streamed rearward through the woods and across an open field. Brewer's Battalion ended its retreat at the main Confederate line, where it reformed and occupied a position on the left of Browne's Brigade between the 45th Virginia and Beckley's Battalion.[177] On the far left, Captain James F. Jones, commander of 120 Niter and Mining Battalion troops, retreated into the breastworks held by Beuhring Jones's brigade on the left. Captain Francis Thornton, acting major of the 36th Virginia, ordered Captain Jones to place his miners into a vacant position in the open ground atop the bluffs on the extreme left of the Confederate line. Posted beyond the woods, the miners gathered the few logs and rails at hand and constructed a short breastwork that barely sheltered a prone soldier.[178]

Although the day had started off slowly for General Imboden, the Army of the Valley District had gained some extra time through the determined actions of men such as Major Henry Brewer, Captain John Opie and Lieutenant Carter Berkeley. As a result of their delaying actions, General Jones now had the opportunity he so desired to challenge Hunter in open field combat.

Chapter 5

"Every One Held His Position"

G eneral David Hunter went into battle at Piedmont believing that he was facing General John D. Imboden's slightly reinforced command. U.S. Grant had informed Hunter that Breckinridge's infantry had departed the valley to join Lee in the defense of Richmond. As late as June 3, Federal intelligence reports estimated Imboden's strength at 2,500 troops, including the local reserves and a gathering force of Maryland Confederates. Hence, Hunter logically concluded that only Imboden, slightly reinforced, stood between the Army of the Shenandoah and Staunton. But logic failed Hunter, because Grant had no reliable intelligence sources in southwest Virginia and east Tennessee. This blind spot in the Federal intelligence-gathering mechanism allowed General Jones to shift a significant Confederate force to the valley undetected.[179]

After the Union forces drove off Berkeley's artillery and Brewer's troops, a brief calm settled over the Piedmont battlefield. The early morning rain and cloud cover had given way to crisp blue skies and bright rays of sunshine beaming down on the rolling green farmlands situated in the shadows of the looming Blue Ridge Mountains. Hunter and his staff rode out "some distance" in front of DuPont's batteries to a ridge overlooking the battlefield. No sooner did Hunter's party appear on the cleared spur than the Confederate gunners opened fire. They scanned the field, which Colonel Strother described from the Union perspective:

> *The enemy's position was strong and well chosen. It was on a conclave of wooded hills commanding an open valley between and open, gentle slopes in front. On our right in advance of the village of Piedmont was a line*

of log and rail defenses very advantageously located in the edge of a forest and just behind the rise of a smooth, open hill so that troops moving over this hill could be mowed down by musketry from the works at short range and to prevent artillery from being used against them. The left flank of this palisade rested on a steep and impracticable bluff sixty feet high and washed at its base by the Shenandoah.[180]

Satisfied with his view of the battlefield, Hunter retired "into an adjoining wood where a vengeful shell pursued him." DuPont's guns then opened fire and quickly silenced the offending Confederate pieces. Hunter then watched the developing battle on the west side of the Staunton Road.[181]

The first demonstration against the main Confederate line occurred when Stahel advanced Wynkoop's brigade against the Confederate left "to see if it could be turned." The Confederate left rested near a horseshoe bend in the Middle River where steep bluffs lined the river's north bank. Moving west into the river bend, the ground leveled out into rolling fields conducive to mounted operations. Behind the western reaches of the bluffs, an open flood plain appeared to invite attack on the left rear of the Confederate line. Wynkoop selected Major Henry Myers's Ringgold Battalion, a small but rugged outfit from southwest Pennsylvania, for the mission. Myers formed the battalion into line of battle in an open ravine. The Pennsylvanians charged and galloped out of the ravine toward the Confederate left. They drove the Confederate skirmishers back and then hit the Confederate flank, anchored on a prominent eminence known locally as "Sheep Hill." From the Federal position, it appeared that no Confederate forces occupied the flood plain behind Sheep Hill.[182]

In actuality, part of the 36th Virginia and Captain Jones's Niter and Mining Battalion easily covered the position behind Sheep Hill. Their left flank extended almost to the river, leaving no room for the Pennsylvanians to get around the Confederate flank. When the Ringgolds appeared, the 36th Virginia and Captain Jones's miners fired into the ranks of the Federal horsemen, forcing them to retire. Myers charged twice more but met the same result. The Ringgolds sullenly retraced their steps back to the wooded ravine. Upon their return, Colonel Wynkoop sarcastically called to them, "You will let a dozen bushwhackers run the Ringgold Cavalry?" Major Myers, his blood up from the combat, replied sharply, "There is good fighting in there for your whole brigade if you will only take them in."[183]

On Wynkoop's left flank, Colonel Augustus Moor had quickly reformed his brigade after his successful attack against Brewer's Battalion. He

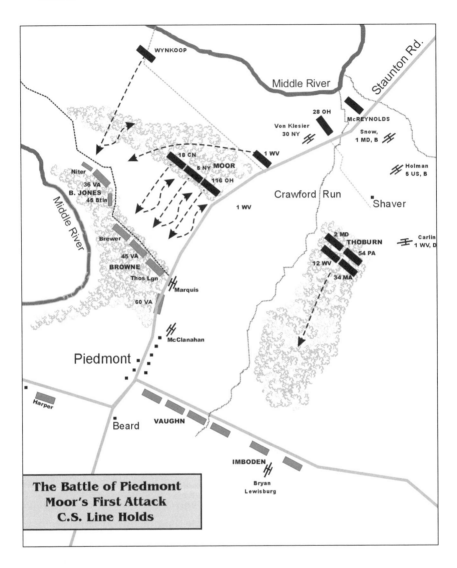

The Battle of Piedmont
Moor's First Attack
C.S. Line Holds

advanced through the woods until reaching their southern extremity, where he came to an open field. Looking across the field, Moor saw the Confederate breastworks extending across the front of the second wood lot. He ordered his men to fire at the Confederate fortifications, but their volleys elicited no response. Moor concluded that they "could walk right over the rail pen" and conferred with Sullivan on their next move. Hoping to build on the momentum of Moor's initial advance, Sullivan determined "to storm them [the breastworks] and ascertain whether or not there was any force behind them."[184]

View of the Confederate line from the perspective of Moor's brigade. *Scott C. Patchan.*

Moor led his brigade out of the woods and through the clover-covered fields toward the Confederate fortifications situated along the opposing wood line. On his right flank, Ely's New Englanders marched out of the woods and entered a wheat field, where the Virginians cut them down like wheat before a scythe. From the rising ground near the Middle River bluffs, Beckley's 45th Battalion delivered a plunging fire into the Federals' exposed right flank. This raking fire forced the 18th Connecticut leftward, crowding it into the 5th New York. The Confederate fire inflicted a deadly toll and stymied the New Englanders. Confusion reigned in their ranks; Colonel Ely had his horse shot out from under him, and his unit quickly lost its cohesion. Ely ordered a retreat, but his troops were already streaming back into the timber.[185]

In the center of Moor's line, Lieutenant Colonel Edward Murray's 1st Battalion, 5th New York Heavy Artillery acting as infantry advanced directly toward Lieutenant Colonel Alexander M. Davis's 45th Virginia. With its left wing covered by the bald hill between the two battle lines, the New Yorkers moved forward in unison with the 116th Ohio on their left and the 18th Connecticut on their right until the New Englanders buckled under the intense musketry on their right. Then, the 5th New York came under an enfilading fire on its right flank that sent the "Heavies" rushing back to the woods.[186]

On Moor's left, the 692 men of Colonel James Washburn's 116th Ohio moved through a field of clover toward the Confederate line. The Buckeyes benefited from the partial cover of a low bald rise for the first one hundred yards of their advance. However, when the Ohioans ascended the hill and their heads and torsos cleared the elevation's crest, Colonel James Love's Thomas Legion poured a galling fire into the Buckeyes. They charged onward, but the Confederates delivered a steady fire, inflicting significant casualties on the Ohioans. One Thomas Legionnaire wrote home, "We never fired at longer range than seventy five yards." Washburn had his horse shot out from under him, and many of his men fell just in front of the Confederate works. Overwhelmed by the intense, close-range musketry of the Thomas Legion, the 116th Ohio withdrew to the slight cover of a rise of ground. There, Washburn and Lieutenant Colonel Thomas F. Wildes reorganized the regiment under fire from Confederate artillery.[187]

While Moor was still advancing, Sullivan dashed back into the woods and retrieved Lieutenant Colonel Jacob Weddle's 1st West Virginia Infantry, situated in reserve behind the 116th Ohio. Sullivan ordered Weddle's regiment to extend Moor's line to the right, and the Mountaineers marched

Moor's brigade charged across these fields from left to right but were twice stopped near the trees and silos in the middle of the picture by Browne's brigade, posted in the distance on the right. *Scott C. Patchan.*

through the woods behind Moor's brigade as it assaulted the Confederate infantry. When Weddle reached Moor's right flank, the 1st West Virginia advanced about one hundred yards into the open field toward Beuhring Jones's brigade and the Niter and Mining Battalion atop the steep bluffs. Weddle ordered the regiment to halt and commence firing. Before they fired a single round, the Confederates leveled "some well directed volleys" into the 1st West Virginia. The West Virginia troops "delivered and received a heavy fire" for a short time, but the "blinding, death dealing deluge of bullets" from Beuhring Jones's Virginians forced Weddle's Mountaineers back to the woods. From the comparative shelter of the trees, the 1st West Virginia fired at the Confederates but dared not challenge Jones's brigade again.[188]

In the end, Moor's attack never had any real chance to succeed, as the Confederates behind the breastworks slightly outnumbered Moor's attacking force. Moor attacked with three regiments totaling 1,600 men. The Confederates defending this portion of the line, Browne's Brigade, numbered more than 1,400 well-protected muskets supported by the 150 men of Beckley's 45th Virginia Battalion on the left. With only a miniscule manpower advantage, Moor lacked the overwhelming odds necessary to launch a successful frontal assault with Civil War weapons and tactics.[189]

Moor's linear assault formation also lessened the chance for success. Moor's men advanced in a single line of battle composed of two ranks of soldiers, but the Confederate defenders spread out along the breastworks and wood line. As a result, Moor's advancing line barely covered the entire front of Browne's Brigade. The protected Confederates cared little for alignment and easily picked apart the tight Federal formations as they approached. The accuracy and range of the Springfield and Enfield rifles (the main infantry weapons used at Piedmont) gave the Confederates the firepower to resist more than twice their number as the defenders had done on many Civil War battlefields. Although the war was in its third year, Hunter, like many generals both Union and Confederate, persisted in attempting frontal assaults against prepared defensive positions until the very end of the war.

Simultaneously with Moor's attack against the Confederate left wing, Sullivan advanced Thoburn's brigade through Shaver's woods on the east side of the Staunton Road. The woods bore to the left and carried these Federals toward Imboden's Brigade on the Confederate right. With two companies from both the 1st West Virginia and 54th Pennsylvania screening the advance, Thoburn's Federals slowly picked their way southward through the woods. As the brigade skirmishers cautiously neared the southern edge of the woods, rousing strains of "Bonnie Blue Flag" emanated from a brass band stationed with Imboden's Brigade. Skirmishers from Colonel George Imboden's 18th Virginia Cavalry opened fire on the Pennsylvanians, who shot back and reported the enemy's presence to Campbell. He quickly recognized that Thoburn's left flank lay completely open to an attack by the overlapping position of Imboden's Brigade and rushed this information to the West Virginian.[190]

Thoburn halted immediately and discovered that he was more than half a mile in advance of Moor's brigade, with Imboden's and Vaughn's commands deployed behind "barricades of fence rails extending for three fourths of a mile in length." Instead of attacking, Thoburn pulled back three hundred feet into the woods, leaving five companies in front of the Confederate right wing to screen his position. He reported his situation to Hunter via an aide, who quickly returned "with orders to hold my ground until the 1st Brigade [Moor's] advanced," and presumably resume the advance when Moor did. Meanwhile, as Thoburn's regiments retired deeper into the trees, the 2nd Maryland Eastern Shore lost sight of the regiment in its front and ended up stumbling blindly toward the Confederate line. Thoburn perceived the danger and righted the inexperienced Marylanders before any mishap occurred.[191]

While Thoburn waited for Moor to renew the attack, Captain Thomas Bryan spotted Thoburn's brigade maneuvering through an opening in the timber. Bryan's Lewisburg artillery roared into action, firing four guns blindly into the woods where he calculated the Federals would be. In spite of the handicap, some of Bryan's shells found their mark. The Confederate projectiles screamed through the treetops, clipping off branches that crashed into the Federal troops below. This affected Thoburn and his troops more psychologically than physically. Lieutenant George B. Caldwell of the 12th West Virginia recalled "the tremendous explosion of shell, the profuse rain of case shot [and] the fall[ing] of trees and limbs amid the wounded and dying." For all of the consternation that Bryan's artillery created, Thoburn's brigade suffered relatively few casualties.[192]

At the same time, Captain Marquis' inexperienced gunners had been firing at Moor's infantry in their front and at DuPont's batteries on the right. To the credit of young artillerists, Lieutenant Gottlieb Sheifley of the 116th Ohio observed the numerous flashes of Marquis' guns as they fired at "an astonishingly rapid rate." Shell fragments struck Sheifley in the left thigh, laming him for a while. A short while later, a second fragment "smashed in three ribs" on Sheifley's right breast and knocked him down "as completely as I ever was in my life."[193]

General Jones saw the need for more artillery on his left wing and bolstered Marquis' Battery with two guns from Bryan's Lewisburg Artillery. A twelve-pound howitzer and a three-inch rifled gun swung into battery on the Staunton Road just to the right of Marquis' Battery. Once in position, the Virginians fired on Von Kleiser's guns in their front. Marquis' Battery fired at the Union batteries with its twenty-pound Parrott gun, firing sixty-four rounds from that gun alone. At one point, Jones, dressed in plain civilian garb, carelessly rode his horse right in front of Marquis' guns, causing the gunners to halt their firing and wonder why a farmer was wandering the battlefield.[194]

Upon the repulse of Moor's advance, Hunter and his staff retired to the Shaver farmhouse. The plain wooden frame structure sat about two-thirds of the way down the southern face of the spur containing DuPont's artillery. Its position above Crawford Run provided Hunter and his staff a clear view of the battlefield. Hunter's cavalry escorts tied their horses to trees in an orchard behind the house to conceal them from Confederate artillerists. Upon entering the home, Hunter's staff found "some skulkers plundering and two women crying bitterly." The officers literally kicked the soldiers out of the house and calmed the women, who were members of the Dunkard Church. Hunter learned that the home's owner was hiding in the cellar with his younger children while the women struggled with the plunderers. Several staff officers retrieved Mr. Shaver from the basement, and Hunter berated him for leaving the women upstairs with the marauders while he hid in the cellar. Shaver promptly declared himself "a dunkard preacher and a

The Shaver House served as Hunter's headquarters during the Battle of Piedmont. *Scott C. Patchan.*

85

Union man" and implored Hunter not to let his horses eat the bark from the apple trees. With men dying in battle just outside and the "fate of an army uncertain," Strother noted that Shaver's request did not sit well with the officers, and an appalled cavalry officer "cursed the fellow and ordered him into the cellar."[195]

Hunter and staff quickly put all thought of Shaver aside and conducted the business of managing an army in battle. Although Moor's assault had failed, Hunter remained determined to achieve victory. To that end, he directed DuPont to silence the enemy's batteries. The Union cannons occupied an advantageous position; with four batteries forming an arc that partially encircled the right flank of Jones's advanced left wing. The shells fired from the guns along the arc converged on the left wing of the Confederate position. The guns situated on the extreme left of the arc partially enfiladed the breastworks north of Piedmont. This proved particularly problematic (and lethal) for Colonel Browne's Brigade and Marquis' Battery, which were subjected to the accurate fire of DuPont's skilled gunners. Hunter's unleashing of the Federal artillery ultimately proved to be the first step toward Union victory at Piedmont.[196]

On the far right of DuPont's arc, Captain Alfred Von Kleiser's 30th New York Independent Battery occupied the right end of the arc on some high ground behind Moor's brigade. From this position, Von Kleiser's four bronze, smoothbore Napoleon cannons possessed a line of fire loosely parallel to Staunton Road. To Von Kleiser's left and rear, Snow's Battery B, 1st Maryland Light Artillery, unlimbered its six three-inch rifled guns on the high ground immediately east of the Staunton Road. About 250 yards east of Snow, Holman's Battery B, 5th United States Light Artillery, rolled into position, occupying the heights behind the Shaver House. Carlin's West Virginia Battery occupied the extreme left of the arc in front of the Confederate right wing. Even Shearer's repaired section of horse artillery eventually rejoined the fight.[197]

DuPont established his command post on an elevation between Snow's and Holman's Batteries where he possessed a commanding view of the battlefield. Using a system of mounted orderlies, DuPont maintained firm fire control over his guns and coordinated their efforts toward a larger purpose throughout the battle than an individual battery commander could do acting on his own. DuPont's first orders directed the gunners to disregard Bryan's Lewisburg Artillery on the Confederate right flank and McClanahan's guns in front of the village of Piedmont. Instead, DuPont concentrated the fire of all twenty-two Union guns on Marquis' "Boy Battery."[198]

"Every One Held His Position"

On the far left of DuPont's arc, Captain John Carlin's Battery D, 1st West Virginia, rolled into battery in Shaver's orchard and readied for action. After receiving instructions from DuPont, Carlin studied the Confederate position "long and earnestly" and then ordered his men to load the cannons with case shot timed to a six-second fuse. After all of the guns were loaded, Carlin discussed the distance, windage and elevation with one of his sergeants and then called out, "No. 1, Fire!" The gun roared and sent its projectile hurtling toward the Confederate line. Carlin peered through his field glasses and watched until the shell exploded. He quickly computed the adjustments needed to hit his intended target and then turned to the next gunner, giving him the precise factors to improve the accuracy of the next shot. No sooner had the gun fired than the captain began his routine for the third gun. As he concentrated on aiming the third piece, the gunner on number four grew jumpy waiting for his methodical captain and fired before Carlin gave the order. "Who fired that gun? Who fired that gun?" roared Carlin. He quickly went back to work, and after each gun had fired two rounds in the slow and careful manner directed by Carlin, they were dropping their shells right on target. Satisfied with his work, Carlin called out, "Now boys, block up the wheels with rails and give it to them."[199]

Marquis' inexperienced artillerists had little chance against the concentrated barrage from DuPont's battle-wise veterans. Von Kleiser's Napoleons fired straight up the road and hammered Marquis from the front. At the same time, DuPont's eighteen three-inch rifles ripped into the young battery from the east with varying degrees of both direct and enfilading fire. The brutal Federal fire killed six of Marquis' young gunners and wounded at least one other. Eventually, Marquis' artillerists finally relented to the terrible pounding and raced to the rear, abandoning their guns. Eventually, some extra horses and men from Bryan's Lewisburg Artillery bravely rode into the maelstrom and pulled Marquis' guns to safety south of the Cross Road.[200] With Marquis' Battery out of the picture, DuPont shifted his fire toward the Lewisburg section of short-range guns that Jones had recently positioned near Marquis' Battery. The Union gunners pummeled the Lewisburg artillerists and forced them to withdraw up the Staunton Road and take shelter behind a log cabin located in a field west of the road. The Union artillery fire followed the Virginians, riddling the log house and preventing the Southerners from firing back without unduly exposing their guns to destruction.[201]

Immediately after unlimbering in their new position, the gunners of the Lewisburg section noticed a target at which they could fire while concealed behind the cabin. It was Thoburn's brigade, maneuvering through Shaver's woods east down in the Crawford Run ravine. As the Virginians fired away, General Jones saw the gunners, and by all outward appearances, it seemed that they were firing at trees with no definite target. Jones rode over and asked what they were firing at. Upon learning the nature of the target, Jones replied, "Those people are doing us no harm; fire at that battery in the orchard [Carlin's]." The Virginians informed Jones that their guns lacked the range to hit that Federal battery. After some more discussion on potential targets and positions, Jones directed the Lewisburg men to take their cannons to a safer position in the southwest quadrant of the intersection of the Staunton and Cross Roads.[202]

After eliminating the Lewisburg section as a factor in the battle, DuPont targeted McClanahan's six-gun battery situated near the northeastern fringe of Piedmont. McClanahan's normally resolute gunners proved to be no match for the concentric fire of twenty-two well-handled Federal guns. With percussion shells exploding all around the cannons and having already endured several casualties, the Texan realized that his position was untenable and withdrew to the intersection of the Cross Road and the Staunton Road. There, he went into battery on the left flank of Vaughn's Brigade. With McClanahan's retreat, the exacting and concentrated fire of the Union cannons had forced all of the Confederate batteries supporting Jones's left wing from the front line, leaving the Confederate infantry with no effective artillery support and stripping the gap between Browne and Vaughn of the eight guns that had been covering the opening.[203]

Nevertheless, DuPont was not yet finished with his work. With the exception of Von Kleiser's shorter-ranged Napoleons, the Union batteries hammered away at the remaining four guns of Bryan's Lewisburg Artillery posted with Imboden on the Confederate right. As Von Kleiser's Napoleons lacked the range to strike Bryan's position, DuPont ordered the German to cease firing. Unlike the other Confederate batteries, the Lewisburg Artillery offered stiffer opposition to the Union gunners. A shell from Bryan's twenty-pound Parrott rifle exploded in the midst of Snow's Maryland Battery, the shell fragments killing three horses and wounding one man. The Marylanders responded with their six three-inch rifles and succeeded in knocking out the offending Parrott rifle, when a solid shot bent its axle and immobilized the gun. Ultimately, DuPont did not completely silence Bryan, but did limit him to firing intermittently to avoid exposure to the Union artillery fire.[204]

Sixty years after the war, DuPont still marveled at the "precision" of his artillery:

The concentration and accuracy of the fire rendered the Confederate batteries absolutely useless in very short order and drove them all off the field save one...The precision of the fire was wonderful. An examination of the field after the battle showed hundreds of furrows, made by our projectiles, crossing each other diagonally on the ground where the Confederate batteries were posted. The positions of the hostile batteries were marked also by fragments of wheels and other materiel, dead horses, abandoned harness, projectiles and bloody clothing.[205]

Having impeded the Confederate artillery's effectiveness, the Union gunners shelled the Confederate infantry with near impunity. The Union artillerists especially punished the 60th Virginia Infantry in its new position along the Staunton Road. Von Kleiser's Napoleons and Snow's three-inch rifles enfiladed the 60th Virginia's left flank. Simultaneously, Carlin and Holman added their firepower, and the Federal artillery barrage became more than human flesh could endure. Captain James Johnston allowed his men to fall back into the woods several yards from the road. As luck had it, "Grumble" Jones rode by shortly after the Virginians had abandoned their crucial position in the gap between Vaughn and Browne. Jones dashed up to Johnston and ordered him to return his troops back into position along the road. He complied, but the merciless firing of DuPont's artillery forced the 60th Virginia to scramble for the cover of the forest once more. Johnston determined to hold his regiment in readiness to return to its assigned position in the event of an attack "rather than submit to a useless slaughter of his men."[206]

While DuPont's artillery pounded the Confederate position, Moor reconnoitered the "more elevated ground" on his extreme right with Peale's skirmishers. Colonel Ely of the 18th Connecticut had noted that some artillery could severely damage the Confederate works and accordingly requested artillery support. Moor submitted the request to Hunter's headquarters, and DuPont soon sent two Napoleons from Von Kleiser's Battery. The Prussian artillerist arrived ahead of his guns and joined Moor on his right flank. Lieutenant Colonel Jacob Weddle of the 1st West Virginia saw the German captain and pointed out a depression in the ridge "of sufficient width to accommodate the working of two guns" within short range of the Confederate position. Von Kleiser quickly headed to the suggested spot and examined it closely. The veteran artillerist immediately recognized that he had been afforded the rare opportunity of operating his guns against infantry at close range from a well-protected position. He excitedly turned to Weddle and said, in his German-accented voice, "Never you mind, colonel, wait a little, I'll show you something." Von Kleiser retrieved his two twelve-pound Napoleon cannons, brought them to the selected position and unlimbered them for action.[207]

Von Kleiser quickly made good on his promise to Weddle. The Napoleons fired solid shot at the Confederate breastworks at point-blank range of only five hundred yards across the field.[208] The Germans fired, and their projectiles "made a hole through the rail pen you could drive a horse through," thought one Connecticut soldier. Amidst a shower of splintering wood, the Confederates rushed out of the death trap "like bees swarming out of a hive." The shells burst among Beuhring Jones's Virginians with "every shot telling" and raining death down on Beuhring Jones's Virginians. The colonel quickly tired of watching his men suffer without artillery support and informed General Jones of the developing situation on the left via courier, suggesting that "some artillery would render great service in engaging that of the enemy in my front." At the very least, some counter-battery fire would divert Von Kleiser's attention away from the suffering Confederate infantry. However, the Confederate artillery had already been roughly handled and were so far to the rear that they could be of no immediate assistance, so General Jones tersely replied, "Hold your position."[209]

Although Von Kleiser's guns continually punished Lieutenant Colonel Fife's 36th Virginia, it remained in or near the breastworks with "Spartan resolution." However, Colonel Jones considered the Virginians' sacrifice "so apparently useless" that he sent a second plea to General Jones. This time, the general permitted Colonel Jones to withdraw the exposed portion of his line behind the river bluffs. Grumble emphasized that Colonel Jones must hold the Virginians in readiness to reoccupy the original line without delay should the Federals make another attack. The brigade commander relayed the orders to Fife, who promptly moved the unprotected companies of the 36th Virginia behind the bluffs.[210]

Although Jones had held Hunter at bay thus far in the battle, the cantankerous Virginian evidently recognized the damage that the Union artillery was inflicting on his infantry. Jones realized that he had to reposition his battle line to save his infantry from further damage and unite the two wings of his army. According to Sergeant Milton Humphreys of the Lewisburg section, the general rode up to the detached section of that battery about thirty minutes after it had withdrawn beyond the Cross Road and personally led these two guns forward to support the Confederate left wing, placing them in position behind Colonel Beuhring Jones's brigade.[211]

As Humphrey told it (and there is absolutely no evidence to the contrary), Grumble Jones called the two sergeants aside and explained his strategy and their role in it:

"Every One Held His Position"

I am going to withdraw the infantry from these woods to the edge of those [Jones pointed to the woods situated on the south side of the Cross Road as he spoke], *where they will be in line with the dismounted cavalry. You are to remain here, reserve your fire till the movement is made, and enfilade the enemy with cannister if they press closely after. Hold your position with confidence; you will be amply protected by infantry.*[212]

Jones then galloped away toward the Confederate infantry to begin a tactical retreat to a superior location. However, ensuing events quickly altered his decision.

Meanwhile, Hunter had by no means ceded the initiative and had Sullivan making arrangements to resume offensive operations. Lieutenant Colonel Gottfried Becker's 28th Ohio shifted from its position supporting the artillery to reinforce Moor's battle line. The veterans of the 28th Ohio provided a much-needed boost to Moor's bruised brigade. These well-drilled soldiers had experienced combat on several occasions yet had endured sustainable combat losses that did not bleed the regiment of its best men, leaving its combat efficiency intact. However, on June 5, 1864, one question loomed over the Ohioans' heads like a dark cloud. Their enlistments expired soon, and this normally dependable regiment marched into battle with much incentive to place self-preservation above their military duty. Thus far in 1864, the Union army's short-timers had proven themselves to be unreliable on many occasions.[213]

Color guard and band of the 28th Ohio; Colonel August Moor is standing in front at far left. *Antietam Battlefield.*

The formation of Moor's line had changed slightly since the first attack. The bloodied 116th Ohio still manned the left flank, but now the fresh 28th Ohio occupied the brigade's left center. The Germans' arrival forced the balance of the brigade to shift to the right. The 5th New York held the right-center position, and the 18th Connecticut occupied the space on the right of the New Yorkers, with the 1st West Virginia in support. In a swale behind Moor's brigade, Colonel Wynkoop's Pennsylvania mounted troops waited in anticipation to exploit any break in the Southern lines.[214]

A bugler sounded the advance; Moor's brigade moved out of the woods and into the open meadow. Sullivan rode his horse up and down the battle line, shouting words of encouragement to his men as they moved through the field. Although some had accused him of cowardice during the New Market Campaign, Sullivan had three horses shot out from under him and won laurels for gallantry at Piedmont. Moor led his brigade to within 150 yards of the Confederate works, where it came under a "withering and steady fire of musketry and artillery." "It was no sport or pastime now," recalled an Ohioan. "The boys, who had yesterday been so frolicsome and gay, now wore the serious aspect of thoughtful and determined veterans."[215]

From behind the rail breastworks, Browne's Carolinians and Virginians poured "a galling fire" into the exposed bluecoats as they moved across the open meadow. The Union men fell in droves from the deadly and accurate fire of the Confederates. The 116th Ohio "reeled, staggered and almost broke and fled," but the steady example of the regiment's color guard inspired the men to maintain order in the ranks. The 116th Ohio's color guard suffered horrendously in this attack from the withering Confederate musketry. A bullet struck Color Sergeant Reese Williams in his side as he bore the Stars and Stripes. Williams clutched the flag and bore it aloft until he fainted from loss of blood. When Williams went down, Color Sergeant David Barrett, himself already wounded in the arm and carrying the regimental colors with his good arm, grabbed Old Glory and continued to lead the advance bearing both flags.[216]

For ten minutes, the 116th Ohio held its ground stubbornly and slugged it out with the Southerners, but the Ohioans, already dazed from their earlier repulse, began to give way. With their comrades dying all around them, the bloodied Buckeyes finally broke and streamed to the rear seeking shelter. They fell back to the cover of a rise of ground, where they "halted and lay down to await Thoburn's coming, as we ought to have done in the first place," in the opinion of Lieutenant Colonel Thomas F. Wildes. The 116th Ohio lost 181 men killed and wounded at Piedmont—more than any other unit in Hunter's army.[217]

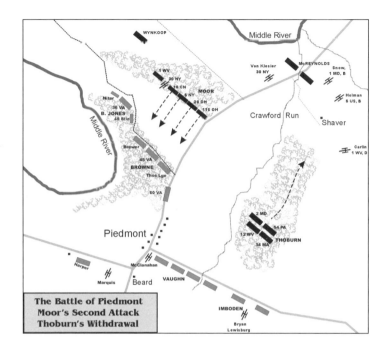

The Battle of Piedmont
Moor's Second Attack
Thoburn's Withdrawal

On Moor's right flank, the 18th Connecticut charged across the clearing toward Brewer's Battalion on Browne's right. Colonel Ely reported, "The soldiers fought desperately and at some disadvantage, being entirely in the open field." Brewer's Virginians pounded the New Englanders with a vicious musketry, assisted by an enfilading fire from Beckley's Battalion to their left. Owing to the heavy loss, Ely ordered the 18th Connecticut to retreat to the woods under the covering fire of Von Kleiser's guns. To the left of Ely's regiment, the 5th New York met the same fate and tumbled back to the woods in confusion. The Confederate success had its cost; Lieutenant Colonel Henry Beckley fell seriously wounded, elevating Major Blake L. Woodson of Botetourt County to command of the battalion. Several Virginians then carried Beckley from the field to a hospital at New Hope a few miles to the south.[218]

In the center of Moor's battle line, Lieutenant Colonel Becker gave the order to advance, and 581 resolute German Americans of the 28th Ohio emerged from the woods and trudged toward the Confederate line. When the Ohioans crested the bald rise in front of the Confederate lines, Browne's 45th Virginia greeted them with a deadly volley. In quick secession, the 28th Ohio lost two color-bearers killed and three more wounded. A Confederate bullet found its mark and killed Major Ernest Schache, the highest-ranking Union officer slain in the battle. Suffering as much if not more than the

Photo taken from the perspective of Colonel William Browne's Brigade. As Moor's Ohioans crested the ridge containing the twin silos, Browne's Virginians and North Carolinians opened fire, mowing them down. The 28th Ohio resisted the Confederate counterattack from a position near the silos and trees. *Scott C. Patchan.*

other regiments of Moor's brigade, the 28th Ohio seemed to be on the verge of being driven from the field like the others who were falling back to their left and right.[219]

The situation appeared bleak for the Army of the Shenandoah, and the crisis of the battle was at hand. Both flanks of Moor's brigade had collapsed, and the jubilant Confederate troops launched a determined attack with ear-splitting yells. The Confederates taunted the Union soldiers with cries of "New Market...New Market." But the words New Market proved to be as foreign to the Germans of the 28th Ohio as these men were to the country for which they fought. Although several regiments had fallen back under the tremendous Confederate musketry, Moor ordered the regiment to lie down and fire at the Confederates. The men obeyed like the veterans they were and loosed a volley into the attacking Confederates.[220] The 28th Ohio's Lieutenant Henry Ocker described the scene in a letter to his mother in Diepholz, Germany, written shortly after the battle:

> *The first brigade, of which our regiment was a part, was ordered to advance by our colonel, and, reaching a bald hill, we stopped. Here we were received by a murderous musket fire, and to obtain better cover, the regiment went down flat on their bellies and loaded the muskets lying on their backs. The other regiments of the brigade to our right and left could with this fire hardly hold their line and made off, leaving us behind alone, fighting with six to seven rebel regiments plus artillery. Our artillery by their excellent case shot fire, helped a great deal during the battle, but the horrible mass of fire-spitting rifles which were aimed at the front of our regiment, brought us a great loss of men, dead and wounded, but no one gave ground, every one held his position.[221]*

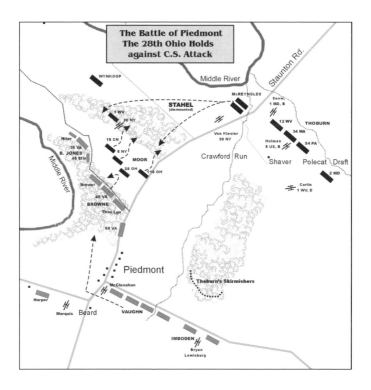

The steady fire of the 28th Ohio stalled the Confederate attackers before they could gain any momentum. The 45th Virginia's Captain Charles Fudge fell seriously wounded as he led his men forward in the charge. Von Kleiser's advanced section of Napoleons supported the Ohioans and prevented Beuhring Jones's Virginians from attacking the Ohioan's right flank. The fire of DuPont's rifled batteries on the Shaver Farm kept the Thomas Legion from leaving its works and attacking the 28th Ohio's left. Unable to make any headway, the Confederates retreated and carried several wounded Union soldiers back to the safety of the Confederate lines and, ultimately, on to field hospitals in New Hope two miles to the rear.[222]

Isolated and alone, the 28th Ohio maintained its advanced position for thirty minutes, while the other regiments reorganized, sheltered by the timber. The 28th Ohio exchanged fire with Davis's 45th Virginia. In spite of the furious musketry, the 28th Ohio stood firm. Three-quarters of an hour after the assault began, Moor ordered the Ohioans to retire to the wood line, as a new line of battle had been established, and the danger of being swept from the field had passed. The German Americans crawled rearward on their stomachs, sometimes stopping to fire at the Confederates. After reaching a safe spot, the Buckeyes stood up, made a right about-face and marched into the woods to rejoin their brigade.[223]

The performance of the 28th Ohio at Piedmont eliminated any doubts about the regiment's reliability during its last days of service. With thoughts of joyous reunions with family and friends lurking in their minds, the soldiers of the 28th Ohio had every reason to hold back. But as fate is often cruel, many of these brave men never returned home to see the smiling faces of family and friends. The 28th Ohio lost 33 men killed and 105 wounded out of 581 combatants; 7 out of 21 officers fell dead or wounded. Seventy-two bullets and shell fragments had perforated the regimental colors by the time the fighting had stopped. Lieutenant Ocker, a veteran of Antietam and South Mountain, considered Piedmont "the hardest and bloodiest" battle that his regiment ever fought and one that brought "the 28th Ohio much honor."[224]

While the Ohioans were still on the firing line, an observant Hunter rushed a staff officer to Stahel with orders to dismount part of his division and bolster Moor's battered brigade. The officer "galloped furiously" to Stahel's position in a hollow behind Moor's brigade. An onlooking cavalryman saw the messenger approaching and, given the situation, anticipated "another skedaddle down the valley." At the time, "Everything seemed to indicate that our men were being driven back," recalled the trooper. But Hunter was cut from a different bolt than his predecessors and was giving no thought to retreat. Instead, his staff officer shouted to Stahel, "For God's sake, dismount and help the infantry!" The Hungarian quickly dismounted several regiments from Colonel Andrew McReynolds's brigade, including the 1st Maryland PHB Cavalry, 1st Veteran Cavalry, the 21st New York Cavalry and the 14th Pennsylvania Cavalry.[225]

Stahel led his dismounted troopers through the woods, where the wounded of both sides lay strewn on the ground. Bullets whistled through the air, and stragglers pressed toward the rear, but the horsemen continued forward until they reached the edge of the timber. There they found Moor's infantry "sheltering themselves behind trees and logs as well as possible." By the time the horse soldiers reached the front, the firing had died down to an occasional shot. They quickly spread out and took cover behind trees and logs along the edge of the woods. The horse soldiers of the 1st Veteran Cavalry fired a few Spencer rounds into the Confederate's rail works "just for luck" but soon ceased wasting their ammunition against the protected Southerners.[226]

On the right of Moor's brigade, Stahel personally led the dismounted portion of Colonel Tibbits's 21st New York and 14th Pennsylvania. Stahel's horse soldiers maintained a "desultory but constant skirmishing fire." During the course of this combat, a Confederate bullet struck Stahel's left shoulder,

This photo is taken from the position of the 28th Ohio and is looking toward the bluffs of the Middle River. *Scott C. Patchan.*

inflicting "a contused wound of a painful character" before glancing off the bone. Although greatly shocked by the blow, Stahel walked a short distance to the rear without assistance where he laid down while the surgeon bandaged his wound. For the time being, Colonel Andrew McReynolds assumed command of the cavalry division.[227]

On the Union left flank, Thoburn's brigade had not advanced in conjunction with Moor, rendering the German's assault futile. Thoburn had experienced defeats at Second Manassas, Port Republic and New Market and grew uneasy about his situation at Piedmont. He had gone into battle lacking confidence in Hunter's leadership as a result of his policy of living off the land and liberal foraging guidelines. Before the army had marched out of its camp at Port Republic that very morning, Thoburn wrote in his diary: "It is a bad condition in which to go forth to meet enemy, as we expect to. Such mismanagement does not promise well for effective results."[228]

Thoburn's pessimistic mindset at Piedmont did little to advance the Union cause thus far in the battle. Instead of advancing with Moor as the plan seemed to have been, Thoburn awaited the outcome of the assault instead of supporting it. When Moor failed, Thoburn concluded "that I was doing no good where I was and that I should be needed on the right." As such, he ordered his regimental commanders to withdraw to the high ground behind DuPont's batteries, leaving only his skirmishers directly in front of the Confederate right wing. Colonel Rodgers of the 2nd Maryland Eastern Shore observed that Thoburn, though "a brave and excellent man," had grown very excited at Moor's repulse. To Thoburn it signified the beginning of another Union defeat. When the West Virginian informed his officers of Moor's setback and ordered the withdrawal, his excited manner had a "disagreeable effect" on the men. Private William B. Stark of the 34th Massachusetts "supposed the battle was lost." One by one, Thoburn pulled his regiments back to the heights behind the Shaver House, where they supported DuPont's artillery and waited for further instructions.[229]

At some point during or shortly after the repulse of Moor's second assault, General Jones abandoned the planned unification of his entire army south of the Cross Road. The sight of the retreating Federal infantry emboldened the aggressive Confederate commander. Instead of withdrawing, he not only maintained his advanced position on the left but also reinforced it from the right wing to launch a counterattack. Jones rushed a courier to General Vaughn with instructions to bring the larger portion of his brigade to the left. At the same time, the 60th Virginia was moved from its position facing eastward along the Staunton Road to form a second line of battle behind Browne's Brigade, presumably at Jones's direction. This movement once again left the gap between Browne's and Vaughn's brigades wide open in the center of the Confederate line. In 1902, a soldier of the 21st Virginia Cavalry claimed that he delivered Imboden a directive from Jones to "operate against the two regiments in front of him." According the old trooper, Imboden supposedly assured him that Jones's orders would be carried out "immediately." However, Major J.J. Lafferty of Imboden's staff more convincingly wrote on June 8, 1864, that "he [Imboden] never received any orders."[230]

Vaughn personally led Major John B. King's 1st Tennessee Cavalry, Major Robert McFarland's detachment of the 39th Tennessee Infantry and Colonel William L. Eakin's 59th Tennessee Infantry to the left wing. A detachment of the 3rd Tennessee Infantry also accompanied Vaughn to the left.[231] As the Tennesseans marched around the southern outskirts of Piedmont toward the timber on the Confederate left wing, they were plainly visible to Hunter, his staff and artillery from the Shaver Farm. When the Tennesseans entered the open space in rear of the left wing, DuPont's rifled batteries welcomed the Tennesseans to the Shenandoah Valley with solid shot and shell. As the column entered the woods, Vaughn galloped up to the 1st Tennessee and shouted words of encouragement to his troops. As the men cheered Vaughn, the Union gunners ranged in on the Tennesseans and renewed their work of destruction, killing and wounding a number of them, including Major Jacob Hays of the 59th Tennessee.[232]

The arrival of the 1st and 59th Tennessee on the left wing surprised Colonel Beuhring Jones. The Confederate left wing had repulsed three distinct Union attacks without wavering. "I cannot conjecture why this was done," wondered Colonel Jones. "I have thought that perhaps, the bearer of the order misunderstood it, as the gap in the line along the road was the place they should have occupied." Colonel Jones had received no orders or explanations as to what was expected of the Tennesseans. Given General Jones's physical presence on the left wing and the removal of the 60th Virginia from its critical position, it is unlikely that all of these units had moved to the positions they ended up in by mistake. General Jones certainly had some design in mind, and his battlefield dispositions are clearly indicative of preparations for a counterattack against Moor's bloodied brigade.[233]

After marching through the woods behind the Confederate line, the 1st Tennessee slipped into the line of battle and occupied a position behind the rail breastworks somewhere in the vicinity of Beuhring Jones's brigade, likely on his right. When Colonel Eakin's 59th Tennessee reached the breastwork, he found it fully occupied. Lacking specific orders once they arrived on the left wing, the 59th Tennessee filed to the left, searching for a vacancy in the line. The troops of the 18th Connecticut observed the Tennesseans moving over the bluff and fired furiously into it. Von Kleiser's Napoleons pounded the Tennesseans as well, but they pressed on, ascended the bluff, passed over the crest and descended to the shelter of the reverse slope. There, the Tennesseans formed their line of battle with their backs against the Middle River on the extreme left of the Confederate line. The balance of the troops Vaughn shifted to the left had not yet reached the battle line but were moving through the woods behind the Confederate left wing.[234]

General Jones had reduced the strength of the Confederate right wing by one-third when he ordered the Tennesseans to his left. The shift left no more than 1,500 troops from the combined commands of Imboden and Vaughn backed by Captain Bryan's three remaining guns on the right wing. When Vaughn departed, he left roughly 400 troops under the command of Lieutenant Colonel David Key. These men belonged to the 43rd Tennessee Infantry and the 12th and 16th Tennessee Cavalry Battalions. On Key's immediate right, Imboden's small cavalry brigade manned the Confederate right flank. As ordered by Jones, Imboden had refused his right flank by deploying flankers who extended the line southward to Round Hill near the village of New Hope. Although his line was paper thin, he faced no threat of attack after Thoburn withdrew his brigade.

"Grumble" Jones had gambled when he realigned his army in an effort to drive Hunter from the battlefield by counterattacking his battered right wing. However, in shifting Vaughn's troops to the left, Jones had overplayed his hand, and "Black Dave" called his bluff.[235]

Chapter 6

"We Lit Right in After Them"

From the Shaver House, Hunter and his staff peered across the gentle vale of Crawford Run toward the Confederate lines beyond the village. They could plainly see Vaughn's Tennesseans marching around Piedmont to reinforce the Confederate left wing. Hunter immediately recognized that Moor's battered brigade would be unlikely to withstand a heavy attack.[236] With no time to reinforce Moor, Hunter decided to strike back hard and prevent Jones from seizing the initiative. Hunter's young chief engineer, Lieutenant John Meigs, had just informed Hunter of the breach in the center of the Confederate line that had been partially occupied by the 60th Virginia before Jones began shifting his troops for a counterattack. Hunter directed Colonel William Starr, the army's provost marshal, "to ride with full speed to Colonel Thoburn and order him to move his brigade across the valley and assail the enemy's open flank." At the same time, Hunter sent Moor orders to attack on the right in conjunction with Thoburn.[237]

At three o'clock in the afternoon, Starr raced over to Thoburn near DuPont's guns and delivered Hunter's order to assail the weak Confederate center. It was the moment that Thoburn had anticipated when he withdrew his command from Shaver's woods, and he wasted no time, immediately placing his command in motion to attack. His brigade did not enter the assault at full strength, as the 2nd Maryland Eastern Shore remained behind to support the artillery and cover the army's left, while the 1st West Virginia was still on the army's opposite flank. Five of Thoburn's companies, about 250 soldiers, remained on the skirmish line in Shaver's woods confronting Imboden's and Key's Confederates and screening the Union left wing.[238]

While Thoburn began his movement toward the gap in Jones's line, Hunter directed DuPont to barrage the Confederate infantry "as a preliminary." The Union artillerists once again concentrated their guns on the Confederate infantry, forcing them to hug the earth for protection and limiting their ability to see, let alone react to Thoburn's approaching brigade. Captain Bryan's three long-range guns on the Confederate right fired intermittently at the Union artillery but were so ineffective that DuPont's gunners ignored them and focused steadfastly on the Southern infantry. While DuPont's rifled guns pummeled the Confederates from Shaver's heights, Von Kleiser's Germans showered the front of the Confederate breastworks from his position with Moor's brigade.[239] Not only did DuPont's artillery inflict significant physical damage on the Confederates, the thundering of the firing cannons and exploding projectiles also exceeded anything the Southerners had previously experienced and proved most demoralizing. Private Isaac G. Hendricks of the Thomas Legion wrote, "Men that was at the battle of Seven Pines say they never heard no harder." He further explained that DuPont's guns "cut the timber all to pieces" and completely severed "great big trees."[240]

As Thoburn moved to attack, Hunter and his staff watched the attack from a knoll. Although shells from Bryan's guns burst nearby, Hunter displayed "remarkable coolness…that elicited the admiration of all his men." The importance of Thoburn's movement was apparent to all, and officers availed themselves of every opportunity to inspire their men. Lieutenant Meigs appeared on the scene and "rode backward and forward along the line encouraging the men to do their duty." One Federal recalled that the "determined expression on the countenances of both men and officers boded no good" for the Confederates. Lieutenant George B. Caldwell, adjutant of the 12th West Virginia, noticed the look of resolve on the men's faces, turned to his commander, Colonel William B. Curtis, and confidently declared, "The boys are full of fight today."[241]

On the Union right, the dismounted cavalry launched a diversion against the extreme Confederate left. Hunter personally enjoined Lieutenant Jonathon L. Rivers of the 1st Maryland PHB "to take about a dozen of his men over to the right of the line and charge into a wheat field and make as much noise as we could to draw their attention from the movement on the left." The Marylanders joined other elements of Stahel's dismounted troopers and charged Colonel Eakin's 59th Tennessee with the Middle River at its back. The Union horsemen went in gamely, but the Tennesseans opened fire and sent them scurrying back into the woods.[242]

On Moor's right flank, Ely's 18th Connecticut attacked well before the rest of the brigade. Ely apparently believed that Von Kleiser's guns had completely demoralized the opposing Confederates. Ely's soldiers advanced over the prostrate forms of dead and wounded Union soldiers lying in a wheat field. The New Englanders charged right up to the holes that Von Kleiser's men had blasted in the breastworks, but as Sergeant George Setchell wrote, "the Rebs were as thick around each hole as flies around a molasses barrel." He also noted that "the lay of the ground was such that the Rebs had a clean sweep at us from the time we left the woods until we got to the openings in the rail pen." Contrary to Ely's expectations, Major Blake Woodson's 45th Battalion and the fresh 1st Tennessee raked the Northerners with a blistering fire. Private Joel L. Henry of the 1st Tennessee recalled that "from the time they [the 18th Connecticut] entered the field until they were repulsed in front of our lines their loss in killed and wounded was fearful."[243]

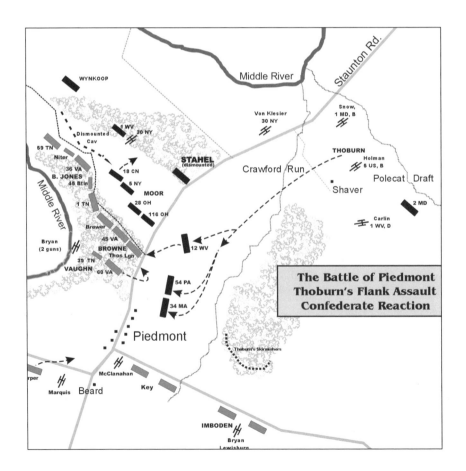

The Battle of Piedmont
Thoburn's Flank Assault
Confederate Reaction

To Ely's left, the balance of Moor's brigade waited a while longer for Thoburn to reach his position before advancing. On Moor's left flank, Colonel Washburn's 116th Ohio advanced and then halted and lay down behind a sheltering swell to await the flanking column's arrival. While in this position, the Ohioans suffered from the sporadic firing of Bryan's Lewisburg Battery that enfiladed the Ohioans' line. Lieutenant Colonel Thomas F. Wildes was in the act of rising from his prone position when a shell whistled in and plowed into the earth "just under his left breast and passed on just beneath the surface under his person till it reached the vicinity of his feet," where it exploded. The ensuing blast severely wounded Captain Wilbert E. Teters and hurled Wildes head over heels into the regimental color guard. The force of the explosion ripped the buttons from his jacket, leaving it in shreds, and severed the sole from his right boot. Moments after the blast, Thoburn's brigade appeared on the left, and the 116th Ohio rose up and advanced. A dazed Wildes limped back to Captain Teters, ordering him to go forward with his company. Only then did the colonel realize the extent of Teters's wound, so he turned around and joined the regiment in its charge toward Browne's Confederate brigade.[244]

As Washburn's Ohioans moved out, wounded color sergeant Reese Williams returned from the field hospital. Comrades had previously carried him to the rear after he had passed out from a bullet wound through the body. When he regained consciousness, he arose from the ground and went directly to his regiment, took hold of the colors and "waved them over his head as cheerfully and coolly as though nothing had happened" when the regiment advanced across the clover field.[245]

To Washburn's right, Lieutenant Colonel Becker ordered the seasoned

Lieutenant Colonel Thomas F. Wildes was a prewar newspaper editor from Athens, Ohio, who would rise to brigade commander during the 1864 Valley Campaign. *USAMHI.*

veterans of the 28th Ohio to fix bayonets and march in line of battle to the crest they had previously held near the Confederate lines. The men readily complied, and "with lots of hurrays and the flags flying high," Becker's Germans rushed toward the Confederate line. To their right, Murray's 5th New York Heavy Artillery joined the movement toward the Confederate works. On the right, the 18th Connecticut, "having fallen to the rear" after its repulse, did not immediately join in the final assault. On the far right, Weddle's 1st West Virginia waited in the wood line before assaulting the daunting heights in its front.[246]

All of the aforementioned activity along Moor's front occurred as Thoburn's brigade was making its final approach through the low ground along Crawford Run toward the breach in the Confederate center. Over on the extreme Union left, Thoburn's five-company skirmish battalion "fired one volley after another to distract the attention of the Confederate right," while his brigade moved to the attack.[247] From the Confederate perspective, the increased activity across the entire front of Hunter's army created a situation that kept Jones and his officers from clearly deciphering Hunter's intentions until it was too late. From the dismounted troopers on the right to the artillery and Thoburn's skirmish battalion on the left, this activity covered Thoburn as his brigade moved stealthily through the Crawford Run ravine toward the gap in the Southern line. With DuPont's batteries laying down a heavy covering fire over the heads of Thoburn's men, the Southerners remained pinned in their positions. Confederate units could not have moved without incurring heavy losses, even if they had detected the coming attack sooner. The Union artillery also prevented Jones from carrying out his own designs.[248]

Thoburn's brigade had nearly reached the position for launching the attack when the Confederates finally detected its presence. His flank movement only became apparent as his command covered the final stretch of ground leading toward his objective. Officers from the Thomas Legion observed Thoburn's final approach and promptly passed the information on to General Jones. Up until that time, he had been in the "finest spirits," very much elated at his success thus far in the battle. Upon receiving the startling news, Jones "bravely ran his horse out between the lines" to personally examine the situation. He immediately comprehended the seriousness of his army's predicament and galloped back to his line. He raced back toward the woods and shouted to the Thomas Legion, "Brave Carolinians, I'll bring you help!"[249]

"Old Grumble" rode rapidly to Captain Johnston's five-hundred-man 60th Virginia Infantry, which was now farther removed from the gap after being moved into position behind the Thomas Legion. At the time, these Virginians were laying down to avoid the Federal artillery projectiles crashing into the woods. Jones ordered Johnston to hurry back to the gap, and the Virginians sprang to their feet and filed to the right. Jones then rushed a courier to his left flank and ordered Vaughn to bring his Tennesseans, some of whom were still moving through the woods toward the Middle River, back to the threatened sector. Vaughn started immediately with McFarland's 39th Tennessee toward the Staunton Road, leaving orders for Colonel Eakin to follow with the 59th Tennessee on the

Major Robert McFarland commanded the 39th Tennessee at the Battle of Piedmont, losing nearly half of his command. *Don Bible Collection.*

extreme left. Jones also ordered Colonel Kenton Harper's Reserves and a section of McClanahan's Battery to hurry forward from their position south of the Cross Road. Then, with no time to spare, Jones dashed back toward the Staunton Road to rally his troops for the coming attack.[250]

Gunfire first erupted along the front of Browne's Brigade when Moor's Ohioans made their appearance. Moments later, Thoburn's brigade appeared on the right flank of the Thomas Legion. Thoburn's brigade had marched through a field of clover in the small vale formed by Crawford Run, his regiments wheeling to the right as they neared their assigned positions for the assault. On Thoburn's right, Curtis's 12th West Virginia had the least distance to cover before it reached the Confederate line. As Curtis swung his regiment around to the right, it directly confronted the angle in the line where the Thomas Legion's refused right flank ran parallel to the Staunton Road. Love's North Carolinians opened fire, halting the West Virginians at a distance of one hundred yards from the Confederate works.[251] The

Mountaineers promptly lay down and returned fire, and the Thomas Legion suddenly found itself engaged on two fronts.[252]

On the left of the 12th West Virginia, Colonel Jacob Campbell's 54th Pennsylvania arrived at the brow of the hill. There the Pennsylvanians lay down in the field and waited for the 34th Massachusetts to come up on the left of the brigade. As the Pennsylvanians waited, Bryan's long-range guns fired sporadically, and one of his rounds knocked a Pennsylvanian out of action. The regiment's principal musician, James Snedden, a fifteen-year-old boy from Edinburgh, Scotland, watched the man fall and requested permission from Campbell to take his place on the firing line. Campbell assented; Snedden picked up his rifle and joined the ranks of his old company. The eager Snedden had barely assumed his position in the battle line when the 34th Massachusetts came up on the Pennsylvanians' left flank, and Thoburn's assault began in earnest.[253]

Only moments before the 34th Massachusetts crested the hill, Captain Johnston's 60th Virginia marched past the right flank of the Thomas Legion. The Virginians advanced out of the woods, crossed the Staunton Road and began deploying into line of battle. They were too late. By the time the Massachusetts soldiers crested the hill, only two companies of the 60th Virginia had deployed into line of battle. Nevertheless, those Virginians who were ready loosed a volley into the 34th Massachusetts at the scant distance of twenty yards. The Confederate volley killed four and wounded several other men, including Color Sergeant John E. Calligan. One of the color corporals threw down his gun and caught the flag before it hit the ground. In spite of the losses, the Confederate rifle fire did not faze Wells's disciplined soldiers.[254] Instead, he ordered a charge, and his men let out a yell "that could have been heard a mile" as they rushed forward, delivering an accurate volley and reloading on the run.[255]

To Wells's right, Campbell's prone 54th Pennsylvania loosed an accurate volley into the deploying left wing of the 60th Virginia, throwing it into confusion. The blast also struck the refused right flank and rear of the Thomas Legion, already under attack from Moor's Ohioans in front and the 12th West Virginia on its flank. Then the Keystone State regiment rose up from the ground, charged and drove the Virginians into the woods behind the Thomas Legion.[256]

When Curtis saw the Pennsylvanians charging on his left, he shouted to the 12th West Virginia, "Go in boys they're whipped!" The West Virginians quickly arose from the ground and dashed toward the Confederate breastworks. The Thomas Legion challenged the West Virginians with a

Thoburn's brigade attacked up the hill from the silos in the low ground on the left toward the house on the right and came under fire in the field in the foreground. *Scott C. Patchan.*

searing volley that stunned their progress. Corporal Joseph S. Halstead, the regimental color-bearer, saw his comrades falling fast and rushed ahead into a "sheet of rebel flame." Nonetheless, he sprinted toward the Confederate fortifications, leaped atop the rails and cried out, "Come on boys, here's where I want you!" Inspired by Halstead's bravery, his comrades swarmed toward the Confederates. Halstead continued over the breastworks but managed only a few steps before a Tarheel gunned him down.[257]

Dozens of West Virginians followed the courageous Halstead and clambered over the rail pens. One Mountaineer climbed upon the breastworks and shouted at the Tarheels, "Look out Johnny's we're coming down on you like a thousand [tons] of brick." The West Virginians leveled their bayonets and tore into the Thomas Legion. A vicious hand-to-hand melee then occurred between the Thomas Legion and the 12th West Virginia. "I saw many have their brains knocked out with clubbed muskets," attested the surgeon of the 12th West Virginia. Many Confederates fled, but most stood their ground and fought back against the converging attacks. The situation quickly became hopeless for the Confederates when soldiers from the 54th Pennsylvania charged through the woods behind the Legion and joined the deadly fracas.[258]

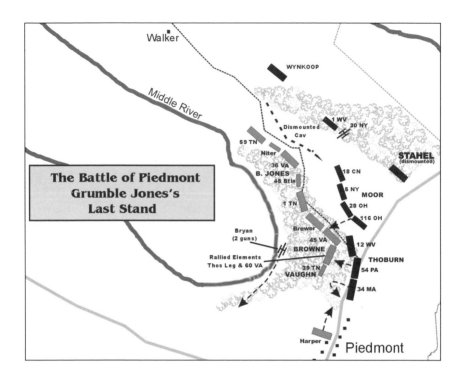

The Battle of Piedmont
Grumble Jones's
Last Stand

When the 60th Virginia broke back into the woods, "Grumble" Jones dashed among the men and rallied a portion of the regiment about thirty yards into the forest. Vaughn arrived on the scene and deployed McFarland's small detachment of the 39th Tennessee before assisting Jones in rallying the broken troops of the 60th Virginia, incurring a flesh wound in the process. The Tennesseans deployed behind a rail fence running through the woods and in conjunction with the more resolute elements of the 60th Virginia "poured lead" into the 34th Massachusetts "like hail stones." For the next fifteen minutes, the two sides stood only a scant twenty yards apart in what one Federal termed "just the prettiest fighting you ever saw, give and take."[259]

Considering the unprepared state of the Confederate center, Jones had almost miraculously managed to at least engage Thoburn's brigade. The situation for these U.S. troops grew precarious when Colonel Kenton Harper's Augusta Reserves advanced down the Staunton Road and "poured a withering fire" into the left flank of the 34th Massachusetts. In less than five minutes, Wells lost Major Harrison Pratt, Captain Andrew Potter, Lieutenant Samuel Woods and fifty enlisted men dead or wounded in the two companies on his left flank. The situation was, admitted one Massachusetts soldier, "nip and tuck with us in the woods."[260]

In spite of the heavy fire, the well-disciplined 34th Massachusetts quickly reacted to the situation. One Bay State soldier on the regiment's besieged left sprinted over to Colonel Wells, who at the time was on the right and reported "the situation of affairs." Reacting quickly, Wells led a detachment from the right to the left. Arriving on his battered flank, Wells roared, "Remember New Market!" above the din of battle as the reinforcements opened fire at Harper's Reserves on the left. Although the 34th Massachusetts men were battling in two directions, they held their ground under the deadly fire, just as they had done at that battle only three weeks ago.[261]

Colonel George D. Wells, 34th Massachusetts. This Harvard Grad and Boston lawyer proved himself to be one of the finest infantry leaders in the Army of the Shenandoah throughout 1864 until his death in an engagement near Cedar Creek on October 13, 1864. *Nick Picerno Collection.*

The New Englanders also received assistance from the 54th Pennsylvania on the right. Colonel Campbell quickly analyzed the situation and realized that the Confederates behind the fence in the woods had "partially" checked the advance of the 34th Massachusetts. Campbell recognized this fence as "the key" to the enemy's position, as it prevented the Bay State regiment from charging into the woods and completely flanking the Confederate position. Campbell promptly led three companies from his left wing to assist the New Englanders, leaving Major Enoch Yutzy in command of the five remaining companies, which were battling Colonel Browne's Confederates.[262]

Campbell's detachment quickly turned toward the Tennesseans and Virginians in front of Wells and ripped a searing volley into their flank. At the same time, Wells steadied his left wing and directed its fire at Harper's Reserves, while the rest of his regiment volleyed into Confederates behind the fence.[263] The pressure on the Confederates became too great, and their line began to crumble. Jones rode into the midst of a group of leaderless troops and called for an officer to assume command and retake the lost ground. At first no one came forward, but a moment later, Lieutenant Monroe Blue, commanding Company K of Harper's regiment, leapt from his horse, waving his sword in the air, and shouted, "General, I will lead them, boys follow me and we will soon have them on the run." Blue placed his cap on his sword, raised it into the air and led the troops in a hopeless counter charge.[264]

Campbell's wing of the 54th Pennsylvania fired into Blue's troops and quickly shattered what little formation they had. Blue attempted to rally them, shouting, "New Market! New Market! Remember New Market!"[265] A captain from the 54th Pennsylvania saw the Confederates assembling around Blue and cried out, "Boys shoot that officer before he starts a rally!" A Pennsylvanian later recalled, "Several of us cut loose at him and he spun around, dropped his sword, and fell to the ground." Blue died instantly, and those Confederates who had been gathering near him quickly vanished from the scene.[266]

At the same time, the precise rifle fire of the 34th Massachusetts unnerved Harper's inexperienced reserves. Seeing the Tennesseans and Virginians on their left in confusion, the reserves soon lost their cohesiveness and began to retreat. Captain Robert Doyle, who had resigned the lieutenant colonelcy of the 62nd Virginia in 1863 to become the Augusta County Commonwealth's attorney, attempted to rally some disheartened reserves, but a Union bullet ended his life. As the last vestige of Confederate resistance evaporated, Grumble Jones succumbed to his combative nature and galloped among the fugitives in a last-grasp attempt to salvage the victory that had seemed almost certain a short time earlier. With his hat in his hand, he cheered the men and urged them to rally and hold their ground. The volume of rifle firing coming from the Federals was tremendous, and Jones soon fell, "stricken dead by loyal vengeance." A Minié ball struck Jones in his temple near his eye and killed him instantly. Vaughn and his horse were struck by five bullets but suffered no serious wounds. However, with Jones's death, the battle had been decided. Upon Jones's death, the Confederate resistance in the immediate vicinity completely dissolved.[267]

In the years after the war, dozens of Union veterans staked claim to being the soldier who fired the fatal shot that killed General Jones. The braggadocio

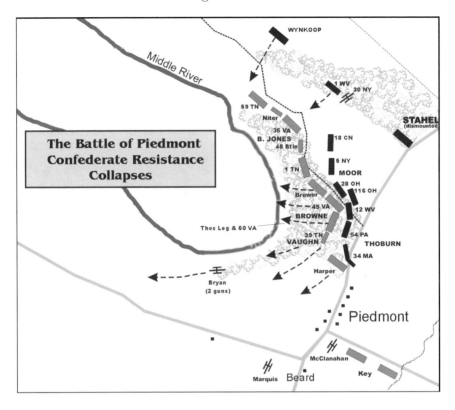

became so outlandish that one Pennsylvanian quipped, "If every boy who later claimed to have shot him had put a bullet in him, why, he would have been so heavy it would have taken a four horse team to have moved his body off of the battlefield."[268] At the time, however, no one stopped to examine Jones's body, nor did his plain attire provide any ready evidence of his rank. Instead Thoburn's self-styled "braves" cheered and swooped through the woods after the retreating Confederates, chasing them toward the bluffs and into the Middle River.[269]

While Thoburn attacked the Confederates in flank and rear, Moor's brigade struck Grumble Jones's left-wing head-on. On the German's left, Lieutenant Colonel Wildes regained his senses, mounted his "coal black steed" and galloped out in front of the 116th Ohio. Seriously wounded Color Sergeant Reese Williams attempted to follow Wildes but was too exhausted, so he kissed the tattered flag and handed it to another soldier. Not wanting to be outdone by Thoburn's brigade, the Buckeyes raced toward the breastworks with shouts of victory, clambered over the breastworks and assisted the 12th West Virginia in mop-up operations against the Thomas Legion.[270]

On Wildes's right, the 28th Ohio leveled its bayonets and charged toward the Confederate fortifications, with the 5th New York on its right. The 45th Virginia and Brewer's Battalion laced the approaching Federals with a searing volley but did not stop Moor's troops. In spite of the Confederates' "most stubborn resistance," the 28th Ohio planted its battle flag on the breastworks and together with the 5th New York fired "a horrible musket volley" into the Virginians that "heavily reduced" their number. A Federal bullet hit Browne's thigh, and another struck Major William Sanders in the chest, inflicting an apparent mortal wound. Major Brewer also went down with a mortal wound, and the entire line started to unravel as the 12th West Virginia and 54th Pennsylvania closed in from the right and rear. One West Virginian ordered the wounded Browne to surrender, but he refused to hand his sword over to an enlisted man. As the Mountaineer raised his rifle to shoot Browne, Colonel Curtis arrived on the scene, and Browne exclaimed, "I will surrender to you!" As the 28th Ohio charged over the ground previously held by the Confederates, one German looked down at a wounded Southern soldier, asking him, "And how doose [sic] you feel now, you damn Rebel?"[271]

Some of Browne's Confederates ran rearward into the arms of Campbell's Pennsylvanians and Wells's Bay State soldiers. The 45th Virginia's color-bearer took off through the woods and headed toward Piedmont with his regiment's battle flag. The Virginian continued through the woods until he came upon a group of Confederates fleeing the 54th Pennsylvania. Seeing them in confusion, the Virginian stopped, waved his flag and shouted, "Rally, Boys, Rally!"

Private Thomas Evans of the 54th Pennsylvania suddenly found himself face to face with the 45th Virginia's color-bearer, who at that moment seemed "about as big as a full grown grizzly bear." For the first time in his military service, Evans suddenly found a good use for his bayonet other than as a candle holder. He whacked the flag staff so hard that it "really stung that Johnny's hands." When he reflexively lowered the flag, Evans grabbed it and pulled, yelling, "Let go Reb!" The two men pulled back and forth and spun around in a circle, struggling for possession of the battle flag. Their melee ended when Evans raised his rifle with one arm and commanded, "Drop that there flag or I will pin you to a tree!" The Virginian promptly surrendered the flag, and Evans turned it over to an officer and sent the prisoner to the rear. The Pennsylvanian received the Medal of Honor later that year for his capture of the flag.[272]

On the right of the 5th New York, Colonel Ely heard the cheering on the left and urged his men to make one more "desperate effort." The New

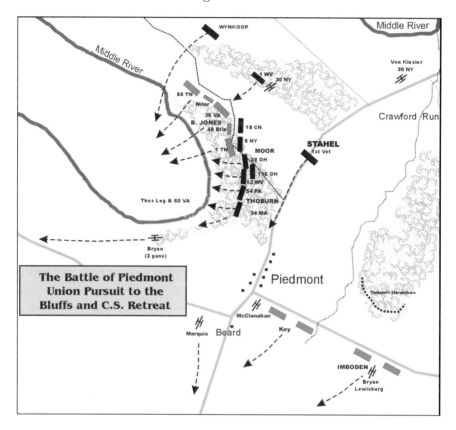

The Battle of Piedmont
Union Pursuit to the
Bluffs and C.S. Retreat

Englanders attacked Major John King's 1st Tennessee Cavalry (dismounted). The Tennesseans fought stubbornly, but their resistance proved futile as the jubilant mass of Federals closed in on their right and rear. Those not captured behind the works attempted to reach the Middle River and became caught in the crossfire between Moor's and Thoburn's U.S. troops. As the Tennesseans ran for the river bluffs, they fell by the dozen. By the time the fighting stopped, the 1st Tennessee had lost at least twelve men killed (including Major King), an unknown number of wounded and eighty-three prisoners. One Tennessean recalled that his regiment lost almost half of the four hundred men the 1st Tennessee took into action.[273]

The intermingled mass of Union infantry quickly turned its attention to Colonel Beuhring Jones's brigade atop the Middle River bluffs. The Union troops became considerably intermingled as they swept over the works, and both Moor's and Thoburn's men closed in on Jones's position from the right flank and the rear. On Jones's right, Major Blake Woodson stood bravely and held the 45th Battalion to its position until a bullet cut him down, and those who could turned and fled into the woods, where fifty-five (more than one-third of the unit's strength) of them ran into the open arms of Thoburn's jubilant troops and became prisoners.[274]

At the same time, the 1st West Virginia's Lieutenant Colonel Weddle shouted, "Boys, there's Colonel Thoburn doubling up the enemy on the right, let's meet him in the defences. Charge!" They raised a "West Virginia yell," sprinted downhill and then charged up the bluffs as the 36th Virginia fired a volley that largely sailed over their heads. The West Virginians struggled up the steep hillside, clambered over the works and engaged the Virginians in close-quarters combat.[275] "Our boys made a desperate stand," related Isaac Prillaman of the 36th Virginia, "but the yanks ran up in our lines & fought hand to hand for 15 minints." In the ensuing melee, the 1st West Virginia captured a battle flag from the 36th Virginia and sent its members fleeing in confusion toward the Middle River. With the entire Confederate line all but dissolved, the men from the Niter and Mining companies looked around and followed the example of the veteran Confederate infantry and joined the retreat.[276]

The victorious blue throng pursued the beaten Southerners toward the Middle River. Individual Confederates turned and fired wildly while on the run but did little harm to their pursuers. Some Confederates fled into the woods in an attempt to escape but ended up running into the arms of the 34th Massachusetts. Sergeant Fountaine G. Shackelford of the 36th Virginia vividly recalled the scene:

> A few others with myself, took straight across the cleared land to the bluff of the river. A squad of twenty or thirty of the enemy appeared and having a load in my gun, I let it drive at the bunch but did not wait to see the result. I then let myself down a few feet, when I was out of sight of the enemy. The bluff being very steep, we had to be very cautious, and use saplings for hand holds to let us down; when down, we then had to cross the river, which we done by wading. As we were in a hurry we lost but little time. After crossing we had something like a half mile to go across an open field exposed to the fire of the enemy.[277]

On the extreme left of the Confederate line, the 59th Tennessee found itself in a hopeless situation. Its commander, Colonel Eakin, rode ahead of his regiment in response to Vaughn's orders and galloped into the retreating mass of fugitives. He attempted to rally the fleeing Confederates, but his pleas fell on deaf ears, and he soon joined the growing list of prisoners. Fortunately

When the Confederate line broke, hundreds of Confederates fled down these slopes toward the Middle River to evade capture. Many of them were gunned down as they crossed the river and into the open flood plain beyond by Union troops on the high ground. *Scott C. Patchan.*

for the retreating Confederates, the 59th Tennessee had remained in position behind Sheep Hill long enough to prevent the Federals on the extreme right from surging across the river and capturing even more prisoners. The Tennesseans fended off an attempt by Stahel's dismounted cavalry and Moor's skirmish battalion under Major Peale to drive the Volunteer State soldiers into the river. The Tennesseans' success proved to be an aberration, for Moor's and Thoburn's brigades united atop the river bluffs and poured a murderous fire into the Confederates in the flood plain. Captain Reuben Clark of the 59th Tennessee had just ordered his company to charge. Then Clark heard U.S. troops yelling, "Surrender, damn you!" Startled, Clark whirled around and saw masses of blue-coated soldiers rushing to seal off the Tennesseans' line of retreat. Clark jumped down the riverbank, splashed through the water and escaped unhurt with another officer, who got away with only "some holes shot in his clothing."[278]

The entire Confederate left wing had collapsed under the weight of Thoburn's and Moor's converging attacks. For most Southerners, the Middle River on the far left was the only available avenue of escape. Hundreds of Confederates stumbled down the bluff and sprinted into the river. From atop the high bluffs, the U.S. soldiers from Moor's brigade joined Thoburn's brigade atop the bluffs, and together they fired down at the retreating Southerners as they attempted to flee across the river and through the cornfield beyond. A Massachusetts soldier informed his father that ninety Confederates died from gunshots as they attempted to escape in the "Bloody Battle of the Ford." As the Confederates fled, Colonel John Wynkoop's two-hundred-man 20th Pennsylvania Cavalry bolted into their midst near the river, swinging sabers overhead and firing pistols and snared several hundred more Confederate prisoners of war.[279]

Some of Wynkoop's horsemen splashed across the Middle River and continued southward in an effort to increase the size of their haul. The Pennsylvanians galloped across the open fields in rapid pursuit of the fleeing Southerners, cheering as they closed in on a squad of men from the 59th Tennessee. Captain Clark, its ranking officer, cried out, "Boys, for God's sake stop and fire on those fellows." The Tennesseans stopped and fired a single volley into the Pennsylvanians as they passed through a gap in a fence. That shot proved to be enough to force the Pennsylvanians to halt and reform, providing the Tennesseans the time they needed to reach the cover of some nearby woods.[280]

Colonel John Wynkoop led the 20th Pennsylvania Cavalry in a charge that netted hundreds of prisoners at the battle's end. *USAMHI.*

While Wynkoop hauled in his prisoners, the Union infantry snared a large number of prisoners on the east bank of the river. James Snedden, the musician who had joined the combat troops of the 54th Pennsylvania, saw Colonel Beuhring Jones attempting to flee along the bank. Snedden demanded the colonel's surrender, and Jones reluctantly handed the Pennsylvanian his sword and two revolvers. Snedden's valor at Piedmont earned him the Medal of Honor.[281]

Over on the Staunton Road, the reserves fled in confusion through Lieutenant Berkeley's two-gun section of artillery, which had just unlimbered and attempted to fire. Captain Walter K. Martin, General Jones's adjutant, peremptorily ordered Berkeley to limber up and save his guns from capture. Berkeley obeyed promptly and rushed his section back toward New Hope. Berkeley later wrote, "I would have lost them I believe had I staid a minute longer. My boys were behaving splendidly and would have stood by the guns until the last."[282]

On the far Confederate left, the detached section of Bryan's Lewisburg Artillery barely evaded capture. The tearing sounds of increased musketry extending southward along the Staunton Road had alerted the artillerists to Thoburn's attack as they waited on the high ground behind the Confederate left. When the Confederate infantry poured out of the woods in confusion, the gunners limbered up and galloped away as Federal bullets began to fall among them. They raced toward the Cross Road and found the 34th Massachusetts blocking their path toward New Hope and Imboden's wing of the army. With no other choice, the Virginians headed west toward Staunton.[283]

They had proceeded only a short distance when a Confederate major rode up to the retreating guns and urged them to unlimber and deploy. Bryan's gunners complied but could not fire as the fleeing Confederate infantry blocked their line of fire. To make matters worse, the gunners soon discovered that some Union infantry had advanced up the flood plain and were ascending the bluff not more than twenty feet away. Seeing that, the major "implored the men to bring the guns off." Once again, these two guns limbered up and raced away, barely escaping as they headed toward Staunton.[284]

Meanwhile, the impetuous Colonel Tibbits yearned for another go at the Confederates. Now in command of a brigade due to Stahel's wounding, Tibbits sought Colonel McReynolds's permission to pursue the beaten Confederate army. McReynolds twice denied Tibbits's request, but things soon changed. At Hunter's urging, General Stahel returned to the front on foot as it "pained his arm too much to ride." He arrived on the front line with his arm in a sling just as Wynkoop's brigade returned with its haul of prisoners. Assisted onto his horse, the Union horse soldiers cheered the resilient Hungarian as he made his way to see McReynolds. Stahel ordered the portly McReynolds to pursue the broken and disorganized enemy.[285]

Soon after Stahel spoke with McReynolds, Tibbits again requested permission to charge up the Staunton Road. Motivated by Stahel's direct order, McReynolds relented and allowed Tibbits to pursue with both the 1st New York and 1st Veteran cavalry regiments. Tibbits immediately gathered up Lieutenant Colonel John S. Platner's 1st Veteran Cavalry, which had just remounted after fighting dismounted with Moor's brigade. He also sent orders to Major Quinn for the 1st New York Cavalry to join in the movement. Quinn requested that his troopers take the rear of the column because his horses were tired. Tibbits approved the request and ordered Quinn's

Major General Julius Stahel rejoined the fight after having his wounds bandaged. He was hit leading his dismounted cavalry into the woods to support the infantry. *From* Deeds of Valor *(1901)*.

regiment to fall in behind the Veterans, keep pace and follow closely.[286]

The New Yorkers arrived at the Cross Road, and Tibbits ordered the 1st Veteran Cavalry to charge up the Staunton Road into the retreating Confederates. Tibbits expected the 1st New York Cavalry to be immediately behind the Veterans and intended to send it around the left to flank the Confederates at New Hope. He was greatly disappointed when they were nowhere to be seen. He sent his adjutant to hurry Quinn forward, but the staff officer failed to return after a few minutes. An infuriated Tibbits rode rapidly down the road and soon found the 1st New York Cavalry "coming up on a slow trot." He demanded an explanation from Quinn to explain why he had not complied with his orders. Quinn responded that "his horses were too worn out to move at a faster gait." Tibbits dressed the major down briefly and then ordered him to press forward, "which he did reluctantly" after wasting much precious time that allowed the Confederates to strengthen their rear guard near New Hope.[287]

General John D. Imboden had watched the Confederate left wing disintegrate and ordered his men to mount up and prepare to cover the retreat. He then rode to see Vaughn under the supposition that he, "being nearest Jones, would have received orders." Imboden found him south of

Piedmont and learned that Jones was dead, leaving Vaughn in command. "We must save all we can of our poor fellows," explained Vaughn. However, he admitted, "I don't know this country, was never in it in my life before. You know it well, I hear, and I will adopt your suggestions." Imboden, a hero during the retreat from Gettysburg, once again stepped forward and gave direction to the floundering remnants of the army at New Hope. He told Vaughn that they must "gain the road as quickly as possible, and if pursued, fight our way back to Mowry's hill," where the enemy could be held in check until night. Imboden requested that Vaughn move his remaining troops to New Hope, leaving guides to lead the way.[288]

Imboden sent orders to his brigade to fall back to the Crumpecker Farm just north of New Hope and then headed there himself. As he arrived on the scene, Captain McClanahan and Lieutenants Parkinson Collett and Hugh H. Fultz were unlimbering four guns of the Staunton Horse Artillery in a field on Crumpecker Farm. Imboden shouted to them, "That's right boys; double shot your guns with canister and we will support you." After ramming charges of canister down their gun tubes, the Virginians waited for the Union cavalry to appear. Their position was located three hundred yards south of the woods that separated them from the Cross Road near Piedmont. Although the woods in front blocked their view, McClanahan's Virginians plainly heard the blaring bugles as the 1st Veteran Cavalry began its charge near Piedmont.

Meanwhile, Lieutenant Colonel George W. Day led the dismounted 12th Tennessee Cavalry Battalion through the woods from its position on the Confederate right toward New Hope. Day noticed Berkeley's section of McClanahan's Battery rushing pell-mell out of the woods with the 1st Veteran in pursuit. Day instantly rushed his troopers up Crumpecker Lane on the west side of the road. Imboden yelled, "Will your men fight?" "Like hell if you give them the chance," replied Day as he positioned them behind the rail fence. He ordered them to hold their fire until the Union horsemen were in short range.[289]

In front of the Confederate rear guard, the road between the two villages was lined with woods from the vicinity of the Cross Road to the Crumpecker Farm north of New Hope. The New Yorkers charged through the trees in column in what one trooper described as "a very foolish charge." Unbeknownst to the 1st Veteran, a substantial rear guard had assembled opposite the southern edge of the woods through which it was charging.[290]

The 1st Veteran Cavalry pounded up the road, chasing hordes of Confederates toward New Hope who then raced into the open on the Crumpecker Farm. The Union horsemen charged after the fugitives, shooting and sabering as they went. The Tennesseans held their fire until the New

Yorkers closed in on the Confederate position, and then the Tennesseans poured a deadly volley into the Federals.[291] Simultaneously, McClanahan's gunners yanked their lanyards, and the cannons belched a storm of canister into the charging blue mass. "The whole head of the Yankee column seemed to melt away," recalled a Virginian. General Imboden described the decimated column as "a mass of groaning men and horses." When the smoke cleared away, the New Yorkers were rapidly disappearing back toward the Union lines.[292]

The stymied New Yorkers reeled in their saddles and then turned and fled in confusion toward Piedmont, barely making it back to the Union lines. Had Imboden's Brigade begun shifting toward New Hope a few minutes sooner, the Virginians likely would have cut off many New Yorkers behind the Confederate lines. As it was, Platner lost eight killed, many wounded and eleven captured in the final charge of the battle. Returning to the Union line, the chagrined Veterans passed by the 1st New York Cavalry, which Tibbits had just managed to get moving forward. Learning the results of Platner's charge, Tibbits realized that McReynolds's and Quinn's recalcitrance had squandered the chance to pursue the beaten Confederates at the most opportune time. Soon after the battle, a bitter member of the 1st Veteran Cavalry wrote, "It is conceded by all who were acquainted with the circumstances that if the 1st Veteran Cavalry had been supported in that charge by a regiment that has been petted and puffed and was ordered to follow in the charge, we would have driven the enemy into our own lines."[293]

The day had proven to be long and bloody, but in the end, Hunter and the dogged Army of the Shenandoah had achieved the most resounding victory that the United States Army had won in the valley to that date. They had also penetrated deeper into the valley than had any U.S. general who preceded Hunter. The effort cost the Union nearly 850 men killed and wounded. The Confederacy suffered more than 600 men killed and wounded and also lost 1,000 unwounded prisoners of war. Among the Union trophies were three Confederate battle flags and two thousand stand of arms.[294]

The strong Confederate rear guard at New Hope dissuaded Hunter from attempting any further pursuit. He ordered his army to bivouac on the battlefield at Piedmont. Strother postulated that "[t]he worthlessness of our cavalry was probably what induced the General to content himself with the affair as it stood."[295]

For the Union enlisted men, the victory "wiped out the disgrace of New Market." With few exceptions, Piedmont was their first victory. Jubilation filled the Union ranks. Cheers resonated across the battlefield, and "[s]tretcher

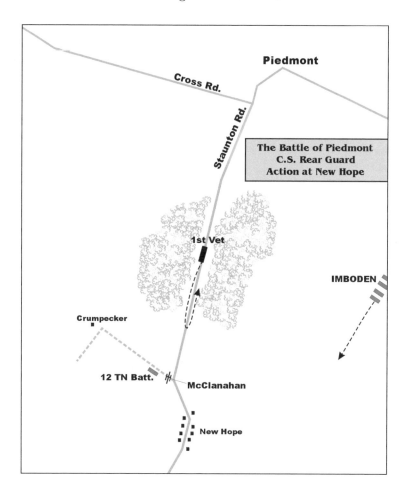

men, ambulance drivers, wounded men, butchers, bummers, all took up the shout and back upon the hill crests Negroes, teamsters, and camp followers re-echoed the joyful shout."[296]

The wounded Union soldiers responded with joy to the news of their victory. The 18th Connecticut's chaplain, Reverend William C. Walker, recalled how "[t]hey cheered, clapped their hands, and those who were able sprang to their feet, threw up their hands and caps, amid shouts and tears of joy cheered again and again for the Union."[297] The celebration proved contagious. Even the ornery General Hunter joined in the merriment. Within the privacy of a farmhouse, Hunter "threw his arms around Halpine and Major Stockton, kissing their cheeks and slapping their backs."[298]

Chapter 7

"I Never Want to See
Such a Sight Again"

The dead and wounded of both sides lay strewn about the battlefield. Piedmont provided most of the Union troops their first post-combat view of a battlefield. They were aghast at the horrors the battlefield revealed when the firing stopped and the adrenaline slowed. The slaughter at Piedmont produced one of the most macabre post-battle scenes the war had known. "There were some of the worst mangled men I ever saw," declared a New Yorker. "Some had their heads shot clear off, others cut in two, one part of the body lay in one place and the other a rod or two from it."[299]

At Hunter's headquarters, the cavalry reported that the Confederate General Jones had been killed. Hunter sent Strother to verify the claim. Strother found a crowd of soldiers gathered around "a body coarsely clothed in a dirty grey suit without any military trappings or insignia about it." Strother noted that the dead man wore "a pair of fine military boots well worn." "His hands were small and white," observed Strother, "and his features, high white forehead, brown beard, and long hair indicated the gentleman and man of the upper class."[300]

Four captured Confederates arrived at the scene with a stretcher to carry Jones's body to a burial sight, as the provost marshal had previously ordered them to do. Strother asked the prisoners if they knew the dead man, to which they replied, "Yes, that is the body of our commander, General William E. Jones." The detail temporarily buried the body of Grumble Jones in a nearby garden. Eventually, Jones was reinterred next to his wife, Eliza, in the cemetery at Glade Spring Presbyterian Church near Abingdon, Virginia. Jones's cavalry brigade was filled with "universal sorrow" over his death.

The Walker House served as a field hospital after the battle ended. *Scott C. Patchan.*

"He was cool in a fight," observed an officer on Imboden's staff, "and the bravest of the brave."[301]

Jones was only one of many casualties wrought by the battle. Colonel Tibbits rode along the Confederate breastworks after the fighting. Behind the rail fortifications, he found more than one hundred wounded Confederates. Tibbits observed "many of them having the flesh torn off the body by splinters from rails" that had been shredded by the Federal shells. The exploding shells also set aflame the flesh of many of the Confederate dead. He also saw a group of wounded Confederates who had crawled into the shade of a tree, and distinctly remembered their "audible prayers and psalm singing," which contrasted starkly with the incessant roar of musketry that had raged all day.[302]

A soldier of the 18th Connecticut observed the same wounded Confederates. He wrote in his diary for June 5, 1864: "I have heard of men being torn in pieces, but I never want to see such a sight again as there was behind their rail pen. It was a real slaughter house." Sergeant Setchell of the same unit remembered: "One poor fellow had been completely skinned the whole length of his back. It must have been done by a piece of rail, as he lay on the ground on his stomach. He was conscious, and could talk with us, but one of the doctors said he would not live a minute if we turned him over."[303]

Men in gray held no monopoly on suffering at Piedmont. Many Union dead lay on the field in front of the Confederate left wing. J.R. Pilkington of the 34[304] Massachusetts vividly recalled the macabre spectacle of the "dead and wounded of the 28th Ohio lying halfway across the clearing near the enemy's line of works," a testament to the stand they had made.[304] Dr. Alexander Neil, regimental surgeon of the 12th West Virginia, gathered up the wounded Mountaineers and had them carried to the field hospitals with the assistance of other members of the medical department. Neil observed that "Rebs and Union lay side by side, praying aloud fervently for God to have mercy on them." When men with green sashes (the green signified a member of the medical department) appeared, scores of wounded begged for help at the same time. That only a few could be helped at a time weighed heavily on the hearts of the medical staff.[305]

The surgeons performed little of their work in the field. For the worst cases, they administered morphine or whiskey to the wounded in the field. The army doctors also ligated bleeding arteries before a wounded soldier was carried to the rear. But most of the time, a surgeon did little more than ensure that the stretcher bearers carefully handled the wounded troops.[306]

Colonel Thoburn and Lieutenant Colonel Weddle of the 1st West Virginia discovered a mortally wounded Confederate who was "probably sixty years of age, and to all appearances was physically wholly unfitted for the exposure and hardships of a soldier's life." The white-haired gentleman proudly informed the officers that he and many others had been taken from their homes in Staunton and forced into the ranks of the Confederate army.[307] "But they couldn't give me the heart to fight against my country, and though in the ranks of its foes, I have never fired a shot against that old flag," explained the dying loyalist.[308] As Thoburn and Weddle rode over the field, they noticed that many of the dead and wounded were "striplings, mere boys, probably forced into the service."[309] Some Marylanders came upon a badly wounded Tennessean who "had no wish to fight against the Union." The man added that he had two sons in the Union army.[310]

Throughout the evening, U.S. soldiers roamed the fields at Piedmont looking for injured comrades and rendered aid to friend and foe alike. Private Charles Lynch of the 18th Connecticut carried an armload of canteens over to the Middle River and filled them for his comrades. Upon his return, he stopped and attended to a wounded Confederate, rinsing his wounded foot with cool water. Lynch also gathered up discarded blankets that he found scattered about the battlefield and carried them to the U.S. field hospital. There, he blanketed wounded comrades to warm them during the coolness of the coming night. The painful sights of a battlefield hospital made Lynch sick, and he declared that he had "[n]o more desire to visit a field hospital after a battle."[311]

Major William C. Sanders of the 45th Virginia had his chest pierced by a bullet that narrowly missed his heart, sliced through his lungs and exited near his spine. Medical personnel left Sanders on the battlefield, believing that he was dead. Sanders spent at least one night on the battlefield before being placed in a wagon and taken to the Crawford Farm for burial. Mr. Crawford examined Sanders closely and realized that he still had a faint pulse. Crawford promptly administered Sanders "half a pint of mountain whiskey, which stimulated his heart and lung action and led to his recovery." He did not succumb to his wound until 1921.[312]

The 45th Virginia's Colonel William E. Browne proved less fortunate than Sanders. After being carried to a field hospital on the Shaver Farm, the Union surgeons treated Browne's leg wound and made him as comfortable as possible on the ground. Captain Henry DuPont knew Browne from their days together as classmates at West Point. When DuPont learned of Browne's plight, he hastened to the Shaver Farm and visited him. When DuPont saw Browne, he was relieved that he did not seem seriously wounded. Browne

Corporal August Gaebe of the 28th Ohio was wounded during the final charge at Piedmont. After spending two days in a barn on the battlefield and two days in a Staunton hospital, Gaebe had the fortune to return home to Cincinnati, where he spent several days with his family, having his wound dressed by his wife. *Larry Strayer Collection.*

talked "almost exclusively" about the tactics of the battle and insisted that "the Union infantry had not been well handled." Believing that Browne would soon be on his way to a prison camp in the North, DuPont gave him the last ten dollars that DuPont had with him. Surprisingly, Browne died that night inside the Shaver House and was buried by the family in a wooden coffin.[313]

One family in east Tennessee suffered double the grief when two sons in the 39th Tennessee were killed at Piedmont. They died instantly on the battlefield, and a local resident buried both privates in his garden. When their father received notice of his sons' deaths, he drove a team of horses and wagon all the way from Tennessee to Piedmont to retrieve their bodies for interment in the family cemetery. When he arrived at Piedmont, the father packed their bodies in salt and began the long and sorrowful journey home with his boys.[314]

In addition to the military personnel, the battle also affected the local civilian population. When the combat ceased, the Beard family realized that their six-year-old boy, Cleave, was missing. Family and friends organized a search party that combed the area looking for the child. They finally found him curled up inside of a tree stump. When asked why he had left his house, young Cleave replied, "I wanted to see the fire'n." But the roar of battle was worse than he had ever imagined, and the frightened child had crawled inside the tree stump.[315]

The Union provost guard herded the Confederate prisoners of war into a makeshift corral on the Shaver Farm. Two prisoners approached their cavalry guards and asked if the Ringgold Battalion was present. When the guard answered affirmatively, the prisoner Allen Hurst of the 45th Virginia asked if he could see his brother, Frank. Another Pennsylvania asked in utter astonishment, "If you are Frank Hurst's brother, what in the hell are you doing in the Confederate army?" Before he answered, Private Henry Burke of Brewer's Battalion asked to see his brother, John, who was also a member of the Ringgold Battalion. Unfortunately, John was at Andersonville Prison Camp, where he died in November 1864.[316]

The ordeal of combat and the resultant defeat had depressed the spirits of the captured Southerners. However, one free-spirited Confederate did his best to alleviate the melancholy aura that had settled over his comrades. He climbed on a tree stump and called everyone to attention. Then, he soothed his comrades' feelings by urging them not to worry, for "[n]ext week the Richmond papers will come out, and we will have gained another glorious victory in the Valley."[317]

Not all of the Confederates on the left wing ended up in the prison pen. A handful who evaded capture actually made it to Staunton. Sergeant E.G. Burum of the Thomas Legion reported that a part of his command reached Staunton at dark. Once in town, he and his comrades had "a great time." Although Burum failed to elaborate on their doings, it seems likely that the Confederates probably got into a large cache of liquor stored in the town. When the Union army occupied Staunton the next day, Hunter's provost marshal destroyed a large quantity of alcohol to prevent its further consumption by the Northern troops.[318]

At New Hope, Vaughn and Imboden scraped together the remnants of their defeated force. Vaughn also performed the unwelcome duty of notifying General Lee of the battle's outcome:

> *Fought the enemy to-day eleven miles from Staunton. Near New Hope now. Have been driven back. I will try to protect Staunton, but unless re-enforcement's come at once I cannot do it. May have to fall back by way of Waynesborough. General W.E. Jones killed.*[319]

Colonel Edwin G. Lee, commander of the military post at Staunton, more succinctly informed General Lee in a concise telegram: "We have been pretty badly whipped...I fear Staunton will go up."[320] By ten o'clock that night, Vaughn withdrew the Confederate force back to Fishersville, seven miles east of Staunton. From there, he informed the authorities in Richmond that his battered force could not prevent Hunter from occupying Staunton, the very thing that General Lee had hoped to avoid when he sent Jones to the Shenandoah Valley.[321]

As night came on, the U.S. soldiers at Piedmont gradually drifted off to sleep beneath the stars. Before turning in for the night, Colonel Joseph Thoburn penned a simple line in his diary reflective of the unspoken thoughts of many men in the Army of the Shenandoah: "We have had a hard fought battle and by the favor of God we have been victorious."[322]

Chapter 8

"The First Federals Ever Here"

S ometime during the night, Vaughn realized the precariousness of his situation. He prudently determined to fall back on Rockfish Gap in the Blue Ridge Mountains.[323] At eight o'clock the next morning, Confederates filed out of Fishersville. They marched fourteen miles through Waynesboro to the Blue Ridge Tunnel at Rockfish Gap, just east of town. From Waynesboro, Vaughn informed Confederate secretary of war James A. Seddon that the Confederate Army of the Valley District numbered "not over 3,000 effective men, including Imboden's cavalry, 800."[324]

Back at Piedmont, Hunter set the United States Army of the Shenandoah in motion toward Staunton at six o'clock that morning. Hunter's ordnance department supplied each man fifty rounds of ammunition before departing camp. The victorious Union troops marched south through Piedmont and New Hope. Morale among the troopers was lofty, with one soldier noting that he was "happy as a big sunflower." The army soon reached a fork in the road located about one and a half miles south of New Hope. The western fork led to Staunton and a junction with Crook, while the eastern branch led to Fishersville and a potential showdown with Vaughn's "wreck of an army." Colonel Strother fervently hoped that Hunter would take the road leading toward Fishersville and "finish" off Vaughn's remaining force. However, Hunter remained focused on the longer-range objectives that Grant had set out for him. To that end, Hunter headed west to Staunton and a junction with Crook and Averell.[325]

After Hunter's decisive victory at Piedmont, his stock had risen in the eyes of the Army of the Shenandoah's soldiers. One West Virginian recalled:

Brigadier General John C. Vaughn assumed command of the Confederate forces after Jones was killed at Piedmont. Criticisms of him at the Battle of Piedmont are rooted more in his prior reputation than in any misdeeds on the battlefield. *USAMHI.*

"Notwithstanding Hunter's lack of popular qualities, now that he had won a victory, he was at this time popular with the boys; and they were disposed to cheer him when he made his appearance before them." Orderly Frank Reader wrote in his diary: "Hunter is adored by his troops now. He showed the finest generalship that ever has been shown in this valley." Hunter had won the men over, and they were in good spirits with which to continue the campaign in the valley.[326]

In military terms, the march to Staunton proved uneventful, as expected when the general marched his army away from Vaughn's force at Fishersville. The Union force encountered a number of civilians who made friendly overtures toward them. Thoburn noted in his diary: "On the way from Piedmont here we found about one half of the families who gave evidence of sympathy and good will toward us." Thoburn believed "if proper rule was exercised over the people of this country, one half of them would be outspoken friends of the Union."[327] Strother voiced a similar opinion: "The people along our route were either very much frightened or very glad to see us." Loyal women waved their kerchiefs and brought buckets of milk and water for the thirsty United States troops. As they neared Staunton, a dozen girls dressed in their best Sunday dresses stood by the side of the road and presented Hunter and his entourage with a bouquet of flowers.[328]

Inside Staunton, fear grew among the townspeople. At the Waddell house, Virginia Waddell was resting on her couch and discussing the prospect of the Federals coming to town with a friend. As they spoke, the Waddells' panic-stricken slave Selena burst into the room with a look for horror etched on her face. She shouted, "They're coming! They're coming! Miss Virginia, they're coming!" The terrified Waddell children raced into the room behind Selena, "screaming with terror." Before long, another slave ran in and shouted, "They shelling the town, and you must fly to the basement!" The whole crowd raced down the stairs into the basement. When they reached the cellar, Virginia stared at her terrified and panicked family and friends, and realizing the "ludicrous" sight they presented, she burst into laughter.[329]

Their fears were much exaggerated, as Mrs. Waddell soon realized, and the Union army did not shell the town. Several officers of Hunter's staff rode in the vanguard with the 15th and 21st New York Cavalry, who entered town after driving off a small body of Confederate cavalry. The Union forces passed the Virginia State Lunatic Asylum, where a large number of African American slaves working at that institution waited eagerly for their liberators. The superintendent warned them not to look into the "brutal eyes of the Yankees" and threatened to lock them in the cells if they fraternized with the Federals. Hunter's adjutant, Lieutenant Colonel Halpine, learned of this and promptly informed the slaves that they were now free and could come or go as they pleased, much to their enthusiasm. They displayed their gratitude by showing the Federals where the Confederates had hidden $300,000 worth of uniforms and army cloth at the asylum.[330]

When the main army reached Staunton about noon, Strother organized a triumphant march into the town. A color guard carried a massive United States flag that was so heavy it nearly broke its staff. Two bands marched with the color guard, playing "Dixie" as they entered Staunton, drawing the attention of the town's curious residents. Then as the people came out to watch and listen, the bands literally changed their tune and belted out patriotic strains of "Hail Columbia" and "Yankee Doodle" as they proceeded through the town. The Union infantry marched immediately behind the color guard and its bands, with Colonel Joseph Thoburn's brigade in the lead. The 1st West Virginia marched at the head of the column, carrying the inverted Confederate battle flag captured from the 36th Virginia at Piedmont. The infantry marched through the town and set up camp one mile west of Staunton. The victorious march into Staunton proved especially satisfying for the many soldiers of Hunter's army that been sent there in 1863 after their capture at Winchester. Then, the residents had derisively laughed and mocked the Connecticut, Ohio and West Virginia troops as they were marched through the town. At the time, the Federals had responded by singing patriotic songs and promising to bring their muskets the next time they came to town. It took nearly a year, but they ultimately made good on their promise, much to the dismay of the people of Staunton.[331]

The procession soon passed the Staunton Bank, where Halpine sat down with Alexander H. Stuart, a former Whig politician, and other local dignitaries. As the bands played "Hail Columbia" and the color guard filed past the bank, Stuart told Halpine, "That's a grand old tune. A grand old tune and a grand old flag. It's long since I have seen the one or heard the other." Halpine quietly observed Stuart's emotions and concluded that "he looked as if he were not sorry."[332]

The people of Staunton were overwhelmingly secessionist in their views. Although the Union army had encountered friends as they marched through the countryside, the town proved anything but amiable to its guests. J. Chapin Warner of the 34th Massachusetts summed it up when he wrote, "Rank secession in Town." Although the people in the town proved less than hospitable to the Federals, they found the natural beauty and splendor of the area most inviting. Samuel Ely of the 20th Pennsylvania Cavalry deemed Staunton "a beautiful place. The roses are in bloom; so many flowers." Private Lynch recorded that "[t]he scenery in this vicinity is grand" and evoked memories of his hometown, Norwich, Connecticut.[333]

The arrival of Hunter's army in Staunton had created great consternation and worry among the civilian populace. Rumors of his incendiary exploits at Newtown and en route from Cedar Creek to Staunton had put the civilian populace in a state of great apprehension. Alexander Stuart led a group of influential citizens to Hunter's headquarters to discuss "the present condition of the town." As he did with the Newtown entourage, Hunter refused to meet them and called on valley native Strother to confer with them. He informed the Stauntonites that "we were warring according to the rules of civilized nations." As such, all "warlike stores, manufactures, and buildings which appertained to the Confederacy would be destroyed." Strother assured them that "private property and noncombatants would be respected," alleviating some of their fears.[334]

Although Strother had reassured the town's leaders about the army's official intentions, he also warned them of the dangers of "an ill disciplined soldiery." The Union troops had made it to Staunton on half rations; many had little or nothing to eat since before the Battle of Piedmont. These hungry soldiers had not been party to Strother's meeting, and the bountiful town of Staunton and its environs provided the troops with ample opportunities to fill their stomachs. As a soldier of the 12th West Virginia related, "It was not long before a certain class of individuals who claim largely in the 'Southern Rights' enterprise, had very urgent calls from 'Yankee mudsills' for flour, bacon and various other articles of subsistence, which were applied to the keeping alive of a species of the human family known in this section as 'Yanks.'"[335]

The most popular prize found in Staunton by the soldiers proved to be a large warehouse filled with tobacco. The Union officers threw open the doors to the warehouse, and hundreds, perhaps thousands of men took advantage of the opportunity to obtain some of the precious and rare (to Federals) tobacco. One New Englander noted, "Every man had all he could carry." When the Army of the Shenandoah abandoned the town several days later, the same soldier recorded, "We left the streets paved with it [tobacco]." Federal troops also took large quantities of the tobacco to the Confederate hospital and distributed it to the wounded Southerners. The recuperating Southerners thanked the Federals, and a few even said, "We're glad you came."[336]

Hunter quickly cast aside the fanfare and diplomacy and got down to the military business of his campaign. His victory at Piedmont was in the past, and he was "very cross" because Crook and Averell had not reported back to him. Hunter received a report that Averell was at Buffalo Gap, ten miles west of Staunton. In response, Hunter promptly sent two signal officers escorted by the 1st Maryland PHB Cavalry to open signal communications with Averell. The Marylanders rode out of Staunton that same evening. As they neared Buffalo Gap, they saw the glimmer of campfires burning along the road in the gap. By the time they reached the gap at daylight the next morning, the camp had been abandoned. It had been occupied by Colonel William L. "Mudwall" Jackson's Brigade, which had just moved off to the south. The scouts moved through the gap and continued on for ten miles but still could not locate Averell or Crook. "Rumor" placed them at Goshen, but no concrete information could be gained, so they turned around and headed back toward Staunton.[337]

The occupation of Staunton brought with it mundane duties to be addressed. Four hundred wounded and sick Confederates were in the town's military hospitals and had to be issued paroles. The Unionists also found large stores of ordnance and commissary supplies that the Confederates had been unable to remove. The army's ordnance and commissary departments distributed all usable supplies to the Union troops. What could not be used was destroyed. Among those items were three cannons and one thousand stands of small arms.[338]

Early on the morning of June 7, Hunter's troops began destroying any infrastructure that could support the Confederate war effort. The work of destruction continued throughout the next four days. The Union army burned all railroad depots and facilities, a woolen mill, steam mill, wagon factory, stables and forage houses. They also destroyed a shoe factory, cutting it to pieces and destroying the machinery because burning it risked spreading the fire to private property.[339] Warehouses, tanneries, blacksmith shops and any other entrepreneurial activity that benefited the Confederate military were destroyed. The destruction created quite a spectacle as the "devouring flames" rolled upward into the sky. While Hunter unhesitatingly destroyed Staunton's military-industrial facilities, his troops did take precautions to avoid the destruction of private residences. When the burning of a carriage shop and the shoe factory would have endangered private property, the citizens were allowed to completely disassemble the workshops to avoid any conflagration to nearby homes. One woman was so worried for the safety of her home that she grabbed an axe and ran across the street to assist with the destruction in a most ludicrous fashion.[340]

The widespread destruction of Staunton's manufacturing capacity and foraging by individual Union troops outraged the citizenry. After Hunter left town, the editor of the *Staunton Vindicator* declared, "The incendiarism and thieving which has characterized this raid of Hen-roost Hunter makes him as deservedly as odious as Beast Butler." The *Richmond Daily Dispatch* described Hunter as "a horrid old wretch, next to Beast Butler." Regardless, Hunter's destruction of Confederate resources in the valley paled in comparison to the devastating campaigns carried out by General Philip H. Sheridan and William T. Sherman in the Shenandoah and Georgia later in 1864.[341]

Hunter decided to march the Army of the Shenandoah west toward Buffalo Gap in the Allegheny Mountains. The movements served several purposes. First, he hoped to facilitate his long-sought junction with Crook while at the same time trapping the small force of Confederate Brigadier General John McCausland who was opposing Crook's advance. Hunter also used the opportunity to destroy the Virginia Central Railroad west of Staunton. Bridges were burned, and the rails and ties torn up and burned for several miles. At ten o'clock that morning, the bulk of the Army of the Shenandoah marched out of Staunton and headed toward Buffalo Gap. The army encountered the signalmen and Maryland cavalry who had scouted Buffalo Gap the previous evening but found no sign of Crook and Averell. Tension began to mount because of their absence seventeen days after Hunter issued the order. Strother described it as "singular and vexatious" that they had not yet appeared. Halpine had already wondered if they could be relied on. Hunter surely seethed when no evidence of Crook's progress could be obtained.[342]

While the army went on its spur-of-the-moment mission, a group of stragglers plundered the town, destroying the press of a local newspaper and otherwise damaging private property and terrorizing civilians. A party of Confederate horsemen stormed into Staunton, capturing two of the stragglers who had remained behind without orders. The three officers who remained in town issuing paroles to the wounded Confederates somehow managed to avoid capture.[343]

Word of the disturbance reached the 20th Pennsylvania Cavalry, which was operating east of Staunton at the time. The Pennsylvanians charged through Staunton and easily drove the small Confederate contingent away. They managed to capture some prisoners, but for the most part the Confederates fled without offering resistance. Meanwhile, the main Federal column halted its march at Hebron Church, five miles west of Staunton. After resting for one hour, Hunter marched his troops back to town, where they arrived at six o'clock that evening.[344] After Hunter returned to Staunton, the scouts who carried Hunter's May 22 orders to Crook returned to the Army of the Shenandoah. They brought word that Crook would arrive in Staunton the next day, fulfilling Hunter's objective.[345]

On June 8, Hunter sent Tibbits's cavalry brigade on a reconnaissance toward Fishersville. Tibbits's horsemen encountered Imboden's Brigade in line of battle between Fishersville and Waynesboro. A brief skirmish ensued before Tibbits fell back toward Staunton, having ascertained that the Confederates had not altogether abandoned the Shenandoah Valley. Along the way, his troopers burned the Virginia Central Railroad Depot at Fishersville. The Union infantry also moved east of Staunton and continued the destruction of the Virginia Central Railroad. The soldiers stacked the wooden railroad ties, placed the steel rails on top of the pile and then fired the wooden ties so that the rails warped in the center, "making them useless." This work continued for the next two days and destroyed many bridges and culverts, including the fifty-foot wooden span over Christian's Creek. While they were out in the countryside, the infantrymen seized any cattle or horses that they came across as part of Hunter's effort to live off the abundance of the Shenandoah Valley.[346]

Earlier in the day, Strother had devised a plan to transport the prisoners to a Northern prison camp. Strother recommended that Colonel Moor's

28th Ohio, soon to be mustered out, escort the 1,040 unwounded prisoners captured at Piedmont to Camp Morton prison in Indianapolis, Indiana. Hunter adopted this course of action, no doubt to the great satisfaction of the Ohioans. On the previous day, Lieutenant Colonel Halpine had sent Colonel Moor a letter expressing General Hunter's appreciation for Moor's services in the recent campaign for Staunton. Hunter expressed "high appreciation" of Moor's "soldierly qualities and services, and his regret at losing you from this command. The masterly management of your brigade at the recent battle of Piedmont on the 5th instant, did no more than sustain the creditable character given of you by your former commanders." Halpine also informed Moor that Hunter "trusts that the service may not permanently lose so good an officer at a time so critical and to this end has written a letter to the Hon. Secretary of War."[347]

Hunter had captured Staunton in accordance with Grant's orders, destroying the railroad and the town's manufacturing establishments. Crook and Averell joined Hunter, albeit later than expected. The Confederates in the valley were unable to oppose Hunter after their devastating losses at Piedmont. Indeed, the time appeared to be right for Hunter to launch the next part of his campaign. Based on the recommendation of Strother and General Averell, Hunter targeted Lynchburg, a vital Confederate supply depot and rail center. Shortly before the Federals left Staunton, Hunter's adjutant Halpine wrote, "We can laugh at anything less than one of Lee's Army Corps to reinforce the valley troops." Unfortunately for Hunter, that was exactly what Lee had in mind. When Hunter reached Lynchburg one week later, reinforcements from Lee's army saved that town from the same sort of destruction that occurred at Staunton.[348]

In the predawn darkness of June 10, 1864, Colonel Augustus Moor assembled his force for the march north with the prisoners captured at Piedmont. Moor's own 28th Ohio formed the bulk of the escort, but it also included detachments of several other regiments. The German's command included 9 officers and 160 men from the 23rd Ohio, a small detachment of the 4th West Virginia and a mounted escort from the 1st Veteran Cavalry. Lieutenant Samuel Shearer's section of Battery G, 1st West Virginia Light Artillery, provided artillery support. Many wounded Union soldiers were present, including Julius Stahel (his wound rendering him unfit for the rigors of field duty) and an "endless string of refugees" that consisted of newly freed slaves and Unionists from the valley who did not wish to remain behind when Hunter departed Staunton.[349]

At four o'clock in the morning, the column marched out of Staunton on the road leading to Buffalo Gap. While the prison escort moved westward,

Hunter held his army at Staunton for another hour to place some distance between Moor and the Confederate force at Waynesboro before moving toward Lexington.[350]

Moor's men marched their prisoners through the mountains of West Virginia until they reached the Baltimore & Ohio Railroad at Webster. From there, they rode the rails to the Ohio River, which they crossed on a ferry. In Ohio, they again boarded the trains and continued through the friendly foothills of southeastern Ohio with no fear of bushwhackers and little chance for the prisoners to escape. The train passed through the peaceful Ohio towns of Cambridge, Zanesville and Newark. What a pleasant sight these towns must have presented to both Union soldiers and Confederate prisoners, who had seen nothing but war and desolation for the past three years. The train chugged deep into the heart of Ohio, passing through Columbus and Dayton. Finally, at six o'clock in the evening of June 21, Colonel Moor's force with its prisoners arrived in Indianapolis, Indiana, their final destination.

The 28th Ohio immediately escorted the prisoners to Camp Morton prison camp. The Ohioans remained there until one o'clock the next morning while the prisoners were processed. The 28th Ohio then marched en masse to Camp Carrington, where they bedded down for the night. On June 23, Governor Morton of Indiana invited Moor to bring his regiment to the state capital. The governor sent a band to Camp Carrington that escorted the 28th Ohio to the capital. There an army chaplain led the men in prayer, and Morton "made a long speech to welcome us home, and praised us on our victory and service to our country." On the return march to Camp Carrington, Moor halted the 28th Ohio at a German beer garden and treated his men "to a few glasses of beer." Having quenched their thirst, the Ohioans returned to Camp Carrington. After a few more days in camp, Moor and the 28th Ohio returned home to Cincinnati and their families.[351]

No homecomings awaited the Confederate prisoners at Camp Morton. They received the poor treatment that had become customary in Civil War prison camps. Many Southerners died in prison and never occasioned a joyous reunion with family and friends at home. The officers suffered the misfortune of being transferred to Johnson's Island, Ohio, where they suffered from intense hunger and Lake Erie's frigid winds that chilled them to the bone as they struggled to keep warm during the long, cold northern Ohio winter.

Chapter 9

Piedmont

A Retrospective

The Battle of Piedmont saw more men killed or wounded than any action of Stonewall Jackson's legendary 1862 Valley Campaign. The casualties at Piedmont likewise eclipsed the losses incurred the previous month at New Market. In spite of Piedmont's ferocity, the dynamic nature of the 1864 summer campaign in the valley overshadowed Piedmont. As the *Official Records* published only four after-action reports on Piedmont, historians lacked the most basic and accessible source material. Piedmont also lacked a star attraction such as Stonewall Jackson, Phil Sheridan or the VMI Corps of Cadets. As a result, few historians researched or wrote on the Battle of Piedmont. For this reason, students of the Civil War have seemingly regarded Piedmont as little more than a skirmish that occurred between the Battle of New Market and the Sheridan/Early Valley Campaign of the late summer.

What was written on Piedmont tended to be largely superficial. Past works drew largely on a few published sources. Such pieces overly relied on the writings of Milton Humphrey, David H. Strother, John D. Imboden and several Federal regimental histories. As a result, the contributions of several officers and regiments have been overlooked. Most importantly, the true significance of Piedmont has dissipated over the years. Although its obscurity can be explained, it cannot be justified. At the time, Piedmont changed the course of the war in Virginia. The Union victory there shattered the only Confederate force capable of offering serious resistance to Hunter's army in the Shenandoah Valley. It also exposed the "Breadbasket of the Confederacy" and the valley's productive assets to Hunter's legions, forcing General Robert E. Lee to send additional forces to stop Hunter.

The Union victory at Piedmont compelled Lee to return Breckinridge's Division to the valley on June 6. Less than one week later, Lee rushed in Jubal A. Early's Corps to prevent Hunter from capturing Lynchburg. In total, Hunter's success at Piedmont drew off ten thousand Confederate infantrymen and three artillery battalions from the Army of Northern Virginia. It is ironic to note that Grant, who said that preventing the Confederates in the Shenandoah Valley from reinforcing Lee would be doing him "good service," was unable to capitalize on this significant reduction in Lee's strength during his initial movement against Petersburg.[352]

By compelling Lee to detach a large force to the valley, Piedmont ultimately shifted much focus of the war in Virginia to the Shenandoah Valley and its adjoining regions as they became the scene of strategic military operations and unprecedented combat. By dispatching Early, Lee had committed himself to fighting on the defensive against Grant. This move also precluded Lee from reinforcing the Confederate forces defending Atlanta against Sherman's army. Instead, Lee gambled that Early's bold actions in the valley would draw off Federal troops from Grant's forces at Richmond and Petersburg and discourage the Northern electorate. Perhaps a peace candidate (one who would end the war and give the South its freedom) might even end up in the White House in the coming elections. Ironically, had Hunter been defeated at Piedmont, Early very likely would have remained with Lee in front of Petersburg, and the ensuing Valley Campaign would have looked very different from the one that actually occurred.

On the Union side, General U.S. Grant's legendary determination and resolve were the decisive factors in the campaign for Staunton. The *New York Herald-Tribune* noted, "Grant had an object in view, as Lee perhaps understands by this time, it was not given up because of one repulse." His unhesitating replacement of Sigel and Hunter's quick resumption of offensive operations caught Lee off guard and led to the victory at Piedmont, which exposed the valley's resources to destruction. Grant and Hunter's quick work caught the Confederates unprepared after Lee allowed Breckinridge to join the Army of Northern Virginia after New Market. The *Richmond Examiner* sarcastically opined that the results of the campaign were simply "the necessary consequence of that wise order which brought Breckinridge to Hanover Junction where he was never needed, leaving the Valley wide open...Staunton, Lexington and perhaps Lynchburg were surrendered with that order."[353]

General David Hunter provided the most successful leadership in the valley that the Union had seen thus far in the war. He quickly rejuvenated the Union forces in the valley, getting them back into action and achieving a decisive victory at Piedmont that decimated the Confederacy's ability to effectively protect the valley. In the ensuing operations, Hunter damaged the valley's railroad communications and capacity to supply provisions for General Lee's army. He seriously impaired Staunton's military-industrial capacity and destroyed the Virginia Central Railroad for a distance of six miles, rendering that line inoperable for more than a month. Dozens of mills of all varieties throughout the valley no longer functioned as a result of the Federal efforts, and Hunter's troops also destroyed and consumed large quantities of foodstuffs on their march from Cedar Creek to Staunton and beyond. Hunter's victory opened the door for even further operations against the "vitals" of the Confederacy. Although these subsequent operations did not capture Lynchburg, Hunter succeeded to such a degree that Grant wrote, "I fail to see that Hunter has not acted with great promptness and great success."[354]

For Hunter's division commanders, Piedmont proved to be the lone bright spot in the lackluster careers of Generals Stahel and Sullivan. The Hungarian acted decisively during the advance from Port Republic and displayed personal bravery on the battlefield. He hurriedly led reinforcements into the morning's cavalry action, prevented Imboden from seriously delaying the Federal march and deployed his cavalry to bolster the sagging Union line during the main battle. Of his contributions on June 5, 1864, Hunter wrote to Secretary of War Stanton, "It is but justice to Major General Stahel to state that in the recent engagement he displayed excellent qualities of coolness and gallantry, and for the final happy result the country is much indebted to his services." For his efforts, Stahel was awarded the Medal of Honor during the 1890s. While the Hungarian fared well at Piedmont, his wound forced him to leave the army.[355] Sullivan appears to have exercised little direct control over his division during the battle, with Hunter often sending orders directly to the brigadiers. Nonetheless, he was on the front lines throughout the fight, providing encouragement and leadership for his men. Even the hard-to-please Strother complimented Sullivan's bravery at Piedmont.[356]

At Piedmont, the brigade and regimental level officers proved to be a major factor in the battle's outcome. Colonel William Badger Tibbits became the Union army's spark plug in the early phases of the battle, pressing his advantage and preventing Imboden's cavalry from regrouping. At the battle's end, Tibbits seemed to be the only one who recognized the importance of timely cavalry pursuit in Stahel's absence. Colonel McReynolds's indecision squandered the opportunity to capture hundreds more prisoners and perhaps much Confederate artillery. Stahel afterward commended Tibbits for his "gallant conduct" and "the faithful and efficient manner in which you discharged your every duty."[357]

Colonel Augustus Moor displayed considerable determination in the execution of his attacks on the Confederate works. The Germans of the 28th Ohio believed that Moor was "the man, who more than any other, saved the day at Piedmont." In spite of the heavy losses, Moor maintained his brigade's cohesion and effectiveness. When orders came for the final attack, Moor led his battered brigade forward and prevented the Confederate infantry from changing front to meet Thoburn's attack. Afterward, Hunter expressed his high regard for Moor's soldierly qualities and regretted that the U.S. Army lost the services of such a man.[358]

Colonel Thoburn likewise received praise for his role in the successful attack, although his actions earlier in the day were tentative. The movement of Thoburn's brigade was quick and decisive. Private David Smith of the 20th Pennsylvania Cavalry deemed it "the quickest and best move made by infantry," that he witnessed during the war. Once the final attack began, he ensured its success by extending his line to the left with the 34th Massachusetts to ensure that it struck the rear of the Confederate flank. One Federal staff officer described the West Virginian as "our fearless, cool

Colonel Augustus Moor commanded the bulk of Hunter's infantry at the Battle of Piedmont. *USAMHI.*

and sound-judging Colonel Joe Thoburn." However, Thoburn had much assistance in his brigade, from the precise leadership of Massachusetts's Colonel George D. Wells to the rugged determination and alertness of Pennsylvania's Colonel Jacob Campbell.[359]

Just as important as the officers, the determination of the Army of the Shenandoah's fighting men contributed decisively to the battle's outcome. The Confederate defenders noted the determined nature of the Federal assaults and the vigor with which the bluecoats advanced. One Confederate historian noted that the Federals advanced "with the same sullen determination which belongs to that eminently bull-dog race." A Confederate participant wrote that Colonel Moor's brigade "three times did what men have refused to do a second time without incurring the imputation of cowardice." More specifically, the discipline and precise drill of Moor's 28th Ohio and Wells's 34th Massachusetts saved the Federal army from another embarrassing defeat in the Shenandoah Valley.[360]

On the Confederate side, General John D. Imboden faced tremendous odds from the outset of Hunter's raid. In early May, Imboden offered an enterprising and successful resistance to Sigel's advance. However, Hunter ran a much tighter ship than his predecessor, and Imboden found little opportunity to strike. Instead, he preserved his command from destruction and monitored Hunter's progress, keeping Richmond and Lee apprised of the developing crisis in the valley. Imboden's prompt and accurate intelligence reports allowed Lee to send reinforcements to the Shenandoah Valley in time to contest Hunter's advance on Staunton.[361]

Grumble Jones found himself leading a makeshift army in the Shenandoah Valley after assuming command of the Department of Western Virginia and Eastern Tennessee under uncertain circumstances. For the first time in his military career, he commanded a combined arms force of infantry, cavalry and artillery. He displayed considerable logistical

Attack of the 18th Connecticut against the Confederates behind the rail fortifications at Piedmont. *William C. Walker, History of the 18th Connecticut Volunteers.*

ability as a department commander, transferring four thousand troops to the valley on short notice while screening Crook's advance out of West Virginia. At Piedmont, he aggressively confronted Hunter's flanking march and staunchly resisted the Federal attacks. In the end, however, Jones's overconfidence and inexperience as a combined arms commander contributed much to the Confederate defeat.[362]

Traditionally, Imboden and Vaughn normally receive the lion's share of the blame for the Confederate defeat at Piedmont. However, Jones bears much responsibility, for he stretched his disparate command beyond its limited capabilities. When he rearranged his troops for a counterattack and ordered Imboden to operate against the Federal left, he simply had asked too much from his makeshift army. Maintaining a firm defensive position would have seemingly guaranteed a Confederate victory, but Jones's confidence in his ability to defeat Hunter did not allow him to remain on the defensive. In fact, victory was so close that some Confederates claimed that the Union wagon trains had turned around in preparation for retreat although there is no confirmation of that claim from Federal sources.[363]

Jones's overconfidence clouded his decision making and caused him to underestimate Hunter's fortitude, providing the Federals one last chance for victory. Hunter, a thirty-six-year Regular Army veteran, took the opening that Jones gave him and snatched victory from the jaws of defeat. While Hunter lacked the combat ability of Philip H. Sheridan or George Thomas, he clearly belonged in a different category than the previous Federal commanders in the Shenandoah Valley such as Banks, Milroy and Sigel. By discounting Hunter's offensive capability and aggressiveness, Jones broke a cardinal rule of warfare and opened the door for a Union victory. Jones's disregard for Hunter also led him to minimize the potential risk posed by the gap in the center of his line. Although he recognized the danger to his army and had taken precautions early in the battle, he abandoned his plan to close the gap by withdrawing his left wing to the south side of the Cross Road (thereby closing the gap). He aggravated the situation by apparently moving the only troops in position to defend this gap (the 60th Virginia) from their position. Ironically, Jones's original plan to realign his forces behind the Cross Road might well have assured a Confederate victory at Piedmont.[364]

Before June 5, 1864, Jones had commanded only one or two cavalry brigades in combat. When the fighting began at Piedmont, he reverted to his traditional role of a brigadier and oversaw the infantry battle against Moor's brigade. For most of the battle, he left Imboden and Vaughn to their own devices. He had two capable brigadiers in Colonels Browne and

Beuhring Jones to manage the infantry fight and could have better spent his time focusing on leadership at a higher level and made better use of his artillery. In stark contrast to Jones, Hunter had stationed his headquarters on some slightly elevated ground in the center of the Federal line of battle. He monitored the progress of the battle from the centrally located Shaver House, issuing orders to his brigade commanders based on the overall situation. Hunter lacked Jones's combat experience but made up for it by maintaining a firm grasp on the actions of his army, exercising leadership at a higher level and leaving tactical details to his subordinates.

Although General Jones committed some important mistakes, no one can question his personal bravery and front-line leadership. He died a hero charging into the leveled rifles of his enemies and leading a last-gasp effort to salvage victory from defeat. Colonel Beuhring Jones wrote, "There is a melancholy satisfaction in believing that the fatal missile found our lamented Chieftain while his countenance was yet flushed with cheering anticipation of victory."[365]

Although Jones's realignment of his troops contributed to the Confederate defeat at Piedmont, his two primary subordinates, Vaughn and Imboden, received the lion's share of the blame. Many ex-Confederates believed that both Imboden and Vaughn had received orders from General Jones to move to his assistance when Thoburn attacked. As the story went, Vaughn and Imboden ignored these orders, and the Federals achieved a resounding victory. Given the low regard in which Vaughn and, to a lesser degree, Imboden have been viewed, few found this theory difficult to accept.

Vaughn's poor reputation made him the primary target for those seeking to cast blame for the South's defeat at Piedmont. Lieutenant Colonel Charles T. O'Ferrall spoke for many when he wrote:

> *It is always disagreeable to me to criticize a fellow-officer, condemn him for any act of commission or omission, but truth forces me in this instance to lay blame at the door of General Vaughan for our defeat at New Hope. He ranked General Imboden, and sat quietly on his horse, awaiting orders, in spite of Imboden's persistent desire and the eagerness of the men to move upon the enemy.*[366]

Unfortunately, false assertions such as this ignored the fact that Vaughn had personally moved with more than half of his brigade to the Confederate left in accordance with General Jones's orders and slightly wounded during Thoburn's attack. Only four hundred of Vaughn's men remained in position after he departed. Furthermore, Vaughn's indictment assumed that Thoburn's brigade had remained in the woods in front of Vaughn and Imboden throughout the entire battle. In actuality, Thoburn had withdrawn at least one hour before his final attack. When Thoburn attacked, he advanced from behind the Union artillery, directly toward the right flank of the Confederate left wing, and wheeled into position at the last minute. The rapidity of this move limited any chance for Vaughn's small force to engage Thoburn.[367]

Those who claimed that Imboden or Vaughn could have checked Thoburn's advance, including Imboden, conveniently forgot that DuPont's artillery commanded the ground that any attack on Thoburn's flank would have to traverse. Additionally, five companies of skirmishers from Thoburn's brigade remained directly in front of their position screening his advance. Additionally, the 2nd Maryland Eastern Shore remained in place behind these skirmishers near DuPont's batteries. When all of these facts are considered, Imboden had little chance of successfully checking Thoburn's assault, and Vaughn had taken the larger part of his brigade to the left wing in compliance with Jones's orders. Viewed in the larger scope of history, the whole argument over who lost the battle for the Confederacy is also one that is steeped in "Lost Cause" mythology. It was the idea that the Union could not have won a battle on its own without errors being committed by Confederate commanders. This view is shortsighted and failed to recognize that Union commanders often won battles through actions of their own such as Thoburn's well-executed flank attack at Piedmont.

Imboden, however, did fail in his delaying action at Mount Meridian. The rapid success of the Union cavalry that morning resulted largely from Imboden being caught off guard. Jones sent Imboden to Mount Meridian with one task in mind: to "retard" Hunter's advance. Jones specifically warned Imboden not to become involved in a serious conflict that might risk losing his small command. However, in the heat of combat, Imboden neglected Jones's admonition and overextended his brigade and fought it in piecemeal fashion.[368] In spite of Jones's clear instructions, Stahel's cavalry caught Imboden by surprise. Imboden later admitted, "We came in collision with his [Stahel's] cavalry so unexpectedly that I became more seriously engaged than I intended or my instructions warranted, and had great difficulty in extricating my command from what, for a little while, was a most perilous position." He had no one to blame for this situation but himself. Captain George Chrisman, commander of a company of Rockingham County mounted reserves, later declared that Imboden was simply surprised at Mount Meridian.[369]

The death of General Jones proved to be a substantial setback to the Confederate hopes in the Shenandoah Valley. Colonel Beuhring Jones believed that "[a] more gallant soldier, or more ardent and inflexible patriot, never laid his life, a voluntary sacrifice upon the altar of liberty." His loss extended beyond even the immediate defeat of Jones's force at Piedmont. In late June 1864, Early regained control of the valley for the Confederacy. He maintained a firm grasp on the entire Shenandoah Valley until September 19, 1864, when he was overwhelmed by Sheridan. The poor performance of Early's cavalry contributed much to the defeat. Early's cavalry lacked a leader to instill discipline as Jones had done with his commands on several occasions during the war. Even Jones's brigade lapsed back into its old ways upon the death of its commander. Given Jones's solid reputation as a disciplinarian and combat commander, it is not far-fetched to believe that Early's cavalry would have behaved differently had it been under Jones's able hand.[370]

In terms of manpower, the Confederacy could ill afford to lose in excess of 1,500 men, as it did at Piedmont. Jones took some of the largest regiments in the Confederacy into battle. When it ended, they were reduced to a mere shadow of the commands they had been only a few hours earlier. The 45th Virginia numbered over 600 men before the fight but counted only 200 men in its ranks afterward. The 1st Tennessee lost in excess of 50 percent of the troops taken into battle. The Confederacy could ill afford to suffer such losses in 1864.

For the Union, the moral uplift after Hunter's victory at Piedmont provided Lincoln supporters at the Republican National Convention in Baltimore some reason for excitement in what might otherwise have been a dismal gathering. This decisive victory in the Union's "Valley of Defeat" provided Lincoln a glimmer of hope and demonstrated that the United States Army could indeed defeat the Confederates in Virginia. Although Grant and Sherman had forced their opponents to retreat, neither had attained a clear-cut victory on the battlefield that spring. Consequently, Hunter's triumph gave Unionists some reason to believe in a final victory for the Union.[371]

Although often overlooked, the Battle of Piedmont intensified the conflict in Virginia's Shenandoah Valley to its highest point thus far in the war. The valley no longer served as a secondary theater, and all of its subsequent battles played a role in the war's outcome. Piedmont served as both a catalyst and precursor of these battles to come. Ironically, these resulting campaigns and battles obscured the courage and dedication displayed at Piedmont. But for the men who fought at Piedmont, nothing would make them forget the tempest that they passed through on June 5, 1864.

The Armies at Piedmont

U.S. Army of the Shenandoah
Major General David Hunter

First Infantry Division
Brigadier General Jeremiah C. Sullivan

First Brigade
Colonel Augustus Moor
18th Connecticut, Colonel William G. Ely
5th New York Heavy Artillery, Lieutenant Colonel Edward Murray
28th Ohio, Lieutenant Colonel Gottfried Becker
116th Ohio, Colonel James Washburn
123rd Ohio, Colonel William Wilson*

Second Brigade
Colonel Joseph Thoburn
2nd Maryland Eastern Shore, Colonel Robert S. Rodgers
34th Massachusetts, Colonel George D. Wells
54th Pennsylvania, Colonel Jacob M. Campbell
1st West Virginia, Lieutenant Colonel Jacob Weddle
4th West Virginia, Lieutenant Colonel James H. Dayton*
12th West Virginia, Colonel William B. Curtis

Artillery Brigade
Captain Henry A. DuPont
1st Maryland Light Artillery, B, Captain Alonzo Snow
30th New York Independent Battery, Captain Alfred von Kleiser
5th U.S. Artillery, B, Lieutenant Charles Holman
1st West Virginia Light Artillery, D, Captain John Carlin

First Cavalry Division
Major General Julius Stahel (w)

First Brigade
Colonel Andrew McReynolds
1st Maryland Potomac Home Brigade, Captain George J.P. Wood
1st New York, Major Timothy Quinn
1st Veteran, Lieutenant Colonel John S. Platner
21st New York, Colonel William B. Tibbits
14th Pennsylvania (detachment), Captain Ashbell F. Duncan

Second Brigade
Colonel John E. Wynkoop
15th New York, Captain Oscar R. Colgrove*
20th Pennsylvania (detachment), Lieutenant Colonel Gabriel Middleton
22nd Pennsylvania (detachment), Major Henry Myers

Horse Artillery
1st West Virginia Light, G (two guns), Lieutenant S.J. Shearer

Served as wagon guards during the Battle of Piedmont.

C.S. ARMY OF THE VALLEY DISTRICT
BRIGADIER GENERAL WILLIAM E. JONES (K)

First Brigade
Colonel Beuhring Jones (p)
36th Virginia, Lieutenant Colonel William E. Fife
60th Virginia, Captain James W. Johnston (w)
45th Virginia Battalion, Lieutenant Colonel Henry Beckley (w)
Lewisburg Artillery, Captain Thomas A. Bryan

Second Brigade
Colonel William E. Browne (mw)
Thomas Legion, Colonel Thomas Love
45th Virginia, Lieutenant Colonel Alexander Davis
Major R. Henry Brewer's Battalion

Vaughn's Brigade
Brigadier General John C. Vaughn
16th Georgia Battalion, Unknown
1st Tennessee, Major John B. King (k)
39th Tennessee, Major Robert McFarland
43rd Tennessee, Lieutenant Colonel David Key
59th Tennessee, Colonel William L. Eakin (p)
12th Tennessee Battalion, Major George W. Day
16th Tennessee Battalion, Unknown

Imboden's Brigade
Brigadier General John D. Imboden
18th Virginia, Colonel George Imboden
23rd Virginia, Colonel Robert White
Captain T. Sturgis Davis's Maryland Battalion
Captain John H. McClanahan's Battery

Reserves
Colonel Kenton Harper's Augusta and Rockbridge Reserves
Captain George Chrisman's Rockingham Reserves
Captain H.B. Harnsberger's Rockingham Reserves
Captain James C. Marquis' Augusta Battery

CASUALTIES AT PIEDMONT

United States Army Casualties

1st Brigade	Killed	Wounded	POW/MIA	Total
18th Connecticut	19	109	--	128[372]
5th New York, HA	8	46	5	59[373]
28th Ohio	27	108	--	135[374]
116th Ohio	54	127	--	181[375]
Brigade Total	108	390	5	503

2nd Brigade	Killed	Wounded	POW/MIA	Total
2nd Maryland, ES	--	6	--	6[376]
34th Massachusetts	13	97	--	110[377]
54th Pennsylvania	2	27	--	29[378]
1st West Virginia	7	36	17	60[379]
12th West Virginia	18	41	2	61[380]
Brigade Total	40	207	19	266
Division Total	148	597	24	769

Artillery	Killed	Wounded	POW/MIA	Total
1st Maryland, B	--	1	--	1[381]
1st West Virginia, D	--	1	--	1[382]
30th New York	1	1	--	2[383]
5th U.S., B	--	--	--	0
Brigade Total	1	3	--	4

FIRST CAVALRY DIVISION

1st Brigade	Killed	Wounded	POW/MIA	Total
1st Maryland, PHB	1	--	--	1[384]
1st New York	2	20	4	26[385]
1st Veteran	10	11	10	31[386]
21st New York	2	4	1	7[387]
14th Pennsylvania	2	1	--	3[388]
Brigade Total	17	36	15	68*

2nd Brigade	Killed	Wounded	POW/MIA	Total
15th New York	--	--	1	1[389]
20th Pennsylvania	--	2	--	2[390]
Ringgold Battalion	--	1	--	1[391]
Brigade Total	--	3	1	4*
Division Total	17	39	16	72

Union Grand Total	166	639	40	845

*Total for this unit is likely understated.

Confederate Casualties

Field and Staff	Killed	Wounded	POW/MIA	Total
	2	--	--	2[392]

1st Brigade	Killed	Wounded	POW/MIA	Total
36th Virginia	29	36	112	177[393]
60th Virginia	19	27	68	114[394]
45th Battalion	2	26	55	83[395]
Brigade Total	50	66	235	374

2nd Brigade	Killed	Wounded	POW/MIA	Total
45th Virginia	14	21	325	360[396]
Thomas Legion	20	30	42	92[397]
Brewer's Battalion	15	28	149	192[398]
Brigade Total	49	79	516	644

Vaughn's Brigade	Killed	Wounded	POW/MIA	Total
1st Tennessee	12	?	83	?
3rd Tennessee	?	?	?	47[399]
39th Tennessee	5	?	10	46
59th Tennessee	2	?	20	?
60th Tennessee	?	1	1	?

12th Georgia Battalion	?	?	1	?[400]
Brigade Total	19	164	115	298[401]
Infantry/Dismounted Total	120	332	866	1,318

Imboden's Brigade	Killed	Wounded	POW/MIA	Total
18th Virginia	1	33	26	60[402]
23rd Virginia	3	8	6	17[403]
62nd Virginia	4	2	1	7
Davis's Battalion	?	?	8	8[404]*
Brigade Total	8	39	41	92

Artillery	Killed	Wounded	POW/MIA	Total
McClanahan's	--	3	3	6[405]
Marquis'	5	1	1	7[406]
Bryan's	--	1	--	1[407]
Brigade Total	5	5	4	14

Reserves	Killed	Wounded	POW/MIA	Total
Harper's Reserves	13	38	24	75[408]
Staunton Provost Guard	--	1	1	2[409]
Total	13	39	25	77

Confederate Total	146	419	936	1,501

The total casualties have been reported for Vaughn's Brigade at the brigade level. The regimental details are incomplete with the exception of prisoners.

UNION AND CONFEDERATE STRENGTHS AT PIEDMONT

The strength of the Confederate army at Piedmont has varied with every person who has written on the battle, including participants. Writers who were sympathetic to the Confederate cause have underestimated the strength of the Confederate army and overestimated the strength of the Union force at Piedmont. In typical "Lost Cause" fashion, General Imboden placed the Confederate strength at 4,200 and the Federal at 11,500. If these odds were correct, a Confederate victory would have been out of the question, which is precisely what Imboden hoped that future generations would conclude. But these were not the odds at Piedmont. Jones took 5,600 effectives and sixteen guns into battle at Piedmont against David Hunter's 290 officers and 7,476 enlisted men (total 7,766) with twenty-four guns, as stated in the *Official Records of the War of the Rebellion.*[410]

Why this is so is a mystery; the numbers are available in several sources. A little bit of analysis shows that these sources are in agreement with one another.

The first and most obvious source is the report of General Vaughn, who assumed command of the army upon the death of Jones. On June 6, 1864, Vaughn stated that they went into the fight with 5,600 officers and men. This number is confirmed by two other important sources.

General Robert E. Lee sent a dispatch to Jefferson Davis in which he forwarded troop strengths that he had received from General Jones. Jones wrote Lee telling him that he had 4,000 infantry and dismounted cavalry with him and 1,000 mounted cavalry following overland. Lee is very specific that this is what Jones had before joining forces with Imboden in Staunton. As the cavalry did not reach the valley in time to participate in the Battle of Piedmont, they should not be counted as part of Jones's force engaged at Piedmont. When Jones's 4,000 are added to Imboden's 1,000 cavalrymen and a few hundred reserves, Jones's force totals to about 5,300 or so, depending on one's definition of "a few hundred." This number is remarkably close to Vaughn's.

Hunter's report, which is corroborated by several other Federal accounts, is the third source. Hunter states that he found papers on Jones's body that revealed the strength of the Confederate force at Piedmont. These papers stated that the Southern force numbered "between 6,000 and 7,000 and 16 guns." These papers probably included the 1,000 men of Jones's own cavalry brigade, which did not participate in the battle but was en route to the valley. If these 1,000 men are subtracted from 6,500 (the average of the two figures given by the papers), the total is 5,500. Once again, Vaughn's figure is confirmed by an outside source.

There is a final piece of evidence that shows that Vaughn's total is more than an educated guess. The papers of Colonel Kenton Harper, commander of a regiment at Piedmont, contain an order from Vaughn dated June 6, 1864. This order notes: "Report your effective aggregate. Report at once and also report the number of effectives before the fight of yesterday." This order shows that Vaughn did not estimate his 5,600 men present at Piedmont but rather called on his regimental commanders for exact information on their troop strength at Piedmont.

Taken as a whole, this evidence shows absolutely no reason to dispute Vaughn's reported troop strength. Rather, all sources closely support the total that Vaughn gives. The following table is the breakdown of the various units that composed the Confederate force at Piedmont. It has been compiled based on trimonthly returns from April 1864 in conjunction with losses incurred before Piedmont. Some of the figures are derived from letters and regimental histories.

B. Jones's Brigade	1,300[411]		
Browne's Brigade	1,500[412]	Imboden's Brigade	1,100[414]
Vaughn's Brigade	1,000[413]	Harper's Reserves	700[415]
Western Virginia	3,800	Valley District	1,800
William E. Jones's army (total)			5,600

Notes

Prologue

1. Grant, *Personal Memoirs*, 478.
2. Ibid.
3. Ibid., 478–79.

Chapter 1

4. Strother, *Virginia Yankee in the Civil War*, 229.
5. Ibid., 230–32; Lynch, *Civil War Diary*, 62.
6. Davis, *Battle of New Market*, 179; Strother, *Virginia Yankee in the Civil War*, 230–32.
7. Lynch, *Civil War Diary*, 62; Beach, *1st New York (Lincoln) Cavalry*, 353; Lincoln, *Life with the 34th Massachusetts Infantry*, 292.
8. J.D. Imboden to Colonel I. Marshall McCue, October 1, 1883 (hereafter cited as MOC; John D. Imboden hereafter abbreviated as JDI); O'Reilly, *Baked Meats of the Funeral*, 328–29; Moulton, *From Fort Lyon to Harper's Ferry*, 196.
9. Malone, *Dictionary of America Biography*, vol. 5, 399–400.
10. O'Reilly, *Baked Meats of the Funeral*, 328–29; Warner, *Generals in Blue*, 243–44.
11. Hunter resigned from the army in 1836 to speculate in real estate but rejoined in 1842, O'Reilly, *Baked Meats of the Funeral*, 328–29; Warner, *Generals in Blue*, 243–44.
12. Warner, *Generals in Blue*, 243–44; Hunter, Report of Service, Record Group 594 (cited hereafter as RG-594), National Archives (cited hereafter as NA); O'Reilly, *Baked Meats of the Funeral*, 333; Malone, *Dictionary of America Biography*, vol. 5, 400; Reed, "Black Dave and His Staff," 47.
13. Reed, *Combined Operations in the Civil War*, 277–80, 288–89, 297–98; Longacre, "General David Hunter," 7–8.
14. Hunter, Report of Service, RG-594, NA.

15. *War of the Rebellion: A Compilation of the Official Records of the Union and Confederate Armies*, series I, 34:1:353 (hereafter cited as *OR*, all from series I).

16. *OR*, 37:1:507; Grant, *Personal Memoirs*, 558.

17. O'Reilly, *Baked Meats of the Funeral*, 328–29; Wells to Mother, May 28, 1864; Laura Lee Diary.

18. *OR*, 37:1:507.

19. Hanchett, *Irish*, 108; *OR*, 37:1:510.

20. *OR*, 37:1:508 and 525.

21. Sell and Walle, *Guide to the Heinrich A. Ratterman Collection*, 133–34; Lang, *Loyal West Virginia*, 106.

22. Reid, *Ohio in the War*, 2:194; Sell and Walle, *Guide to the Heinrich A. Ratterman Collection*, 134.

23. Reid, *Ohio in the War*, 2:194; Sell and Walle, *Guide to the Heinrich A. Ratterman Collection*, 134.

24. *Wheeling Daily Intelligencer*, October 24, 1864; Newton, Nichols and Sprankle, *History of the Pan-Handle*, 253.

25. *Wheeling Daily Intelligencer*, October 24, 1864; Newton, Nichols and Sprankle, *History of the Pan-Handle*, 253.

26. Hennessy, *Return to Bull Run*, 160, 428, 436–37; *Wheeling Daily Intelligencer*, October 24, 1864.

27. Tibbits, Report of Service, RG 94, NA; Tibbits Papers, Diary.

28. *OR*, 37:1:508 and 531.

29. Eby, *Porte Crayon*, 115–16.

30. *OR*, 37:2:510; Gilmor, *Four Years in the Saddle*, 162.

31. *OR*, 37:2:516–17 and 525–26; Hanchett, *Irish*, 114.

32. *OR*, 37:1:517–18.

33. Frank Smith Reader Papers, Diary (cited hereafter as Reader Diary).

34. Lynch, *Civil War Diary*, 62; Lincoln, *Life with the 34th Massachusetts Infantry*, 292; DuPont, *Campaign of 1864*, 52.

35. Beer, *Hunter's Raid*, 6 (hereafter cited as Beer, Thoburn Diary).

36. William B. Stark, Journal, in possession of author.

37. Don Silvius, "The Valley Turnpike," http://www.vagenweb.org/shenandoah/cem/turnpike.html.

38. Henry Ocker to his Mother, June 25, 1864; David Powell Memoirs, 67–68; *OR*, 37:1:528; *New York Times*, June 3, 1864.

39. Harry Gilmor admittedly exercised little control over his command. Shearer's company was no exception. Shearer was commander of Company D, 2nd Maryland Cavalry Battalion, Strother, *Virginia Yankee in the Civil War*, 235–36; Ruffner, "More Trouble than a Brigade," 393; http://www.civilwardata.com/active/hdsquery.dll?SoldierHistory?C&1092985 (subscription).

40. Ruffner, "More Trouble than a Brigade," 395.

41. Ibid.

42. Tucker, *Brigadier General John D. Imboden*, 1; Warner, *Generals in Gray*, 177–78.

43. Delauter, *McNeill's Rangers*, 24–25; Imboden, "Sword, Fire and Halter," 170; Warner, *Generals in Gray*, 177–78; Imboden, "Battle of New Market," 480–83.

44. *OR*, 37:1:745.

45. Ibid., 37:1:746–47.

46. Lafferty, "Battle of New Hope."

47. Colley, "Brig. General William E. Jones," 266–67; Booth, *Personal Reminiscences*, 81.

48. William E. Jones Papers, Library of Virginia.

49. *OR*, 12:2:112.

50. Lewis, *Civil War*, 20.

51. *OR*, 27:2:754.

52. Warner, *Generals in Gray*, 166–67; Colley, "Brig. General William E. Jones," 266–67; Maslowski, "Burning Springs, Va.," 8, 65–66.

53. *OR*, 29:2:771–72.

54. Colley, "Brig. General William E. Jones," 267; Warner, *Generals in Gray*, 166–67; Weaver, *64th Virginia Infantry*, 86.

CHAPTER 2

55. *OR*, 37:1:525; Strother, *Virginia Yankee in the Civil War*, 231.

56. *OR*, 37:1:538; Farrar, *Twenty-Second Pennsylvania Cavalry*, 230.

57. J. Chapin Warner to Father, Mother, Brother and Sister, May 27, 1864; Rodgers, "History of the 2nd Eastern Shore Regiment," 174; George D. Wells to Mrs. R., May 28, 1864; O'Reilly, *Baked Meats of the Funeral*, 299.

58. *OR*, 37:1:110 and 537–38; Strother, *Virginia Yankee in the Civil War*, 236.

59. McIlhenny Diary; *OR*, 37:2:543.

60. *OR*, 37:2:747–48.

61. Beer, Thoburn Diary, 6; Wildes, *Record of the One Hundred and Sixteenth*, 91; Norton, "Red Neck Ties," 36.

62. Rodgers, "History of the 2nd Eastern Shore Regiment," 176–77.

63. Reader Diary, 20.

64. Strother, *Virginia Yankee in the Civil War*, 240; *OR*, 37:1:556; Root, "Report Respecting Capture of Wagon Train at New Town, Va," (cited hereafter as "Report"), RG 594, NA; Gilmor, *Four Years in the Saddle*, 163.

65. Root, "Report," RG 594, NA; Imboden to Colonel Kenton Harper, Letter, June 2, 1864; Gilmor, *Four Years in the Saddle*, 166.

66. Reid, *Ohio in the War*, vol. 2, 690; Record of Events, 160th Ohio, May and June, 1864, RG 94, NA.

67. Strother, *Virginia Yankee in the Civil War*, 240; *OR*, 37:1:556; Root, "Report," RG 94, NA.

68. Stevenson, *Boots and Saddles*, 278; Beach, *1st New York (Lincoln) Cavalry*, 355–56.

69. There is now a marker in the parking lot of the Stephen's City (Newtown) Post Office noting Stearns's actions; Laura Lee Diary; Stevenson, *Boots and Saddles*, 278–79; Beach, *1st New York (Lincoln) Cavalry*, 355–56; Strother, *Virginia Yankee in the Civil War*, 241.

70. Beer, Thoburn Diary, 8; Samuel Ely Diary, 11; Lynch, *Civil War Diary*, 64; Cushman Diary, 406.

71. *OR*, 37:1:552; Beach, *1st New York (Lincoln) Cavalry*, 355.

72. *OR*, 37:1:749.

Chapter 3

73. Brigadier General John H. Morgan's Brigade had been assigned to the Department of Western Virginia on May 2, 1864, but was on an unauthorized raid into Kentucky. Morgan entered Kentucky with "2,600 good men" and returned with "700 scattered fugitives." Morgan's troops are not included in Jones's total force of 8,200. Castel, *Campaign for Atlanta*, 277, 344; *OR*, 37:1:750 and 39:1:79.

74. Petre Jennings Diary, May 14, 1864 (cited hereafter as Jennings Diary); McManus, *Battle of Cloyd's Mountain*, 21–45; Humphreys, *Military Operations*, 58–59.

75. Jenning's Diary; Quesenberry to Dear Father and Mother, May 19, 1864; McManus, *Battle of Cloyd's Mountain*, 54.

76. William W. Stringfield Diary, 210–11; *OR*, 33:1,334–35 and 37:1:745.

77. Vaughn brought no mounted troops to Piedmont, although this assumption continues to be repeated in various forms. Vaughn himself was disappointed that his brigade's horses did not arrive in time for the campaign in Maryland, as he noted that he could have "exchanged" the old horses for new ones in Maryland. He went on to say Colonel James Carter of the 1st Tennessee Cavalry had brought the brigade's horses overland to Winchester and that the brigade would soon be mounted. The horses did not arrive in the Shenandoah Valley until July 17. In fact, no primary source material supports that assertion. J.N. Aiken of the 43rd Tennessee wrote, "The brigade was ordered to leave its horses in South-west Virginia and report to Brig.-Gen. W.E. Jones at Staunton." Colonel N.J. Lillard noted that the brigade was ordered to Staunton with "camp equipage and horses to follow." J.L. Henry of the 1st Tennessee plainly noted in his account that "on reaching Bristol we were dismounted, placed on freight cars…to Staunton." The mounted troops from Grumble Jones's own brigade did not reach Lexington, nearly fifty miles from Piedmont, until June 6. Vaughn's mounted men, even if they did begin riding right away, started at Bristol, seventy miles farther away from Jones's Brigade's starting point. John C. Vaughn to Colonel N.J. Lillard, July 15, 1864; William P. McDowell to My Dear Father, July ?, 1864; Jennings Diary; Burum Diary, Private Collection; Stringfield Diary, NCDAH; James Doggett Diary, Confederate Collection; Aiken, "Forty-Third Tennessee," 525; Henry, "First Tennessee Cavalry at Piedmont."

78. Federal officers found this dispatch on General Jones's body, Hunter's Report of Service, Record Group 594, NA.

79. Rodgers, "History of the 2nd Eastern Shore Regiment," 180; Beer, Thoburn Diary, 8; G. Wells to Dear mother, May 30, 1864.

80. George M'Clelland, "The Battle of Piedmont," *Wheeling Register*, June 21, 1864; McIlhenny Diary, 24; Imboden, "Sword, Fire and Halter," 172; Imboden to My Dearest Mollie, June 10, 1864, USAMHI; Corbin, "Diary of a Virginian Cavalry Man," third series, 213.

81. This skirmish occurred near what is today South Main Street on the campus of James Madison University. "Augusta County: Hunter's Raid, 1864," *Southern Historical Society Papers*, vol. 36, 95–103.

82. Kenton Harper Papers, General Imboden's Special Orders No. 148 and No. 150; *Staunton Spectator*, December 31, 1867.

83. Kenton Harper Papers, General Imboden's Special Orders No. 148 and No. 150.

84. Lincoln, *Life with the 34th Massachusetts Infantry*, 294–95.

85. Beer, Thoburn Diary, 9; Wayland, *History of Rockingham County*, 353; Jed Hotchkiss to Wife, July 3, 1864.

86. Beer, Thoburn Diary, 9.

87. Strother, *Virginia Yankee in the Civil War*, 241; Humphreys, *Military Operations*, 59–60; JDI to Colonel McCue, October 3, 1883; Henry, "First Tennessee Cavalry," 397; Jennings Diary.

88. Strother, *Virginia Yankee in the Civil War*, 241.

89. Reader Diary.

90. Halpine, *Baked Meats*, 302; Halpine, "Battle of Piedmont"; Strother, *Virginia Yankee in the Civil War*, 242; *OR*, 37:1:94.

91. Halpine, *Baked Meats*, 302; Halpine, "Battle of Piedmont."

92. Aten, *Study of Civil War Sites*, 64.

93. Samuel Ely Diary; Farrar, *Twenty-Second Pennsylvania Cavalry*, 235; Beer, Thoburn Diary, 10.

94. JDI, *Annals of the War*, 173.

95. Ibid.; JDI to I. Marshall McCue, Letter, October 1, 1883.

96. "War Path," "Reverse in the Valley," June 18, contained in the *Richmond Sentinel*, June 24, 1864. The pen name of "War Path" was Major John J. Lafferty, who served on Imboden's staff as chief of commissary; JDI, *Annals of the War*, 173; JDI to I. Marshall McCue, Letter, October 1, 1883.

97. *Richmond Sentinel*, June 24, 1864; JDI, *Annals of the War*, 173; JDI to I. Marshall McCue, Letter, October 1, 1883.

98. *Richmond Sentinel*, June 24, 1864; JDI, *Annals of the War*, 173; JDI to I. Marshall McCue, Letter, October 1, 1883.

99. *Richmond Sentinel*, June 24, 1864; JDI, *Annals of the War*, 173; JDI to I. Marshall McCue, Letter, October 1, 1883. "War Path" places Imboden's suggestion to fight at Mowry's Hill as occurring on the morning of June 5, after Imboden's cavalry had been driven back toward Piedmont.

100. JDI, *Annals of the War*, 173; JDI to I. Marshall McCue, Letter, October 1, 1883; Jones to Colonel Kenton Harper, June 4, 1864; Stringfield Diary; Hotchkiss Sketchbook, Library of Congress, 9.

101. *OR*, 37:1:152–53; Warner, *Generals in Gray*, 147; *Richmond Daily Dispatch*, June 14, 1864.

102. Helen S. Ely Papers, Samuel Ely Diary; Farrar, *Twenty-Second Pennsylvania Cavalry*, 235; Norton, *"Red Neck Ties,"* 37.

103. Farrar, *Twenty-Second Pennsylvania Cavalry*, 235.

104. Strother, *Virginia Yankee in the Civil War*, 242; Lynch, *Civil War Diary*, 66; Walker, *History of the Eighteenth Conn. Volunteers*, 229; Ocker to Mother, June 25, 1864.

105. Halpine, "Battle of Piedmont"; Strother, *Virginia Yankee in the Civil War*, 242; Reader Diary.

106. *OR*, 37:1:94; Beer, Thoburn Diary, 10.

107. For purposes of clarity, the road which ran from Port Republic to Piedmont will be referred to as the Staunton Road as the Union troops referred to it. Jed Hotchkiss called it on the Staunton-Port Republic Road on his map of the area.

Others referred to it as the East Road. JDI to I. Marshall McCue, October 1, 1883, MOC; JDI, *Annals of the War*, 174.

108. Henry, "First Tennessee Cavalry," 397.

109. JDI, *Annals of the War*, 174–75; JDI to I. Marshall McCue, Letter, October 1, 1883.

110. JDI, *Annals of the War*, 174–75; JDI to I. Marshall McCue, Letter, October 1, 1883; *Richmond Sentinel*, June 24, 1864.

CHAPTER 4

111. *OR*, 37:1:94; Halpine, "Battle of Piedmont"; Strother, *Virginia Yankee in the Civil War*, 242.

112. Moor, Report on the Battle of Piedmont, June 21, 1864 (cited hereafter as Moor, Report, IHS); Stevenson, *Boots and Saddles*, 279, Beach, *1st New York (Lincoln) Cavalry*, 360; Tibbits, Report of Service, RG 94, NA; Halpine, "Battle of Piedmont"; *OR*, 37:1:94.

113. Record of Events, 15th New York, RG 94, NA; Halpine, "Battle of Piedmont"; *OR*, 37:1:572; Elwood, *Elwoods Stories*, 125.

114. Moor, Report, IHS; Walker, *History of the Eighteenth Conn. Volunteers*, 236; Keyes, *Military History of the 123rd*, 62; Record of Events, 123rd Ohio, Field and Staff, RG 94, NA; Record of Events, 15th New York, RG 94, NA; Thoburn, Report on the Battle of Piedmont, June 7, 1864.

115. The Givens Farm straddles both sides of the road leading out to the Valley Pike. The house is on the south side of the road near the Middle River, Rodgers, "History of the 2nd Eastern Shore Regiment," 279; Beach, *1st New York (Lincoln) Cavalry*, 360; JDI to I. Marshall McCue, Letter, October 1, 1883.

116. JDI to I. Marshall McCue, October 1, 1883, Letter, MOC.

117. Ibid.; George W. Imboden to Mollie, June 10, 1864; Beach, *1st New York (Lincoln) Cavalry*, 360.

118. Stevenson, *Boots and Saddles*, 279–80; Beach, *1st New York (Lincoln) Cavalry*, 360.

119. George D. Imboden to Mollie, Letter, June 10, 1864; Beach, *1st New York (Lincoln) Cavalry*, 360–61; Stevenson, *Boots and Saddles*, 279–80.

120. Fitzsimmons, "Hunter Raid," 393; George D. Imboden to Mollie, Letter, June 10, 1864; Beach, *1st New York (Lincoln) Cavalry*, 360–61; Stevenson, *Boots and Saddles*, 279–80.

121. McIlhenny Diary, 25; Imboden to My Dearest Mollie, June 10, 1864; Beach, "Battle of Piedmont."

122. Tibbits, Report of Service, RG 94, NA; W.B. Tibbits Papers, Diary, New York State Archives; Feit, "Battle of Piedmont"; Slease, *Fourteenth Pennsylvania Cavalry*, 132; Warner, *Generals in Blue*, 505–6.

123. Tibbits, Report of Service, RG 94, NA; Fitzsimmons, "Hunter's Raid," 393; Feit, "Battle of Piedmont"; William B. Tibbits Papers, Diary, New York State Archives (cited hereafter as Tibbits Diary, NYSA); Joseph Waddell Diary, UVA.

124. JDI to I. Marshall McCue, Letter, October 1, 1883.

125. *Richmond Sentinel*, June 24, 1864.

126. Tibbits, Report of Service, RG 94, NA; Feit, "Battle of Piedmont"; Halpine, "Battle of Piedmont."

127. Heatwole, *"Remember Me Is All I Ask,"* 42; JDI to I. Marshall McCue, Letter, October 1, 1883; Berkeley, "Augusta's Battle."

128. Tibbits, Report of Service, RG 94, NA; JDI to I. Marshall McCue, Letter, October 1, 1883.

129. Writing eleven days after the battle, Major Lafferty of Imboden's staff places the 23rd Virginia as being the first regiment to come to the aid of the 18th Virginia, followed by Davis's Battalion, including the reserves. General Imboden's account, as well as that of Lieutenant Colonel O'Ferrall of the 23rd Virginia, confirms that, *Richmond Sentinel*, June 14, 1864; JDI to I. Marshall McCue, Letter, October 1, 1883; O'Ferrall, *Forty Years of Active Service*, 98; For an alternate view, see Heatwole, *"Remember Me Is All I Ask,"* 43, 82.

130. O'Ferrall, *Forty Years of Active Service*, 98; JDI to I. Marshall McCue, Letter, October 1, 1883; Berkeley, "Augusta's Battle."

131. Washington Marsh, "Piedmont Again! A New York Cavalryman's Recollection of the Battle," *National Tribune*, April 18, 1889.

132. Captain John Opie served with the 6th Virginia Cavalry of Major General J.E.B. Stuart's famed Cavalry Corps of the Army of Northern Virginia. At home recuperating from a wound, Opie assumed command of a reserve company, Opie, *Rebel Cavalryman*, 218–19; Joseph Waddell Diary.

133. Opie, *Rebel Cavalryman*, 218–19.

134. Tibbits, Report of Service, RG 94, NA; Opie, *Rebel Cavalryman*, 219.

135. Tibbits, Report of Service, RG 94, NA; Opie, *Rebel Cavalryman*, 219.

136. McIlhenny Diary, 25–26.

137. Berkeley, "Augusta's Battle"; Driver, *Staunton Artillery*, roster.

138. JDI to I. Marshall McCue, Letter, October 1, 1883; B. Jones, Report, 1; Porter, *Composition of Sketches*, 189–90.

139. Hunter's total aggregate present on May 31, 1864, was 9,600. The largest disparity between present for duty and aggregate present is in Stahel's cavalry division. It numbered 2,830 officers and men present for duty, but its aggregate present was 4,227. This is a difference of 1,397 who lacked either horses or other equipment or served on the detachments that frustrated Hunter. Sullivan's infantry division had an aggregate present of 4,851 and 4,400 present for duty, JDI to Colonel I. Marshall McCue, Letter, October 1, 1883; *OR*, 37:1:571.

140. JDI to I. Marshall McCue, Letter, October 1, 1883.

141. Ibid.

142. Berkeley, "Augusta's Battle."

143. Ibid; Opie, *Rebel Cavalryman*, 220.

144. Niter or saltpeter is a critical component of gunpowder. The men in the Niter Mining companies had been previously exempted from combat duty because of the importance of their work to the Confederate war effort. They were brought into active duty due to the urgent nature presented by Hunter's advance. *OR*, 51:1:1,225–26 and 37:1:95; B. Jones, Report, 1.

145. *National Tribune*, March 21, 1895.

146. Tibbits, Report of Service, RG 94, NA; Feit, "Battle of Piedmont"; Stevenson, *Boots and Saddles*, 280.

147. Reader Diary, 240; DuPont, *Campaign of 1864*, 555–56; Berkeley, "Augusta's Battle"; *OR*, 37:1:94–95.

148. Humphreys, *Military Operations*, 65.

149. Ibid., 66–67.

150. B. Jones, Report, 1.

151. Shackelford, "My Recollections of the War"; Isaac Prillaman to Dear Brother; B. Jones, Report, 1.

152. Pendleton, *History of Tazewell County*, 610; B. Jones, Report, 1, 4; Humphreys, *Military Operations*, 67; Weaver, *45th Battalion Infantry*, roster.

153. Shackelford, "My Recollections of the War"; Isaac Prillaman to Dear Brother; B. Jones, Report, 1.

154. Pendleton, *History of Tazewell County*, 610. Brewer's Battalion has not received credit for the services it rendered at Piedmont. Historians have not even acknowledged the unit's presence on the battlefield of Piedmont let alone its brigade affiliation. Stringfield of the Thomas Legion included "a battalion of Virginia cavalry" as part of Browne's Brigade in his diary entry of June 3, 1864, W.W. Stringfield Diary; Scott, *45th Virginia Infantry*, roster; William Henry Browne cadet record, U.S. Military Academy Archives, West Point.

155. H. Hardwick, "Battle of Piedmont: An Account by a Johnny Reb," *National Tribune*, December 13, 1888; B. Jones, Report, 1; Humphreys, *Military Operations*, 67; Kegley, *Wythe County, Virginia*, 401; Stringfield, "Sixty-Ninth Regiment," in *Histories of the Several Regiments*, 747.

156. DuPont, *Campaign of 1864*, 58; Humphreys, *Military Operations*, 68–69; Berkeley, "Augusta's Battle."

157. Henry, "First Tennessee Cavalry"; Lillard, "Third Confederate," 138; Doggett Diary; JDI to I. Marshall McCue, Letter, October 1, 1883; Humphreys, *Military Operations*, 66; B. Jones, Report, 2.

158. Out of all of Vaughn's unites, only the 1st Tennessee Cavalry and the 12th and 14th Tennessee Cavalry battalions had originally recruited as mounted troops. Warner, *Generals in Gray*, 316–17; Manard, "Vaughn's Brigade," 138–42.

159. *OR*, 32:3:843–46.

160. Manard, "Vaughn's Brigade," 141.

161. JDI to I. Marshall McCue, Letter, October 1, 1883.

162. Tibbits, Report of Service, RG 94, NA.

163. Ring, "Lynchburg Raid"; Halpine, "Battle of Piedmont"; DuPont, *Campaign of 1864*, 55.

164. DuPont, *Campaign of 1864*, 56, Holman, DuPont Papers, "Report of the Part Taken by Battery 'B'"; Berkeley, "Augusta's Battle"; David Powell Memoirs, 70–71.

165. JDI to I. Marshall McCue, Letter, October 1, 1883; *OR*, 51:1:1,225–26.

166. B. Jones, Report, 2.

167. Moor, Report, IHS; *OR*, 37:1:94–95; Halpine, "Battle of Piedmont"; David Powell Memoirs, 71; Strother, *Virginia Yankee in the Civil War*, 243.

168. Moor, Report, IHS; Tibbits, Report of Service, Record Group 94, NA; Walker, *History of the Eighteenth Conn. Volunteers*, 236.

169. Setchell, "Sergeant's View of the Battle," 44; Walker, *History of the Eighteenth Conn. Volunteers*, 230; Strother, *Virginia Yankee in the Civil War*, 243.

170. Moor, Report, IHS; *OR*, 37:1:117; Wildes, *Record of the One Hundred and Sixteenth*, 93; Rawling, *History of the First Regiment*, 172.

171. R.S., "From the First Virginia," *Wheeling Daily Intelligencer*, June 17, 1864; *OR*, 37:1:118; Rodgers, "History of the 2nd Eastern Shore Regiment"; Caldwell, "Letter from the 12th West Virginia"; Duff, "Battle of Piedmont."

172. Moor, Report, IHS; Record of Events, 28th Ohio, Field and Staff and Co. F., RG 94, NA; Henry Ocker to Dear Mother, June 25, 1864.

173. Moor, Report, IHS; Setchell, "Sergeant's View of the Battle," 44; Lynch, *Civil War Diary*, 68; Walker, *History of the Eighteenth Conn. Volunteers*, 231–32.

174. B. Jones, Report, 1–2; Moor, Report, IHS; Setchell, "Sergeant's View of the Battle," 44; Lynch, *Civil War Diary*, 68; Walker, *History of the Eighteenth Conn. Volunteers*, 231–32; *OR*, 51:1:1,225–26.

175. *OR*, 37:1:117; Lynch, *Civil War Diary*, 68–69; Setchell, "Sergeant's View of the Battle," 45.

176. Wildes, *Record of the One Hundred and Sixteenth*, 93; Moor, Report, IHS; *OR*, 51:1:1,225–26; Lynch, *Civil War Diary*, 68–69; *OR*, 37:1:117; B. Jones, Report, 2.

177. Samuel Ely Diary; *OR*, 51:1:1,225–26; B. Jones, Report, 2.

178. *OR*, 51:1:1,225–26; B. Jones, Report, 4; Shackelford, "My Recollections of the War."

CHAPTER 5

179. George Crook's Army of the Kanawha had returned to West Virginia before Hunter's campaign commenced on May 26. Strother, *Virginia Yankee in the Civil War*, 241; Crook, *General George Crook*, 115–16.

180. Strother, *Virginia Yankee in the Civil War*, 243.

181. Ibid., 244.

182. Elwood, *Elwoods Stories*, 125.

183. Ibid.; B. Jones, Report, 4; *OR*, 51:1:1,226.

184. Moor, Report, IHS; Halpine, "Battle of Piedmont"; Setchell, "Sergeant's View of the Battle," 46; B. Jones, Report, 2.

185. Companies A and B of the 18th Connecticut remained with Major Henry Peale's skirmishers and did not participate in the main assaults, losing only six men during the course of the entire battle. *OR*, 37:1:117 and 51:1:1,226; Lynch, *Civil War Diary*, 69; Walker, *History of the Eighteenth Conn. Volunteers*, 232; Setchell, "Sergeant's View of the Battle," 45; Hardwick, "Battle of Piedmont"; Tobias Quesenberry to Nancy Quesenberry, Johnny L. Scott Collection.

186. Hubbell, "Battle of Piedmont"; *Reunion of 5th New York Heavy Artillery*, 22.

187. Wildes, *Record of the One Hundred and Sixteenth*, 93; Stringfield Papers, Memoirs and Diary; Stringfield, "Sixty-Ninth Regiment," in *Histories of the Several Regiments*, 746–47; Hendricks to Dear Sir, June 8, 1864, Whitaker Papers (cited hereafter as WP).

188. R.S., "From the First Virginia"; Rawling, *History of the First Regiment*, 173; B. Jones, Report, 4; *OR*, 51:1:1,226; Report of Lieutenant Colonel Jacob Weddle, 1st West Virginia.

189. Humphreys, *Military Operations*, 64–65, 68; Moor Papers, Field Return of the 1st Brigade, 1st Infantry Division, Department of West Virginia, June 3, 1864.

190. Report of Colonel Joseph Thoburn, June 13, 1864, WVDAH, 37:1:118; George Imboden to My Dearest Mollie, June 10, 1864.

191. Thoburn left five companies in front of Imboden's and Vaughn's position. Colonel Campbell reported that they were left there "to keep the skirmish line on the left and guard against surprise from that direction." Judd, "Letter from the 34th Mass. Regiment"; Smith, "Gen. Hunter's Raid"; *OR*, 37:1:119; Thoburn, Report on the Battle of Piedmont, June 14, 1864; Duff, "Battle of Piedmont"; Rodgers, "History of the 2nd Eastern Shore Regiment"; Rodgers, Report on the Battle of Piedmont.

192. *OR*, 37:1:119; Rodgers, "History of the 2nd Eastern Shore Regiment"; Caldwell, "Letter from the 12th West Virginia."

193. Captain Marquis' Battery fared poorly once the Federal artillery turned its attention to his guns but did cause some annoyance to the Union infantry. At this point in the battle, Marquis' guns were the only ones in position to fire on Moor's brigade. The accounts of Moor's brigade clearly indicate that they encountered a heavy artillery fire during their initial advance against the Confederate infantry. Humphreys, *Military Operations*, 68–69; Wildes, *Record of the One Hundred and Sixteenth*, 93; G. Sheifley, "Battle of Piedmont," *National Tribune*, March 14, 1889.

194. Humphreys, *Military Operations*, 68–69; "History of Captain J.C. Marquis's Battery," *Augusta Historical Bulletin* 37 (2001): 68–69.

195. Strother, *Virginia Yankee in the Civil War*, 244.

196. Halpine, "Battle of Piedmont"; DuPont, *Campaign of 1864*, 55–57.

197. DuPont, *Campaign of 1864*, 57–58; Henry DuPont Papers, Lieutenant Charles Holman's Report; Humphreys, *Military Operations*, 67–69.

198. DuPont, *Campaign of 1864*, 57–58; Humphreys, *Military Operations*, 67–69.

199. DuPont, *Campaign of 1864*, 56–57; Henry DuPont Papers, Lieutenant Charles Holman's Report; Record of Events, Company F, 28th Ohio, June 1864, RG 94, NA; M'Clelland, "Battle of Piedmont."

200. *Military Operations*, 70–71.

201. Milton Humphreys does not name the officer. The author assumes that McClanahan, Jones's nominal chief of artillery, or one of his lieutenants gave the order due to the location of the incident. Humphreys, *Military Operations*, 69–71.

202. Ibid.

203. DuPont, *Campaign of 1864*, 59; Humphreys, *Military Operations*, 71; Berkeley, "Augusta's Battle"; Henry DuPont Papers, Lieutenant Charles Holman's Report.

204. DuPont, *Campaign of 1864*, 59–60; Humphreys, *Military Operations*, 72–73; Jones, "Battle of Piedmont"; Record of Events, Battery B, 1st Maryland Light Artillery, June 1864, RG 594; NA; Henry DuPont Papers, Lieutenant Charles Holman's Report.

205. DuPont to My Dear Brewerton, August 10, 1895.

206. B. Jones, Report, 2–3; I.G. Hendricks to Jas. Whitaker, June 8, 1864.

207. Moor, Report, IHS; *OR*, 37:1:118; DuPont, *Campaign of 1864*, 60. DuPont claimed that he personally led the section into position, but he is not supported in his claim but any eyewitnesses. Rawling, *History of the First Regiment*, 173; Duff, "Battle of Piedmont."

208. The maximum range of a Napoleon cannon is 1,200 to 1,400 yards, with its effective range being 800 yards. At 500 yards, Von Kleiser had no problem hitting the Rebel works and easily inflicted severe damage on the Confederate occupants. Although 500 yards is within the maximum rifle range, the depression in the

ground minimized casualties in Von Kleiser's Battery. Von Kleiser lost Private Henry Fink, killed, and Private Joseph Eschowis, wounded. Record of Events, 30th Independent Battery, New York Light Artillery, Battery Return, June 1864, RG 94, NA; *OR*, 37:1:117; Walker, *History of the Eighteenth Conn. Volunteers*, 232.

209. B. Jones, Report, 3; Setchell, "Sergeant's View of the Battle," 46.

210. B. Jones, Report, 3.

211. Humphreys, *Military Operations*, 71–72.

212. Ibid., 72.

213. Anonymous, "Twenty-Eighth Ohio Infantry," Antietam National Battlefield; Dyer, *Compendium of the War of the Rebellion*, 1,509; Record of Events, 28th Ohio Field and Staff, May and June 1864, RG 94, NA.

214. Moor, Report, IHS; *OR*, 37:1:117; Henry Ocker to Mother, June 25, 1864, OHS; Halpine, "Battle of Piedmont"; Rawling, *History of the First Regiment*, 173; William Goudy Diary, WVU; Hubbell, "Battle of Piedmont."

215. Dalzell, *Private Dalzell*, 95; Strother, *Virginia Yankee in the Civil War*, 246; Moor, Report, IHS.

216. Stringfield, Memoirs and Diary; Wildes, *Record of the One Hundred and Sixteenth*, 93, 96; Dalzell, *Private Dalzell*, 94–95.

217. Wildes, *Record of the One Hundred and Sixteenth*, 93–94.

218. Lynch, *Civil War Diary*, 69; B. Jones, Report, 7, VHS; Moor, Report, IHS.

219. Colonel Moor reported: "I led my brigade to within 150 yards of the enemy's position when a withering and steady fire of musketry and artillery was received throwing the 18th Cont. and 5th N.Y. Rgmts on my right and the 116th Ohio on my left into some confusion to the rear after severe loss. The 28th Ohio kept its ground by laying down and keeping up a brisk fire. Thirty minutes after the repulse, I ordered the 28th Rgmt to fall back to its place in the new reformed line." Moor, Report, IHS.

220. The 28th Ohio had successfully used this same tactic at Droop Mountain the previous November. Brigadier General William W. Averell reported: "The success of the infantry attack was chiefly due to Colonel A. Moor, 28th Ohio Volunteer Infantry, in command of the same, whose admirable conduct cannot be too highly commended." *OR*, part 1, 95; DuPont, *Campaign of 1864*, 61; Strother, *Virginia Yankee in the Civil War*, 244; Reid, *Ohio in the War*, vol. 2, 194; Moor, Report, IHS.

221. Henry Ocker to Dear Mother, June 25, 1864.

222. Hunter reported: "At 2 pm. the enemy made a determined attack on the First Brigade, which gallantly sustained itself, assisted by Von Kleiser's battery and a cross-fire from Morton's and Carlin's batteries on our left." *OR*, 37:1:95; Strother, *Virginia Yankee in the Civil War*, 244; Reid, *Ohio in the War*, vol. 2, 194; Moor, Report, IHS; Thompson, Gillespie and Peerg, "Captain Charles A. Fudge."

223. Henry Ocker to Mother, June 25, 1864; Moor, Report, IHS; Reid, *Ohio in the War*, vol. 2, 196.

224. The 28th Ohio's participation in the Battles of South Mountain and Antietam amplified Ocker's assessment of the intensity of the Battle of Piedmont. Reid, *Ohio in the War*, vol. 2, 196; Henry Ocker to Mother, June 25, 1864.

225. Lang, *Loyal West Virginia*, 118; Tibbits, Report of Service, RG 94, NA; Beyer and Keydel, *Deeds of Valor*, 357; Julius Stahel, Report of Service, RG 94, NA; Marsh, "Piedmont Again!"

226. Marsh, "Piedmont Again!"
227. *New York Times*, August 10, 1913; Julius Stahel, Report of Service, RG 94, NA; Halpine, "Battle of Piedmont"; Beyer and Keydel, *Deeds of Valor*, 357; McIlhenny Diary, 26; DuPont, *Campaign of 1864*, 62; Humphreys, *Military Operations*, 103.
228. Beer, Thoburn Diary, 10.
229. *OR*, 37:1:118; Thoburn, Report on the Battle of Piedmont; Rodgers, "History of the 2nd Eastern Shore Regiment"; Rodgers, Report on the Battle of Piedmont; Caldwell, "Letter from the 12th West Virginia"; Hibbs, "Piedmont Fight"; William B. Stark Diary, typescript in possession of the author.
230. The *Richmond Daily Dispatch*, June 10, 1864, stated that Gen. W.E. Jones…, then assumed the offensive. B. Jones, Report, 5; Henry, "First Tennessee Cavalry"; Clark, "War Experience of…," 9 (cited hereafter as Clark, Memoir); Humphreys, *Military Operations*, 81; *Richmond Sentinel*, June 24, 1864.
231. Clark, Memoir; Henry, "First Tennessee Cavalry"; Bible, *Vaughn's Brigade*; Humphreys, *Military Operations*, 81.
232. Henry, "First Tennessee Cavalry"; B. Jones, Report, 5; Clark, Memoir, 9.
233. B. Jones, Report, 5; Henry, "First Tennessee Cavalry."
234. Henry, "First Tennessee Cavalry"; Clark, Memoir, 9; B. Jones, Report, 5; Lynch, *Civil War Diary*, 70.
235. Clark, Memoir, 9; B. Jones, Report, 5.

CHAPTER 6

236. *OR*, 37:1:95; Strother, *Virginia Yankee in the Civil War*, 244; Lang, *Loyal West Virginia*, 117–18.
237. Frank S. Smith Diary; Strother, *Virginia Yankee in the Civil War*, 244; Halpine, "Battle of Piedmont"; David Powell Memoirs, 72; Lang, *Loyal West Virginia*, 118; Tibbits, Report of Service, RG 94, NA; Beyer and Keydel, *Deeds of Valor*, 357; Julius Stahel, Report of Service, RG 94, NA; Marsh, "Piedmont Again!"
238. Strother, *Virginia Yankee in the Civil War*, 244; Beer, Thoburn Diary, 11; Rodgers, "History of the 2nd Eastern Shore Regiment"; Rodgers, Report on the Battle of Piedmont; *OR*, 37:118–19; Lincoln, *Life with the 34th Massachusetts Infantry*, 300; Duff, "Battle of Piedmont."
239. DuPont, *Campaign of 1864*, 61–62; Henry DuPont Papers, Lieutenant Charles Holman's Report; Bryan, "Battle of Piedmont"; John Hamer Memoir; Humphreys, *Military Operations*, 103.
240. Many of the North Carolinians of the Thomas Legion also fought during the Seven Days Battles, Second Manassas and Antietam campaigns as Company L of the 16th North Carolina. Upon organization of the 69th North Carolina, Company L of the 16th North Carolina became Company E in the new unit. Fisher, "Story By a Veteran," 129–30; I.G. Hendricks to Stephen Whitaker, June 8, 1864.
241. Frank S. Reader, "Battle of Piedmont"; Hewitt, *History of the 12th West Virginia*, 130, 137–38; Hanchett, *Irish*, 111–12.
242. McIlhenny, "Coles Maryland Cavalry Battalion," USAMHI; Clark, Memoir, 9.

243. *OR*, 37:1:117; Setchell, "Sergeant's View of the Battle," 46; Henry, "First Tennessee Cavalry."

244. Wildes, *Record of the One Hundred and Sixteenth*, 97; Wildes Pension File, Statements of Colonel James Washburn and Captain Wilbert Teters, NA.

245. Wildes, *Record of the One Hundred and Sixteenth*, 96–97.

246. Henry Ocker to Mother, June 25, 1864; F.F. Hubbell, "The Battle of Piedmont."

247. Duff, "Battle of Piedmont."

248. Ibid.

249. Stringfield, "Sixty-Ninth Regiment," in *Histories of the Several Regiments*, vol. 2, 747.

250. Carter Berkeley's 1904 account places Jones as riding back beyond the Cross Road to order Harper's Reserves forward. Considering the time and distance factors, it seems unlikely that Jones could have observed Thoburn's final approach march, rode to the 60th Virginia and Harper's regiment and then be in the thick of the fight and killed back near his original position. B. Jones, Report, 6–7; Berkeley, "Augusta's Battle"; Clark, Memoir, 9; Stringfield, "Sixty-Ninth Regiment," in *Histories of the Several Regiments*, vol. 2, 747.

251. Hewitt, *History of the 12th West Virginia*, 131–32; Hibbs, "Piedmont Fight"; Caldwell, "Letter from the 12th West Virginia."

252. Private I.H. Hendricks wrote that Thoburn's attack "exposed our Legion to a cross fire while we was fighting them in our front." This clearly indicated that Moor's brigade attacked before Thoburn made contact. I.G. Hendricks to Jas. Whitaker, June 8, 1864.

253. *OR*, 37:1:118; John Hamer Memoir; Bryan, "Battle of Piedmont"; Kauffman, "Jonas Kauffman Diary," 108; Beyer and Keydel, *Deeds of Valor*, 356.

254. *OR*, 37:1:118; Lincoln, *Life with the 34th Massachusetts Infantry*, 299–300; Headley, "Report of the Service of the 34th Massachusetts," 367.

255. B. Jones, Report, 6; Burum Diary, Private Collection, San Francisco; I.G. Hendricks to Jas. Whitaker, June 8, 1864.

256. *OR*, 37:1:118; John Hamer Memoir; Bryan, "Battle of Piedmont"; Beyer and Keydel, *Deeds of Valor*, 356; Evans, "Capture the Flag," 14; John Hamer Memoir; Bryan, "Battle of Piedmont."

257. Curtis Papers, Curtis's Account of the Battle of Piedmont; Hewitt, *History of the 12th West Virginia*, 138; Caldwell, "Letter from the 12th West Virginia"; Hibbs, "Piedmont Fight."

258. Hewitt, *History of the 12th West Virginia*, 138; Caldwell, "Letter from the 12th West Virginia"; Stringfield Papers, Diary and Memoir; Hibbs, "Piedmont Fight"; Alexander Neil to My Dear Friends, June 8, 1864; Mowrer, *History of the Organization and Service*, 16; Feit, "Battle of Piedmont."

259. Colonel Jacob Campbell of the 54th Pennsylvanian reported: "About 100 yards from the front of the woods was a fence running from the left of the line, and parallel with it, extending along the front of the regiment on my left (34th Massachusetts). Along this fence to protect their flank the enemy had a strong force posted. This appeared to be the key to their position, and they held it most obstinately for some time, partially checking the advance of the regiment in front of them." The 3rd Tennessee may have been among the troops defending this line. Its colonel reported losing 47 men killed and wounded at Piedmont. *OR*,

37:1:118; *Northampton (MA) Free Press*, June 28, 1864; Moulton, *From Fort Lyon to Harper's Ferry*, 201; Lincoln, *Life with the 34th Massachusetts Infantry*, 306; Smith, "Gen. Hunter's Raid."

260. *Northampton (MA) Free Press*, June 28, 1864; Moulton, *From Fort Lyon to Harper's Ferry*, 201; Lincoln, *Life with the 34th Massachusetts Infantry*, 306.

261. *Springfield Republican*, August 2, 1886; *Northampton (MA) Free Press*, June 28, 1864; Lincoln, *Life with the 34th Massachusetts Infantry*, 306; Headley, "Report of the Service of the 34th Massachusetts," 367; Moulton, *From Fort Lyon to Harper's Ferry*, 201.

262. Feit, "Battle of Piedmont"; Warner Chapin to Father, June 5, 1864; Mowrer, *History of the Organization and Service*, 16; *OR*, 37:1:118.

263. Feit, "Battle of Piedmont"; *OR*, 37:1:118; Lincoln, *Life with the 34th Massachusetts Infantry*, 306; Headley, "Report of the Service of the 34th Massachusetts," 367; Oates, *Hanging Rock Rebel*, 265; John Hamer Memoir; Bryan, "Battle of Piedmont"; Kauffman, "Jonas Kauffman Diary," 108.

264. Blue, 265.

265. Ibid.; Evans, "Capture the Flag," 14; Kauffman, "Jonas Kauffman Diary," 108.

266. Evans, "Capture the Flag," 14; *OR*, 37:1:118.

267. Humphreys, *Military Operations*, 74, Berkeley, "Augusta's Battle"; Stringfield, "Sixty-Ninth Regiment," in *Histories of the Several Regiments*, 747; Stringfield Papers, Diary and Memoir; B. Jones, Report, 6; *Richmond Sentinel*, June 14, 1864.

268. Most Union regiments implied or claimed outright that a member had fired the shot that killed Grumble Jones. Evans, "Capture the Flag," 15; Wildes, *Record of the One Hundred and Sixteenth*, 99; Walker, *History of the Eighteenth Conn. Volunteers*, 236; Lincoln, *Life with the 34th Massachusetts Infantry*, 306; Moulton, *From Fort Lyon to Harper's Ferry*, 201.

269. *OR*, 37:1:118–19; Lincoln, *Life with the 34th Massachusetts Infantry*, 306; Caldwell, "Letter from the 12th West Virginia"; Hewitt, *History of the 12th West Virginia*, 138.

270. Moor's brigade veered to the west during the final charge to avoid fratricide. Moor, Report, IHS; David Powell Memoirs; Wildes, *Record of the One Hundred and Sixteenth*, 94, 96; Dalzell, *Private Dalzell*, 97; *Athens (OH) Messenger*, June 23, 1864; Tobias Quesenberry to Dear Father and Mother, J.L. Scott Collection; Petre Jennings Diary; Scott, *45th Virginia Infantry*, 41.

271. Record of Events, 28th Ohio Field and Staff and Company F, May and June 1864, RG 94, NA; Moor, Report, IHS; Reid, *Ohio in the War*, vol. 2, 196; Compiled Service Records of Confederate Soldiers From the State of Virginia, 45th Virginia, RG 109; Porter, *Composition of Sketches*, 189–90.

272. Evans, "Capture the Flag," 14–15.

273. Lynch, *Civil War Diary*, 70; Henry, "First Tennessee Cavalry"; Compiled Service Records for Confederate Soldiers from the State of Tennessee, 1st Tennessee Cavalry, RG 109; Carter, "First Tennessee Cavalry," 607–8.

274. Moor, Report, IHS; Graham, *History of the 5th New York*, 22; Wildes, *Record of the One Hundred and Sixteenth*, 99.

275. Ibid.; Beer, Thoburn Diary, 11.

276. Isaac Prillaman to Brother; Rawling, *History of the First Regiment*, 174, Beer, Thoburn Diary, 11; Lieutenant Colonel Jacob Weddle, 12th West Virginia, Report on the Battle of Piedmont.

277. Shackelford, "My Recollections of the War."

278. B. Jones, Report, 7; Clark, Memoir, 9.

279. *OR*, 37:1:95 and 119; Clark, Memoir, 9; Halpine, "Battle of Piedmont"; J. Chapin Warner to Father and Mother, June 5, 1864.

280. Clark, Memoir, 9.

281. *OR*, 37:1:119; Beyer and Keydel, *Deeds of Valor*, 356.

282. Berkeley, "Augusta's Battle."

283. Humphreys, *Military Operations*, 75–76.

284. Ibid.

285. Stahel, Report of Service, RG 94, NA; Tibbits, Report of Service, RG 94, NA; Halpine, "Battle of Piedmont."

286. Tibbits, Report of Service, RG 94, NA.

287. Ibid.; Marsh, "Piedmont Again!"

288. JDI, *Annals of the War*, 175; JDI to I. Marshall McCue, Letter, October 1, 1883.

289. Calvin C. Hart, "Parkinson Collett"; Richardson, "Services of W.W. Charles."

290. John C. Lewis, "Prisoners at Piedmont," *National Tribune*, June 2, 1892; Berkeley, "Augusta's Battle," Calvin C. Hart, "Parkinson Collett."

291. Manard, "Vaughn's Brigade," 141; Richardson, "Application of Membership," 91.

292. Hart, "Parkinson Collett"; Berkeley, "Augusta's Battle."

293. JDI to I. Marshall McCue, Letter, October 1, 1883; Hart, "Parkinson Collett"; Richardson, "Application of Membership," 91; Lewis, "Prisoners at Piedmont"; Marsh, "Piedmont Again!"; Strother, *Virginia Yankee in the Civil War*, 245; "Earnest," "1st Veteran Cavalry."

294. Major W.W. Stringfield wrote that four guns belonging to Marquis' Battery and supported by his command were captured. Col. Joseph Thoburn, Report of the 2nd Brigade at Piedmont; Frank S. Reader Diary; Wildes, *Record of the One Hundred and Sixteenth*, 94; Charles Halpine Diary; W.W. Stringfield, Sixty Ninth Regiment, 747.

295. Strother, *Virginia Yankee in the Civil War*, 245.

296. Ibid.

297. Walker, *History of the Eighteenth Conn. Volunteers*, 241.

298. The Battles of Opequon and Cedar Creek, fought in the fall of 1864, exceeded the casualties at Piedmont, but the armies were three to four times larger then. Hanchett, *Irish*, 116.

Chapter 7

299. Wisewell, "From the 1st Veteran Cavalry."

300. Strother, *Virginia Yankee in the Civil War*, 245–46.

301. Ibid., 245; B. Jones, Report, 8–9; Colley, "Brig. General William E. Jones"; J. Kelly Bennette Diary, UNC; *Richmond Sentinel*, June 14, 1864.

302. Reader Diary; Tibbits, Report of Service, RG 94, NA.

303. Cushman Papers, Diary; Setchell, "Sergeant's View of the Battle," 46.

304. Pilkington, "They Killed General Jones."

305. Alexander Neil to My Dear Friends, June 8, 1864.

306. Ibid.

307. Rawling, *History of the First Regiment*, 176–77.
308. Ibid.
309. Ibid., 177.
310. Rodgers, "History of the 2nd Eastern Shore Regiment," 193.
311. Lynch, *Civil War Diary*, 70.
312. "His Original Jacket," Records of the Virginia Prohibition Commission, 1916–34, Library of Virginia, Richmond, Virginia.
313. DuPont, *Campaign of 1864*, 63–64; Walker, *History of the Eighteenth Conn. Volunteers*, 235; Caldwell, "Letter from the 12th West Virginia."
314. Johnston and Williams, *Hard Times*; Bible, *Vaughn's Brigade*.
315. Clem, "Old Homes of August County," 43.
316. Farrar, *Twenty-Second Pennsylvania Cavalry*, 237.
317. Feit, "Battle of Piedmont."
318. Burum underlined "time" in his diary. Burum Diary, June 5, 1864.
319. *OR*, 37:1:150.
320. Ibid., 37:1:151.
321. Ibid., 37:1:150–51.
322. Beer, Thoburn Diary, 11.

Chapter 8

323. JDI, *Annals of the War*, 175; JDI to I. Marshall McCue, Letter, October 1, 1883; O'Ferrall, *Forty Years of Active Service*, 100–101.
324. *OR*, 37:1:151.
325. Ibid., 37:1:95; Strother, *Virginia Yankee in the Civil War*, 246.
326. Reader was obviously referring only to Federal generals in the Shenandoah Valley. Hewitt, *History of the 12th West Virginia*, 141; Reader Diary.
327. Beer, Thoburn Diary, 11.
328. Strother, *Virginia Yankee in the Civil War*, 246.
329. Joseph Waddell Diary.
330. *New York Herald-Tribune*, June 23, 1864.
331. Strother, *Virginia Yankee in the Civil War*, 246–47; Walker, *History of the Eighteenth Conn. Volunteers*, 244.
332. Strother, *Virginia Yankee in the Civil War*, 246–47; Halpine, *Baked Meats*, 304.
333. J. Chapin Warner, Letter, June 7, 1864.
334. Strother, *Virginia Yankee in the Civil War*, 247; Hanchett, *Irish*, 116–17.
335. F.A.C., "From Staunton, June 8, 1864."
336. David Cushman Diary, 408; Lynch, *Civil War Diary*, 73.
337. Hanchett, *Irish*, 116–17; McInhenny Diary.
338. *OR*, 37:1:95–96.
339. Strother, *Virginia Yankee in the Civil War*, 248, *OR*, 37:1:95–96; *Staunton Republican Vindicator*, July 8, 1864.
340. Strother, *Virginia Yankee in the Civil War*, 248–49; F.A.C., "From Staunton, June 8, 1864"; Joseph Waddell Diary, UVA.
341. *Staunton Vindicator*, July 8, 1864; *Richmond Daily Dispatch*, June 14, 1864.
342. Strother, *Virginia Yankee in the Civil War*, 249; Hanchett, *Irish*, 115; Lynch, *Civil War Diary*, 72; John J. Carter Diary; *OR*, 37:1:153.

343. Reader Diary; Samuel Ely Diary.

344. Samuel Ely Diary; Diary of John Wesley Woods; Jacob Campbell Diary.

345. Strother, *Virginia Yankee in the Civil War*, 249; Reader Diary.

346. Tibbits Papers, Diary; Corbin, "Diary of a Virginian Cavalry Man," 213; Lynch, *Civil War Diary*, 72, *OR*, 37:1:153; *Richmond Daily Dispatch*, June 11, 1864.

347. Strother, *Virginia Yankee in the Civil War*, 250; Chas. Halpine to Colonel A. Moor, Staunton, June 8, 1864.

348. Charles G. Halpine Papers, Diary.

349. Augustus Moor, Moor's Report and a History of the 28th Ohio; R.B. Hayes, Diary, vol. 4, 473.

350. Multiple sources place the number of prisoners who left at more than 1,000. When they reached Camp Morton in Indiana, only 940 were present. Moving through the wilds of West Virginia, it is not unreasonable that some would manage to slip away, especially as many of the Confederates were natives of that region. Augustus Moor, Moor's Report and a History of the 28th Ohio; Strother, "Report on Operations of the Army of West Virginia."

351. Henry Ocker to Mother, Letter, June 25, 1864; Reid, *Ohio in the War*, vol. 2, 196.

CHAPTER 9

352. *OR*, 37:1:507.

353. *New York Herald-Tribune*, June 14, 1864; *Richmond Examiner*, June 13, 1864.

354. *OR*, 37:1:94–95, 152–53, 507, 543, 598; Grant, *Personal Memoirs*, 558; Halpine, "Battle of Piedmont."

355. David Hunter to Julius Stahel, June 9, 1864, NA.

356. Halpine, "Battle of Piedmont"; Rodgers, "History of the 2nd Eastern Shore Regiment"; Keyes, *Military History of the 123rd*, 62; Strother, *Virginia Yankee in the Civil War*, 246.

357. Julius Stahel to Colonel W.B. Tibbits, August 29, 1864, RG 94, NA.

358. *OR*, 37:1:95; Halpine to Colonel A. Moor, June 8, 1864.

359. Beer, Thoburn Diary, 11; Caldwell, "Letter from the 12th West Virginia"; Smith, "Battle of New Market."

360. Peyton, *History of Augusta County*, 234–35; Humphreys, *Military Operations*, 78.

361. *OR*, 37:1:744–51.

362. Dowdey and Mannarin, *Wartime Papers of R.E. Lee*, 767.

363. No Union sources confirm that claim. Henry, "First Tennessee Cavalry"; Clark, Memoir, 9; W. McDowell to Father, July 25, 1864, Robert Driver Collection; B. Jones, Report, 6.

364. James R. Love to John C. Breckinridge, October 15, 1864; JDI, *Annals of the War*, 173; JDI to I. Marshall McCue, Letter, October 1, 1883.

365. B. Jones, Report, 9.

366. O'Ferrall, *Forty Years of Active Service*, 100.

367. B. Jones, Report, 9; Rodgers, "History of the 2nd Eastern Shore Regiment"; Stevenson, *Boots and Saddles*, 281.

368. JDI to I. Marshall McCue, Letter, October 1, 1883; JDI, *Annals of the War*, 173–74.

369. JDI, *Annals of the War*, 174.
370. B. Jones, Report, 8.
371. Beach, *1st New York (Lincoln) Cavalry*, 364–65.

APPENDIX

372. 18th Connecticut, Record of Events, Regimental Return, RG 594, NA.
373. *New York Herald Tribune*, June 24, 1864.
374. Reid, *Ohio in the War*, 196.
375. Wildes, *Record of the One Hundred and Sixteenth*, 94.
376. Robert S. Rodgers Papers, History of the 2nd Maryland, Eastern Shore, Duke.
377. Lincoln, *Life with the 34th Massachusetts Infantry*, 300.
378. *OR*, 37:2:119.
379. Record of Events, 1st West Virginia, RG 94, NA.
380. *Wheeling Daily Intelligencer*, June 21, 1864.
381. Record of Events, Battery B, 1st Maryland Light Artillery, RG 94, NA.
382. Record of Events, Battery D, 1st West Virginia Light Artillery, RG 94, NA.
383. Record of Events, 30th New York Independent Battery, RG 94, NA.
384. Partial count based upon a narrative source naming a soldier killed, wounded or captured at Piedmont. McIlhenny, USAMHI.
385. Phisterer, vol. I, 729.
386. Phisterer, vol. II, 1,163.
387. Phisterer, vol. II, 1,054.
388. Partial count based upon a narrative source naming a soldier killed, wounded or captured at Piedmont. William B. Tibbits, Report of Service, RG 94, NA.
389. Phisterer, vol. II, 999.
390. Partial count based upon a narrative source naming a soldier killed, wounded or captured at Piedmont. Smith, "Battle of New Market."
391. Partial count based upon a narrative source naming a soldier killed, wounded or captured at Piedmont. Elwood, 196.
392. General W.E. Jones and Major Henry Brewer are the two officers listed as killed under the heading field and staff.
393. Compiled Service Records, 36th Virginia, NA.
394. Compiled Service Records, 60th Virginia, NA.
395. Jeffry Weaver, author of a history on the 45th Battalion, wrote, "using known strength totals, casualties in other battles, and known desertions, it would appear that the 23 men were probably killed or wounded at Piedmont." These twenty-three men have been added into the wounded column.
396. The killed and wounded in the 45th Virginia appears to be low. Tobias Quesenberry noted that his company suffered eight men killed and wounded. If Quesenberry's company is representative of the whole regiment, then the recorded loss of the 45th Virginia is less than half of those actually killed and wounded. The 45th Virginia probably lost forty to fifty more men killed and wounded than the compiled service record indicates.

397. The POWs are from the Cam Morton, Indiana, Prisoner of War Rolls in the National Archives. The killed and wounded are as reported by Major W.W. Stringfield in Clark's *North Carolina Regiments.*

398. The casualties in Brewer's battalion are derived from the compiled service records of the dismounted cavalry units, which composed the unit and the prisoner of war rolls from Cam Morton prison camp. Brewer's command included many convalescents from the hospitals in Staunton. This total does not include the killed and wounded for those convalescents—only the captured from the POW rolls. The same is true for the Maryland line troops. As such, Brewer's battalion lost a significantly higher number of men killed and wounded at Piedmont than what is stated. Only the number in the POW figure can be considered reliable. Major Stephen Halsey noted, "Our dearly beloved General W.E. Jones having been killed at Piedmont below Staunton…and that part of the Brigade with him almost annihilated in the severe engagement, left our Brigade a shadow of its former self." Anslum L. Watts, a member of the 21st Virginia Cavalry who fought with Brewer, wrote, "[o]f the 500 of us dismounted cavalry men in that battle [Piedmont], only 100 were left."

399. Lillard, "Third Confederate," 138.

400. Paul Chronic of Georgia has conducted a thorough study of the 16th Georgia Battalion and its records and is the source of the casualties for that regiment.

401. William McDowell reported Vaughn's casualties as 298 total. Cam Morton POW rolls show that 115 men from Vaughn's Brigade were captured at Piedmont. The number listed as killed shows only those men who were known to have been killed. The wounded total is merely the number of prisoners and known killed subtracted from the brigade total.

402. Delauter, *McNeill's Rangers,* 23–25.

403. Compiled Service Record, 23rd Virginia Cavalry, NA.

404. Cam Morton Prisoner of War Roll, NA.

405. Compiled Service Record and Camp Morton Prisoner of War Roll, NA; American Civil War Research Data Base.

406. These figures are courtesy of Bob Driver, who his currently working on the regimental history for the Virginia Reserve units for H.E. Howard's Virginia Regimental Series. Mr. Driver obtained his information from the NA and other sources.

407. Jennings Diary, Handley Library, Winchester, Virginia.

408. These figures are courtesy of Bob Driver, who his currently working on the regimental history for the Virginia Reserve units for H.E. Howard's Virginia Regimental Series. Mr. Driver obtained his information from the NA and other sources.

409. Compiled Service Records, Virginia Home Guards, NA.

410. *OR,* 37:1:151, 571, 755.

411. The April 30, 1864 trimonthly return put B. Jones's brigade strength at 99 officers and 1,548 effective men present for duty. This amounts to a total of 1,647 officers and men. The brigade, including the Lewisburg Battery, lost 301 officers and men at Cloyd's Mountain on May 9. This left a total of 1,346 officers and men after the battle. These units remained in southwest Virginia after the battle and recuperated. Assuming that men returning from wounds offsets desertions,

1,300 men present at Piedmont is a conservative estimate of B. Jones's brigade strength. *OR*, 4:1,334–35.

412. Browne's strength is calculated at the regimental level. The 45th Virginia numbered 42 officers and 749 effective men present for duty on April 30, 1864. This totals 791 effective officers and men. The 45th lost 174 officers and men at Cloyd's Mountain, leaving 617 effectives after the battle. Vernon Crowe, author of a well-researched regimental history on the Thomas Legion, wrote that the Legion took 390 men to Piedmont. Anslum Lynch Watts wrote that he was one of 500 dismounted cavalrymen from "Grumble" Jones's Brigade at Piedmont. The 45th Virginia, Thomas Legion and Grumble's dismounted men total 1,507 men of Browne's Brigade at Piedmont.

413. There are no definitive figures available on Vaughn's Brigade. As of April 16, 1864, Vaughn had 1,726 men in his brigade. This number cannot be used for Piedmont because an unknown number of Vaughn's men remained in Tennessee. As it is known for certain that W.E. Jones brought 4,000 troops total from southwest Virginia and east Tennessee, the number of Vaughn's men at Piedmont can be derived by subtracting B. Jones's and Browne's totals from W.E. Jones's 4,000 men. This computes Vaughn's total at about 1,000 or more men at Piedmont. After the battle, Vaughn's Brigade numbered at about 700 to 800 men. Most accounts give Vaughn credit for having only 600 to 800 men present at Piedmont, but this is not possible as the brigade numbered 819 men on June 15, 1864, meaning that the strength at Piedmont was at least 1,000 men, if not higher. Gordon, *Last Confederate General*, 217.

414. Imboden, "Sword, Fire and the Halter," 173.

415. *OR*, 37:1:154.

Bibliography

MANUSCRIPTS

American Antiquarian Society, Worcester, Massachusetts
David F. Cushman to Miss Caroline D. Cushman, Letter, June 8, 1864.
David F. Cushman, Diary, 1864.

Antietam National Battlefield, Sharpsburg, Maryland
Recruits of 28th Ohio to E.M. Stanton, May 1864.

The Bucks County (Pennsylvania) Historical Society
Helen H. Ely Papers, Samuel Ely Diary, 1864.

Cincinnati Historical Society
Morning Report of Captain Louis Frey's Co. D, 28th Ohio.
Register of Deaths, Co. D, 28th Ohio.

Duke University Special Collections Library, Durham, North Carolina
H.A. DuPont to Brewerton, Letter, August 10, 1895.
H.A. DuPont to Brewerton, Letter, February 4, 1896.
H.A. DuPont to Brewerton, Letter, October 1, 1895.
J.P. Sanger to H.A. DuPont, Letter, March 3, 1896.
Lyman Walter Vere Kennon Papers.
Robert S. Rodgers, Report on the Battle of Piedmont, June 7, 1864.
Robert S. Rodgers, History of the 2nd Maryland Eastern Shore, written manuscript history.
Major S.P. Halsey, 21st Virginia Cavalry, to John W. Daniel, June 4, 1905.

East Carolina Manuscript Collection, Greenville, North Carolina
George Duncan Wells, Letterbook, 1864.

Bibliography

Fredericksburg-Spotsylvania National Military Park
  Isaac Prillaman to Brother, Letter, July 30, 1864.

Georgia Department of Archives and History, Atlanta
  Reuben Grove Clark, "War Experience of...," memoir.

Hagley Museum, Wilmington, Delaware
  Charles Holman, Report of Part Taken by Battery "B" 5th U.S. Artillery in the
  Battles of Piedmont and Lynchburg.
  H.A. DuPont to Mother, Letter, June 8, 1864.

Handley Library, Winchester, Virginia
  Petre Jennings, Diary, 1864.

The Historical Society of Montgomery County, Pennsylvania
  John Wesley Woods, Diary, 1864–65.

Huntington Library, San Marino, California
  Thomas Evans Diary.
  Charles Halpine Diary.

Illinois Historical Survey, Urbana, Illinois, Ratterman Collection
  Anonymous, Draft History of the 28th Ohio.
  Augustus Moor, "Field Return of the 1st Brigade," June 6, 1864.
  Augustus Moor, "Field Return of the 1st Brigade," June 3, 1864.
  Augustus Moor, Report on the Battle of Piedmont, June 21, 1864.
  Charles G. Halpine to Colonel A. Moor, Letter, June 8, 1864.
  Charles G. Halpine to Colonel A. Moor, Letter, June 9, 1864.

Jarnagin Collection, Indianapolis, Indiana
  John J. Jarnagin to Cousin Livie, Letter, June 16, 1864.

The John P. Sheffy III Collection, Alexandria, Virginia
  J.P. Sheffy to My Darling Wife, Letter, June 9, 1864.
  J.P. Sheffy to My Darling Wife, Letter, June 27, 1864.

The Library of Virginia, Richmond
  Records of the Prohibition Commission, 1916–1934
    Alexander M. Davis, "His Original Jacket."

Massachusetts Historical Society, Boston
  J. Chapin Warner to Dear Father..., Letter, June 5, 1864.
  J. Chapin Warner to Dear Father..., Letter, May 25, 1864.
  J. Chapin Warner to Dear Father..., Letter, May 23, 1864.

McClung Collection, Lawson-McGhee Library, Knoxville, Tennessee
  William W. Stringfield, "Memoirs of the Civil War," no date.

BIBLIOGRAPHY

Miscellaneous Private Collections
Anslum Lynch Watts, "Reminiscences of My Civil War Days."
Tobias Quesenberry to Father, Letter, June 20, 1864.
William P. McDowell to My Dear Father, Letter, July 5, 1864.

The Mrs. Ernestine B. Leas Collection, Fresno, California
Absalom J. Burum, Diary, 1864–65.

Museum of the Confederacy, Richmond, Virginia
John D. Imboden to Colonel I. Marshall McCue, Letter on the Battle of Piedmont, Virginia, October 1, 1883.

National Archives, Washington, D.C.
A. Moor to Brigadier General Carrington, June 28, 1864.
Colonel D.H. Strother, "Report on Operations of the Army of West Virginia May 21–August 9, 1864."
D. Hunter to Colonel D.H. Strother, Letter, July 13, 1865.
D. Hunter to Major General H.W. Halleck, Letter, June 9, 1864.
J.D. Imboden to W.E. Jones, Letter, June 1, 1864.
Augustus Root, "Report Respecting Capture of Wagon Train at New Town, Va."
Julius Stahel, Report of Service, October 23, 1873.
W.B. Tibbits, Report of Service, March 18, 1874.
Record of Events
18th Connecticut, Regimental Return, June 1864.
15th New York Cavalry, Field and Staff, May and June 1864.
1st Maryland Light Artillery, Battery B, May and June 1864.
1st West Virginia, Field and Staff, May and June 1864.
1st West Virginia Light Artillery, Battery D, May and June 1864.
4th West Virginia, I Company, May and June 1864.
116th Ohio, Field and Staff, April 30 to Aug 31, 1864.
160th Ohio, Regimental Return, May and June 1864.
123rd Ohio, Field and Staff, May and June 1864.
2nd Maryland Eastern Shore, Field and Staff, May and June 1864.
2nd Maryland Eastern Shore, G Company, May and June 1864.
2nd Maryland Potomac Home Brigade, Field and Staff, May and June 1864.
30th Independent Battery New York Light Artillery, Battery Return, May and June 1864.
12th West Virginia, Field and Staff, May and June 1864.
28th Ohio, F Company, May and June, 1864.
28th Ohio, Field and Staff, May and June 1864.

North Carolina Division of Archives and History, Raleigh
I.G. Hendricks to Jas. Whitaker, Letter, June 8, 1864.
W.W. Stringfield, Diary, 1862–65.
W.W. Stringfield, memoirs.

BIBLIOGRAPHY

Ohio Historical Society, Columbus, Ohio
Henry Ocker to Mother, Letter, June 25, 1864.

Pennsylvania Division of Archives and Manuscripts
John J. Carter Diary.

Private Collections
Robert Driver, Brownsburg, Virginia
W. McDowell to Father, July 25, 1864.
Scott C. Patchan, Haymarket, Virginia
William Stark Journal, typescript.

Tennessee State Library and Archives, Nashville
James P. Doggett, Diary, 1864.

University of North Carolina, Chapel Hill, Southern Historical Collection
J. Kelly Bennette Diary, 1864.
Kenton Harper, Military Papers, June–September 1864.

University of Virginia, Charlottesville
Alexander Neil Papers, Neil to Dear Friends, June 8, 1864.
John D. Imboden Papers, Imboden to Colonel Harper, June 2, 1864.
Joseph Waddell Diary.

U.S. Army Military History Institute, Archives, Carlisle, Pennsylvania
Civil War Times Illustrated Collection
William McIhenny, Diary, 1860–64.
David Powel Memoirs, 1861–65.
Harrisburg Civil War Round Table Collection
John Hamer Papers, memoirs.
Civil War Miscellaneous Collection
James W. Mulligan to Wife, Letter, August 15, 1864.
Lyman S. Walker, Diary, 1864.
Albert Artman, Diary, 1864.
Lewis Leigh Collection
George D. Imboden to Mollie, Letter, June 10, 1864.

Virginia Historical Society, Richmond
B.H. Jones, Report on the Battle of Piedmont, no date.

West Virginia Department of Archives and History
Col. Joseph Thoburn, 2nd Brigade, Report on the Battle of Piedmont, June 13, 1864.
Col. Robert S. Rodgers, 2nd Maryland E.S., Report on the Battle of Piedmont, June 7, 1864.
Lt. Col. Jacob Weddle, 1st West Virginia, Report on the Battle of Piedmont, June 8, 1864.

West Virginia University, Morgantown
Frank Smith Reader Diary (5th West Virginia Cavalry).
Jacob M. Campbell, Diary, 1864.
William B. Curtis Papers.
William Goudy, Diary, 1861–65.

Nᴀʀʀᴀᴛɪᴠᴇs, Mᴇᴍᴏɪʀs, Dɪᴀʀɪᴇs ᴀɴᴅ Lᴇᴛᴛᴇʀs

Aiken, J.N. "Forty-Third Tennessee Infantry." *The Military Annals of Tennessee, Confederate.* Ed. John Berrien Lindsley. Nashville, TN: J.M. Lindsley and Co. Publishers, 1886.

Beach, William H. "Battle of Piedmont." *National Tribune*, March 24, 1904.

Beer, Thomas, ed. *Hunter's Raid, 1864, From the Diary of Colonel Joseph Thoburn.* Wheeling, PA: privately published, 1914.

Bell, Jerome. "Never Did Run." *National Tribune*, April 11, 1895.

Berkeley, F. Carter. "Augusta's Battle." *Staunton Spectator and Vindicator*, July 29, 1904.

Booth, George Wilson. *Personal Reminiscences of a Maryland Soldier in the War Between the States 1861–1865.* Baltimore, MD: Press of Fleet, McGinly and Co., 1898.

Bradford, W.M. "Thirty-Ninth Tennessee Infantry." *The Military Annals of Tennessee, Confederate.* Ed. John Berrien Lindsley. Nashville, TN: J.M. Lindsley and Co. Publishers, 1886.

Brooks, Charles U. "Opposing Johnny Reb." *National Tribune*, August 9, 1900.

Bryan, David R. "Battle of Piedmont." *National Tribune*, August 25, 1904.

C., F.A. "From Staunton, June 8, 1864." *Wheeling Daily Intelligencer*, June 20, 1864.

Caldwell, G.B. "Letter from the 12th West Virginia Regiment, June 8, 1864." *Wheeling Daily Intelligencer*, June 21, 1864.

Carter, James E. "The First Tennessee Cavalry." *The Military Annals of Tennessee, Confederate.* John Berrien Lindsley. Nashville, TN: J.M. Lindsley and Co. Publishers, 1886.

Colley, Thomas W. "Brig. General William E. Jones." *Confederate Veteran* 9 (1903).

Corbin, Henry. "Diary of a Virginian Cavalry Man, 1863–4." *Historical Magazine* 2 (1873).

Crook, George. *General George Crook: His Autobiography.* Norman: University of Oklahoma Press, n.d.

Dalzell, James M. *Private Dalzell: His Autobiography and Comic War Papers.* Cincinnati, OH: Robert Clarke & Co. 1888.

Dillon, Philip H. "A Civil War Battle With a Strange Sequel 50 Years Later." *New York Times*, August 10, 1913.

Dowdey, Clifford, and Louis H. Mannarin, eds. *The Wartime Papers of R.E. Lee.* New York: Little, Brown, 1961.

Duff, John F. "Battle of Piedmont." *National Tribune*, December 7, 1900.

DuPont, H.A. *The Campaign of 1864 in the Valley of Virginia and the Expedition to Lynchburg.* New York: National Americana Society, 1925.

"Earnest." "The 1st Veteran Cavalry in the Fight at Piedmont." *New York Tribune*, July 1, 1864.

Eby, Cecil D., ed. *A Virginia Yankee in the Civil War: The Diaries of David Hunter Strother.* Chapel Hill: University of North Carolina Press, 1961.

Elwood, John W. *Elwoods Stories of the Old Ringgold Cavalry, 1847–1865: The First Three Year Cavalry of the Civil War.* Coal Center, PA: self-published, 1914.

Evans, Thomas J. "Capture the Flag." *Kepi,* December 1983–January 1984.

Feit, John. "The Battle of Piedmont." *National Tribune,* March 21, 1895.

Fisher, Spencer. "Story By a Veteran." *The Early History of Haywood County.* Comp. W. Clark Medford. Waynesville, North Carolina, 1961.

Fitzsimons, Charles. "'The Hunter Raid.' November 4, 1885." *Military Essays and Recollections. Papers Read Before the Commandery of the State of Illinois, Military Order of the Loyal Legion of the United States.* Chicago, IL: Cozzens & Beaton Company, 1907.

Gilmor, Harry. *Four Years in the Saddle.* New York: Harper and Brothers, Publishers, 1866.

Grant, Ulysses S. *Personal Memoirs of U.S. Grant; Selected Letters, 1839–1865.* New York: Literary Classics of the United States, Inc., 1990.

Halpine, Charles G. "The Battle of Piedmont—Some Further Details of the March and the Action, Correspondence of the N.Y. Tribune." *Wheeling Daily Intelligencer,* June 21, 1864.

Hardwick, W.H. "Battle of Piedmont." *National Tribune,* December 13, 1888.

———. "An Ex-Confederate." *National Tribune,* January 17, 1889.

Headley, P.C. "Report of the Service of the 34th Massachusetts." *Massachusetts in the Confederatelion.* Boston, MA: Walker, Fuller and Co., 1866.

Henry, J.L. "First Tennessee Cavalry at Piedmont." *Confederate Veteran Magazine,* 22: 397.

Hibbs, T.W. "The Piedmont Fight." *National Tribune,* September 13, 1900.

Hubbell, F.F. "The Battle of Piedmont." *National Tribune,* August 1, 1901.

Humphreys, Milton W. *Military Operations, 1861–1864.* Gauley Bridge, WV: Cotton Hill Publications, n.d.

I., C.X.V. "From the 116th Regiment." *Athens (OH) Messenger,* June 23, 1864.

Imboden, John D. "The Battle of New Market." *Battles and Leaders of the Civil War.* Vol. 4. *The Way to Appomattox.* Eds. Robert U. Johnson and Clarence C. Buel. New York: Century Magazine, 1887–88.

———. "The Battle of Piedmont." *Confederate Veteran* 31 (1923) and 21 (1924).

———. "Fire, Sword and the Halter." *The Annals of the War Written by Leading Participants, North and South. Philadelphia Weekly Times.* Dayton, OH: Morningside, 1988.

Johnston, Jane Echols, and Brenda Lynn Williams. *Hard Times 1861–1865, A Collection of Confederate Letters, Court Minutes, Soldier Records, and Local Lore from Craig County, VA.* New Castle, VA: privately published, 1987.

Jones, Beuhring H. "No Chance." *Confederate Veteran* (September 1917).

———. "Written After His First Breakfast on Rats." *Confederate Veteran* (September 1915).

Judd, Frederick A.C. "Letter from the 34th Mass. Regiment." *Northampton (MA) Free Press,* June 28, 1864.

Kauffman, Jonas B. "Jonas Kauffman Diary." *History of Cambria County, Pennsylvania.* Ed. Henry Wilson Storey. New York: Lewis Publishing Company, 1907.

Lafferty, J.J. "Battle of New Hope." *The Richmond Sentinel.* June 14, 1864.

Lang, Theodore F. *Loyal West Virginia, From 1861 to 1865.* Baltimore, MD: Deutsch Publishing Co., 1895.

Lillard, N.J. "Third Confederate." *The Military Annals of Tennessee, Confederate.* John Berrien Lindsley. Nashville, TN: J.M. Lindsley and Co. Publishers, 1886.

Lynch, Charles H. *Civil War Diary 1862–1865 of Charles H. Lynch, 18th Conn. Vols.* Hartford, CT: Case, Lockwood and Brainard Co., 1915.

Manard, B.G. "Vaughn's Brigade." *The Military Annals of Tennessee, Confederate.* John Berrien Lindsley. Nashville, TN: J.M. Lindsley and Co. Publishers, 1886.

Marsh, Washington. "Piedmont Again." *National Tribune*, April 18, 1889.

McClellan, George W. "Battle of Piedmont—West Virginia Troops Engaged." *Wheeling Register*, June 21, 1891.

Moulton, Charles H. *Fort Lyon to Harper's Ferry.* Shippensburg, PA: White Mane Publishing Co., Inc., 1987.

Oates, Dan, ed. *Hanging Rock Confederate: Lieutenant John Blue's War in West Virginia & the Shenandoah Valley.* Shippensburg, PA: Bard Street Press, 1994.

O'Ferrall, Charles T. *Forty Years of Active Service.* New York: Neale Publishing Company, 1904.

Opie, John N. *A Rebel Cavalryman with Lee, Stuart and Jackson.* Chicago, IL: W.B. Conkey Company, 1899.

O'Reilly, Miles, Private (Charles G. Halpine). *Baked Meats of the Funderal: A Collection of Essays, Poems, Speeches, Histories and Banquets.* New York: Carleton, 1866.

Pilkington, J.R. "They Killed General Jones." *National Tribune*, February 29, 1895.

R.S., Company C, 1st West Virginia. "From the First West Virginia." *Wheeling Daily Intelligencer*, June 17, 1864.

Reader, Frank S. "Battle of Piedmont." *National Tribune*, November 22, 1888.

Ring, Charles M. "The Lynchburg Raid." *National Tribune*, July 28, 1892.

Setchell, George Case. "A Sergeant's View of the Battle of Piedmont." *Civil War Times Illustrated* (May 1963): 42–47.

Shakleford, Fountain G. "My Recollections of the War." *Nicholas (WV) Chronicle*, July 27, 1895, and August 10, 1895.

Sheifley, G. "Battle of Piedmont." *National Tribune*, March 14, 1889.

Smith, David H. "The Battle of New Market, Va." *National Tribune*, August 27, 1885.

Smith, Edwin B. "Gen. Hunter's Raid Up the Valley of the Shenandoah." *Springfield Republican*, August 2, 1886.

Snedden, James. "A Rebel General the Musician's Prisoner." *Deeds of Valor: How America's Civil War Heroes Won the Congressional Medal of Honor.* Eds. W.F. Beyer and O.F. Keydel. Detroit, MI: Perrien-Keydel Company, 1901.

Soley, Alexis C. "Gen. Hunter's Raid Up the Shenandoah." *Springfield Republican*, October 25, 1886.

Stephen, Asbery. *The Diary of Pvt. Asbery Stephen in Andersonville.* Bloomington, IN: Monroe County Historical Society, 1973.

Stringfield, W.W. "Sixty-Ninth Regiment." *Histories of the Several Regiments and Battalions from North Carolina in the Great War—1861–1865.* Ed. Walter Clark. Raleigh, NC: E.M. Uzzell, Printer, 1901.

Swearinger, S.M. "Where General Jones Was Killed." *National Tribune*, May 12, 1904.

Thompson, C.A., G.W. Gillespie and H.G. Peerg Sr. "Captain Charles A. Fudge." *Confederate Veteran* 21 (1913): 32–33.

Williams, Charles Richard, ed. *Diary and Letters of Rutherford B. Hayes.* Vol. 2. Columbus: Ohio State Archeological and Historical Society, 1922.

Wisewell, Charlie. "From the 1st Veteran Cavalry." *Seneca Falls Reveille*, July 1864.

UNIT HISTORIES

Armstrong, Richard. *19th and 20th Virginia Cavalry.* Lynchburg, VA: H.E. Howard, Inc., 1994.

Beach, William H. *The First New York (Lincoln) Cavalry, From April 19, 1861 to July 7, 1865.* New York: Lincoln Cavalry Association, 1902.

Driver, Robert J., Jr. *14th Virginia Cavalry.* Lynchburg, VA: H.E. Howard, Inc., 1988.

―――. *The Staunton Artillery—McClanahan's Battery.* Lynchburg, VA: H.E. Howard, Inc., 1987.

Farrar, Samuel Clarke. *The Twenty-Second Pennsylvania Cavalry and the Ringgold Battalion, 1861–1865.* Pittsburgh, PA: published under the auspices of the Twenty-Second Pennsylvania Ringgold Cavalry Association, 1911.

Graham, John H. *History of the 5th New York Heavy Artillery Regiment.* New York: Gazlay Brothers Printers, 1891.

Hewitt, William. *The History of the 12th West Virginia Volunteer Infantry: The Part It Took in the War of the Rebellion, 1861–1865.* N.p.: Published by the Twelfth West Virginia Infantry Association, 1892.

Jones, J. Lem. "The Battle of Piedmont." *National Tribune,* January 3, 1889.

Keyes, C.M. *The Military History of the 123rd Regiment Ohio Volunteer Infantry.* Sandusky, OH: Register Steam Press, 1874.

Lincoln, William S. *Life with the 34th Massachusetts Infantry in the War of the Rebellion.* Worcester, MA: Press of Noyes, Snow and Company, 1879.

Mowrer, G.H. *History of the Organization and Service During the War of the Rebellion of Co. A, 14th Pennsylvania Cavalry.* N.p.: n.d.

Norton, Chauncey S. *"The Red Neck Ties," or the History of the Fifteenth New York Volunteer Cavalry.* Ithaca, NY: Journal Book and Job Printing House, 1891.

Olson, John E. *21st Virginia Cavalry.* Lynchburg, VA: H.E. Howard, Inc., 1989.

Rawling, C.J. *History of the First Regiment Virginia Infantry.* Philadelphia, PA: J.B. Lippincott Company, 1887.

Reader, Frank S. *History of the Fifth West Virginia Cavalry, Formerly the Second Virginia Infantry, and of Battery G., First West Va. Light Artillery.* New Brighton, PA: Daily News, 1890.

Reid, Whitelaw. *Ohio in the War: Her Statesmen, Generals and Soldiers.* 2 vols. Cincinnati, OH: Moore, Wilstach & Baldwin, 1868.

Richardson, Virginia Charles. "Application of Membership United Daughters of the Confederacy, Sam Davis Chapter, Morristown, Tennessee." *Distant Crossroads,* July 1991.

―――. "Services of W.W. Charles, 12th Tennessee Cavalry Battalion." *Distant Crossroads,* July 1991.

Scott, J.L. *45th Virginia Infantry.* Lynchburg, VA: H.E. Howard, Inc., 1989.

―――. *36th and 37th Battalions Virginia Cavalry.* Lynchburg, VA: H.E. Howard, Inc., 1986.

―――. *36th Virginia Infantry.* Lynchburg, VA: H.E. Howard, Inc., 1987.

Slease, William D. *The Fourteenth Pennsylvania Cavalry in the Civil War.* Pittsburgh, PA: Art Engraving & Printing Company, 1915.

Stevenson, James H. *Boots and Saddles: A History of the First Volunteer Cavalry of the War known as the First New York (Lincoln) Cavalry.* Harrisburg, PA: Patriot Publishing Company, 1879.

BIBLIOGRAPHY

Walker, William C., Chaplain. *History of the Eighteenth Conn. Volunteers in the War or the Union.* Norwich, CT: The Committee, 1885.

Weaver, Jeffrey C. *45th Battalion Virginia Infantry: Smith and Count's Battalions of Partisan Rangers.* Lynchburg, VA: H.E. Howard, Inc., 1994.

———. *64th Virginia Infantry.* Lynchburg, VA: H.E. Howard, Inc., 1992.

———. *22nd Virginia Cavalry.* Lynchburg, VA: H.E. Howard, Inc., 1992.

Wildes, Thos. F. *Record of the One Hundred and Sixteenth Regiment Ohio Infantry Volunteers in War of the Rebellion.* Sandusky, OH: I.F. Mack & Bro., Printers, 1884.

Williams, George T. *Company A, 37th Battalion Virginia Cavalry.* Roanoke, VA: R.H. Fishburne, 1910.

SECONDARY SOURCES

Aten, Laurence E., ed. *Study of Civil War Sites in the Shenandoah Valley of Virginia.* Washington, D.C.: U.S. Department of the Interior, 1992.

Bennett, Charles W., Jr. *Four Years with the 54th: The Military History of Franklin Bennett, 54th Pennsylvania Volunteer Regiment, 1861–1865.* Richmond, VA: Charles W. Bennett, Jr., 1985.

Bible, R. Donahue. *Vaughn's Brigade at Piedmont.* Mohwak, TN: privately published by the author, 1994.

Castel, Albert D. *The Campaign for Atlanta.* Lawrence: Kansas University Press, 1991.

Clem, Gladys B. "Old Homes of August County: 'Belmont Farm.'" *Augusta Historical Bulletin* (Spring 1981): 43.

Crow, Vernon H. *Storm in the Mountains: Thomas' Confederate Legion of Cherokee Indians and Mountaineers.* Cherokee, NC: Press of the Museum of the Cherokee Indian, 1982.

Davis, William C. *The Battle of New Market.* Baton Rouge: Louisiana State University Press, 1975.

Delauter, Roger. *McNeill's Rangers.* Lynchburg, TN: H.E. Howard, Inc., 1986.

Dyer, Frederick H. *A Compendium of the War of the Rebellion.* New York: Thomas Yoseloff, 1959.

Dyer, Gustavus W., and John Trotwood Moore. *The Tennessee Civil War Veterans Questionnaires.* Easley, SC: Southern Historical Press, 1985.

Eby, Cecil D., Jr. *Porte Crayon: The Life of David Hunter Strother, Writer of the Old South.* Chapel Hill: University of North Carolina Press, 1960.

Gordon, Larry. *The Last Confederate General: John C. Vaughn and His East Tennessee Cavalry.* Minneapolis, MN: Zenith Press, 2009.

Hanchett, William. *Irish: Charles G. Halpine in Civil War America.* Syracuse, NY: Syracuse University Press, 1970.

Hart, Calvin C. "Parkinson Collett." *Confederate Veteran* 19 (1911).

Heatwole, John L. *"Remember Me Is All I Ask": Chrisman's Boy Company, History of the Civil War Service of Company 1, 3rd Battalion, Virginia Mounted Reserves.* Bridgewater, VA: Mountain and Valley Publishing, 2000.

Hennessy, John J. *Return to Bull Run: The Campaign and Battle of Second Manassas.* New York: Simon and Schuster, 1993.

Kegley, Mary B. *Wythe County, Virginia: A Bicentennial History.* Marceline, MO: Walsworth Publishing, Inc., 1989.

Longacre, Edward G. "General David Hunter." *Civil War Times Illustrated* 16:9 (January 1978).

Mahr, Theodore C. *Early's Valley Campaign: The Battle of Cedar Creek, Showdown in the Shenandoah, October 1–30, 1864.* Lynchburg, VA: H.E. Howard, Inc., 1992.

Malone, Dumas, ed. *Dictionary of America Biography.* Vol. 5. New York: Charles Scribner's Sons, 1929–31.

Maslowski, Andy. "Burning Springs, Va." *America's Civil War,* September 1988.

May, Clarence E. *Life Under Four Flags in North River Basin of Virginia.* Bridgewater, VA: McClure Press, 1982.

McManus, Howard Rollins. *The Battle of Cloyd's Mountain; The Virginia and Tennessee Railroad Raid, April 29–May 19, 1864.* Lynchburg, VA: H.E. Howard, Inc., 1989.

Miller, William J. *Mapping for Stonewall: The Civil War Service of Jed Hotchkiss.* Washington, D.C.: Elliot and Clark Publishing, 1993.

Newton, J.H., G.G. Nichols and A.G. Sprankle. *History of the Pan-Handle, Being Historical Collections of the Counties of Ohio, Brooke, Marshall and Hancock, West Virginia.* Wheeling, WV: L.A. Caldwell, 1897.

Ohio General Assembly. *Official Roster of the Soldiers of the State of Ohio in the War of the Rebellion, 1861–1866.* Cincinnati: Ohio Valley Publishing and Manufacturing, 1886.

Pendleton, William C. *History of Tazewell County and Southwest Virginia: 1748–1920.* Richmond, VA: W.C. Hill Printing Company, 1920.

Peyton, J. Lewis. *History of Augusta County, Virginia.* Bridgewater, VA: C.J. Carrier Company, 1953.

Phisterer, Frederick. *New York in the War of the Rebellion, 1861 to 1865.* Albany, NY: J.B. Lyon, Co., State Printers, 1912.

Porter, Duval. *A Composition of Sketches of the Public Men of Virginia,* 189-190. Richmond: Whittet and Shepperson, 1920.

Reed, Rowena. *Combined Operations in the Civil War.* Lincoln: University of Nebraska Press, 1993.

Reed, Thomas J. "Black Dave and His Staff." *America's Civil War,* July 1989.

Robertson, James I. *Soldiers Blue and Gray.* New York: Warner Books, 1988.

Ruffner, Kevin Conley. "'More Trouble than a Brigade': Harry Gilmor's 2d Maryland Cavalry in the Shenandoah Valley." *Maryland Historical Magazine* 89 (Winter 1994): 393.

Sell, Donna Christine, and Dennis Francis Walle. *Guide to the Heinrich A. Ratterman Collection of German American Manuscripts.* Urbana: University of Illinois Library and the Graduate School of Library Science, 1979.

Tucker, Spencer C. *Brigadier General John D. Imboden: Confederate Commander in the Shenandoah.* Louisville: University Press of Kentucky, 2003.

Waddell, Joseph A. *Annals of Augusta County, Virginia from 1726 to 1871.* Bridgewater, VA: C.J. Carrier Company, 1902.

Warner, Ezra. *Generals in Blue: Lives of the Union Commanders.* Baton Rouge: Louisiana State University Press, 1964.

———. *Generals in Gray: Lives of the Confederate Commanders.* Baton Rouge: Louisiana State University Press, 1959.

Wayland, John Walter. *A History of Rockingham County.* Dayton, VA: Ruebush-Elkins Co., 1912.

Wert, Jeffry D. *From Winchester to Cedar Creek.* New York: Simon and Schuster, 1987.

Williams, T. Harry. *The Civil War Volunteer Officer: Hayes of the 23rd.* New York: Knopf, 1965.

Index

About the Author

S cott C. Patchan is a leading authority on the 1864 Shenandoah Valley Campaign. He has written several books on the American Civil War, most recently *Shenandoah Summer: The 1864 Valley Campaign* and *Second Manassas: Longstreet's Attack and the Struggle for Chinn Ridge*. He is a much sought-after tour guide and has also composed dozens of articles on the Civil War, including feature essays on all major battles of the 1864 Valley Campaign for *Blue and Gray* magazine. He also served as a writer and historical consultant for Time-Life's *Voices of the Civil War: Shenandoah 1864*. He sits on the Shenandoah Valley Battlefield Foundation's Resource Protection Committee and the Kernstown Battlefield Association Board of Directors. Scott is also a two-time president of Bull Run Civil War Round Table.

Visit us at
www.historypress.net